Camp Harmony

THE ASIAN AMERICAN EXPERIENCE

Series Editor
Roger Daniels

Camp Harmony

Seattle's Japanese Americans and the Puyallup Assembly Center

LOUIS FISET

UNIVERSITY OF ILLINOIS PRESS

Urbana and Chicago

Library of Congress Cataloging-in-Publication Data
Fiset, Louis.
Camp Harmony : Seattle's Japanese Americans and the Puyallup
Assembly Center / Louis Fiset.
p.   cm. — (The Asian American experience)
Includes bibliographical references and index.
ISBN 978-0-252-03491-6 (cloth : alk. paper)
ISBN 978-0-252-07672-5 (paper : alk. paper)
1. Japanese Americans—Evacuation and relocation, 1942–1945.
2. Puyallup Assembly Center (Puyallup, Wash.) 3. Japanese
Americans—Washington (State)—Seattle—History—20th
century. 4. World War, 1939–1945—Washington (State)—Seattle.
5. Seattle (Wash.)—Ethnic relations—History—20th century.
6. Seattle (Wash.)—History—20th century. I. Title.
D769.8.A6F48   2009
940.53'1779778—dc22   2009015034

To Richard C. Berner,
University of Washington archivist,
whose vision for a Japanese American
collection made this book possible.

Contents

List of Illustrations

List of Tables

Foreword

Although the vast majority of Japanese Americans who were incarcerated under military auspices during World War II began their traumatic experience in one of the fifteen temporary assembly centers on the West Coast from western Washington to central Arizona, relatively little scholarly attention has focused on these places. Now Louis Fiset's careful study of the hastily thrown together camp on the state fairgrounds at Puyallup and the people herded into it not only gives us the first detailed history of that place, but also provides other scholars a reference point for the studies of other centers, which are sure to come.

Dubbed "Camp Harmony," the place served as a holding pen for the more than seven thousand men, women, and children from Seattle and other parts of western Washington who were cooped up there for more than four and a half months until a more isolated place of confinement could be constructed for them in southern Idaho.

Fiset begins his story with an account of the thriving ethnic enclave in downtown Seattle, which its inhabitants called *nihonmachi* and polite outsiders called Japantown, and shows us how, in the weeks after December 7, 1941, its residents—two out of three of them U.S. citizens—had their civil and human rights methodically stripped away.

He then describes the plans that the government made to have an orderly episode of what we now call ethnic cleansing and the efforts the Japanese American community made to mitigate the circumstances that had been unimaginable only months before. This meant cooperating with their oppressors, a decision some questioned, then and later. In Seattle a few Japanese American leaders collaborated with the army and other government officials and continued to play that role in Camp Harmony itself. For a time they enjoyed an extraordinary amount of authority over the mundane details of captivity without having any say about release. While the extent of this arrangement in Seattle and at Puyallup may have been more encompassing than at other camps for Japanese Americans, similar arrangements had and have been developed in the systems of non-judicial incarceration developed by other nations.

Fiset, whose first academic career was as a university research dentist, pays particular attention to the health care and public health issues involved and provides a detailed account of the service provided by Japanese American medical professionals who were themselves prisoners.

Too much of what has been written about the wartime Japanese American experience describes those who experienced it as if they were patient, passive victims. Fiset's book shows us how misleading that image is. To be sure there was no mass resistance: it is frightening to think of what men like General DeWitt and his subordinate, western Washington native Karl Bendetsen, might have ordered if that had occurred. But clearly the incarcerated people were active agents in making their four and a half months in places like Camp Harmony and much longer periods in the camps of the War Relocation Authority (WRA) as tolerable as possible under the circumstances.

Roger Daniels

Acknowledgments

The efforts of a number of individuals helped bring this book to fruition. First, University of Washington Libraries archivist Richard C. Berner's vision in the 1970s enabled the university to pursue a collection of papers of individuals and organizations important to the incarceration experience of Pacific Northwest Nikkei, accessions that might otherwise have headed to the dumpster. This study relies on documents contained within what became known as the Japanese American Collection.

The careful readings and comments of five anonymous readers, each bringing to the manuscript a different perspective, helped reduce inconsistencies and factual errors, expand underrepresented topics, and enable my narrators to speak more with their own voices, all serving to enrich the story of Camp Harmony. Professor Roger Daniels, an advocate of this book from its fragile beginning, offered documentation, bibliographies, historical perspective, and ongoing commentary throughout the years of its creation, while asking only for good scholarship in return.

I thank the survivors of the Camp Harmony experience who generously shared with me memories of their incarceration, many of them painful. They helped guide me through their long days as inmates separated from daily life in the sidewalks and streets of Puyallup by the thickness of a barbed wire fence: Kenji Okuda, Sally (Shimanaka) Kazama, Sharon (Tanagi) Aburano, Margaret (Baba) Yasuda, Elmer Tazuma, Tamako (Inouye) Tokuda. I wish to especially acknowledge narrators Shigeko (Sese) Uno, Nobuko (Yanigamachi) Suzuki, Eddie Sato, Bill Hosokawa, Shosuke Sasaki, and Jim Akutsu, who did not live to see publication of this book.

My wife, Joan, took time from her busy professional life to read every page of the manuscript and its major revisions, offering insightful comments, queries, and edits everywhere.

Finally, I want to make note of my Calico Louise, whose daily routine shifting from one side of my long desk to the other following the sun's rays occasionally resulted in a stroll across my keyboard, reminding me this project was a labor of love and I should take myself less seriously than I often do.

Camp Harmony

Introduction

On August 31, 1896, the Nippon Yusen Kaisha (NYK) steamer *Miiki Maru* docked at Schwabacher Wharf on Seattle's Elliott Bay waterfront, arriving from Yokohama via Hawaii. The crew discharged 8 passengers, 253 immigrants, and a modest cargo of tea, silk goods, camphor, and other exotic items from Asia. Yachts and boats of all descriptions at anchor in the harbor, fireworks, a brass band, and steam whistles blowing the length of the waterfront all combined to cheer on the welcome event.[1]

Railroad entrepreneur James J. Hill, who brought the Great Northern Railroad to Seattle in 1893, saw Japan as a rapidly modernizing and industrializing nation with potential to become a consumer of surplus U.S. agricultural and manufactured products that he could ship to the Pacific Northwest profitably. Hill signed an agreement with NYK establishing monthly service between Hong Kong, Japanese ports, and Seattle.[2]

The *Miiki Maru* returned to Yokohama in September carrying lumber, flour, raw cotton, heavy hardware, and other goods loaded from Great Northern rail cars, thus completing its first run between Japan and Seattle, NYK's only North American port of call.

The result put Seattle in competition with San Francisco, Los Angeles, and Victoria for transpacific shipment of commerce, lifting hopes in the region that the Pacific Northwest might become the commercial gateway to Asia. Riding the enthusiasm, two years later Osaka Shosen Kaisha (OSK Line) inaugurated its first ocean route to North America, providing service linking Hong Kong and Tacoma.

Although this commercial venture with Japan was new to Seattle, Seattle residents already had some experience with Japanese people. In 1890, Washington's 127 Japanese immigrants resided in King County, all but 2 in Seattle. In the ensuing 10 years, the city's Nikkei population rose to 2,990, most coming after 1896 when Seattle became a stepping-off place for many immigrants coming to North America.

Most early arrivals worked in agriculture and the railroad, lumber, and fishing industries, helping fill the void left by an aging Chinese population that had arrived in the American West prior to the exclusion of Chinese laborers in 1882. Japanese-run labor contracting firms recruited the workers while working directly with agents for American companies. Two of the earliest contractors promoting direct labor emigration to the West Coast were the Tacoma Construction and Maintenance Company and the Oriental Trading Company of Seattle, both established in 1898.[3]

The contractors funneled most immigrant laborers into section gangs throughout the West created to maintain the tracks and rail beds laid down by Hill's Great Northern Railroad and its competitor, Northern Pacific. In 1898 alone, the Oriental Trading Company of Seattle supplied Great Northern with more than 800 workers. A branch office established the following year in Yokohama helped raise that number to more than 2,000 annually. In the fiscal year ending June 1900, almost half the 12,635 Japanese admitted to the country entered through the Pacific Northwest.[4]

While the railroads absorbed most of the early workers, the contractors also supplied men for lumber, fishing, and agricultural interests. As a result, Japanese immigrants provided labor to sawmill towns in coastal areas of Washington and the western slopes of the Cascade range, such as Port Blakely, Port Townsend, Enumclaw, Onalaska, Snoqualmie Falls, and Selleck, as well as other communities surrounding Seattle and Tacoma within reach of a crosscut saw.

Immigrant field hands went onto farms in the Kent, White River, and Puyallup River valleys, as well as to Bainbridge Island in Puget Sound west of Seattle and the Bellevue area to the east. Later, many started up their own truck farms on plots averaging less than forty acres, where they employed innovative farming methods brought from Japan that allowed them to compete head to head with white farmers working larger tracts of land.[5] Labor contractors also helped a smaller number of laborers find work in the salmon canneries of Puget Sound and Alaska.

Supplying immigrant labor to the Pacific Northwest and the American West was fraught with political problems. Responding to pressure from a growing backlash in the United States over a sudden increase in laborers from Japan, in 1900 Japan's Foreign Ministry first instituted a quota system, then stopped issuing passports to labor emigrants altogether. The ensuing labor shortage caused labor contractors to look to Hawaii as an alternate source for their clients' labor needs. Japanese immigrants working in the sugarcane fields were promised higher wages on the mainland, often double what they were earning in Hawaii. By offering higher wages the two Puget Sound–based Japanese laborer contractors competed with contractors in San Francisco for the bulk of these workers.[6]

However, sugar planters, fearing loss of their Japanese labor force, helped bring an end to the practice in 1907 in the midst of widespread calls for total exclusion of the Japanese. This did not occur, however, before 38,000 left the islands for the mainland, many of them arriving in the Pacific Northwest.[7]

By this time, the majority of Japanese laborers in the United States worked under the labor-contracting system. Ten thousand were employed by the railroads in the western states, 2,200 worked in the sawmills in Oregon and Washington, and 3,600 labored in the salmon canneries of Alaska, Oregon, and Washington. An additional 8,000 agricultural workers tilled the fertile soils of the Pacific Northwest.[8]

Most Japanese immigrant laborers, including those in the Pacific Northwest, came to America to make quick money then return to Japan. Some did, but for most, wages were too low to enable a triumphant return home. As the immigrant population grew and communities began to form in the coastal cities of the United States, the country became more attractive; many men began to think of settling down.[9]

While many laborers were dispersed from Washington throughout the American West, Seattle and, to a lesser extent Tacoma, became congregating points for immigrants seeking common cultural experiences. A Japanese settlement began to rise up south of Yesler Street in the vicinity of Seattle's 1854 pioneer settlement. Between 1900 and 1910, Seattle's Japanese population doubled in size, to 6,127.

During this period of growth social and commercial institutions created by and for the immigrant Japanese community began to appear in the city. The Seattle Japanese Baptist Church was organized in 1899, with the Seattle Buddhist Church following two years later. By 1908, most major Japanese Christian churches were well established.

The Oriental-American Bank, first of three branches of Japanese banks, opened in 1905. Two local Japanese banks soon followed. Tokyo-based trading firms, such as Mitsui and Company, opened offices on the waterfront to handle transpacific commerce, while nearby, small entrepreneurs catering to both Japanese immigrants and immigrant and migrant whites opened minor hotels and lodging houses, grocery stores, and dry-cleaning establishments.[10]

By 1908, two Japanese-language newspapers served the Japanese community; professionals such as doctors, dentists, lawyers, and translators opened offices in the growing *nihonmachi*. Business and cultural associations emerged.

In the meantime, in 1900 males in the Japanese population in the United States outnumbered females 22,311 to 958 (22:1 ratio), with many of the women prostitutes and unmarried. Only 410 married women existed in all of Japanese immigrant society, with few American-born children, or Nisei, arising from those unions.[11] Among Washington's 5,566 Japanese residents, only 51 children had been born on U.S. soil. As a result, many men with plans to settle in the United States and start families sought wives in Japan. Those who could afford the expense of money and time traveled to Japan to find their wives, while other bachelors resorted to the so-called picture bride practice by which parents, relatives, or other "go-betweens" in Japan picked the bride after an exchange of photographs and information about the immigrant's life in America.[12] The net effect was that by 1910, 13 percent of Washington's Nikkei were female and, by 1920, 35 percent. The number of American-born children from these unions increased from 6 percent of the overall Nikkei population in 1910 to 25 percent in 1920.[13]

Exclusionists attacked the picture bride system for being barbaric, for violating earlier agreements with Japan to curtail labor immigration, and for leading to overpopulation with offspring who were automatically U.S. citizens. In 1920, advocates in Washington, D.C., pressured Japan's Foreign Ministry to cease issuing passports to picture brides. Four years later, passage of the Immigration Act of 1924 brought an end to Japanese immigration altogether.[14]

These exclusionary measures, coupled with the economic depression years of the 1930s, resulted in a migration out of Washington to California or a return to Japan with emigration elsewhere. Not surprisingly, Washington's Nikkei population declined by 18 percent between 1930 and 1940, to 14,565. By 1940, however, as diplomatic tensions between the United States and Japan escalated, nearly half of Seattle's 6,975 Nikkei were female and the Nisei, now comprising 60 percent, were poised to begin assuming leadership of the community from their immigrant Issei elders. However, even with their numbers now in the majority, the average age of the second generation was only eighteen.

Thus, the Issei still dominated political, economic, cultural, and intellectual activity within the community as the decade of the 1940s began.

World War II dramatically interrupted this gradual generational shift of power. By mid-May 1942, Seattle's Japantown was emptied of its Nikkei residents, the entire community herded off under military guard to a makeshift incarceration compound thirty miles south of the city, on Puyallup's western Washington fairgrounds. By the end of June, only a few dozen Nikkei—long-term inpatients—remained "free" within western Washington's exclusion zone.

This study examines the experience of more than seven thousand Seattle and Puget Sound region Nikkei during their four-month incarceration at the so-called Puyallup Assembly Center, one of sixteen army-run centers in Washington, Oregon, California, and Arizona set up as holding pens until permanent relocation centers could be built to accommodate them. The book offers a detailed field study of an assembly center, the first of its kind, which army publicists referred to as "Camp Harmony" even before the first inmate arrived. Using archival sources, contemporaneous accounts, and narratives provided by eyewitnesses, it focuses on the people who were incarcerated, their response to the experience, and the place of their imprisonment.

I selected the Puyallup Assembly Center as a case study because of long-time residence in the Puget Sound region, access to some of the survivors, and availability of productive archival sources at the nearby University of Washington.

In many respects the Puyallup Assembly Center was typical of the centers, thereby enabling it to serve as a model for studies of the other sites. With the exception of Manzanar, built from scratch in the Owens Valley two hundred miles east of Los Angeles, the assembly centers arose in urban or semi-urban locales with a significant Nikkei presence. Existing public places such as fairgrounds, racetracks, and livestock pavilions provided acreage and infrastructure needed to quickly assemble the centers. Built as temporary shelters, the centers offered few amenities and meager health and social services. Inmates ate in mess halls, slept in noisy barracks, and enjoyed little privacy. Although some employment and volunteer opportunities existed, most inmates spent their days in relative idleness. The army, through its arm, the Wartime Civil Control Administration (WCCA), oversaw all centers, while civilian government appointees ran the day-to-day operations. The inmates themselves helped provide order and served as liaisons between the residents and the Caucasian administration. And few of the imprisoned population departed the assembly centers during the centers' four months of existence.[15]

On the other hand, notable dissimilarities exist between Camp Harmony and the other centers. For example, nearly 80 percent of the center's population consisted of urban people while half the Nikkei residing on the West Coast at the outbreak of the war lived and worked in rural or semi-rural areas. The layout of the center was characterized by four distinct shelter areas separated from one another by city streets, adding difficulty to administration of the center. A Seattle Nisei-led administration that was established undemocratically prior to exile of the city's Nikkei and designated to serve as an interface with army administrators ruled the inmates with an iron fist. Dissension arising among the residents as a result abated only with the group being neutralized by the center's civilian manager with help from the army. This experience led to abolishment of self-government in the other assembly centers.

*   *   *

The chapters that follow explore the Seattle Nikkei experience from the time the United States entered the Pacific war in December 1941 until the en masse transfer of the Puyallup Assembly Center's inmates to the Minidoka Relocation Center came to an end in September 1942.

Chapter 1 provides a historical prewar sketch of Seattle's *nihonmachi,* a community shared with the other racial minorities in the city, the Chinese, Filipinos, and African Americans. Journalist Jimmie Sakamoto emerged as a community leader who would rise to prominence after the bombing of Pearl Harbor. Chapter 2 narrates ways in which Seattleites of all kinds reacted to the shocking news of Pearl Harbor and how the government began to improvise plans to "do something" about the Japanese living on the Pacific coast, beginning with the arrest of Issei community leaders. The Nikkei began to mobilize, with Sakamoto heading the Emergency Defense Council later to form the nucleus of Nisei leaders at the Puyallup Assembly Center. Seattle's residents started to speak out for and against the Nikkei. Chapter 3 describes and analyzes how both captors and captives made preparations for a mandated and often poorly planned exile. It highlights the difficulties of moving.

Chapter 4 describes and analyzes the creation of the Puyallup Assembly Center and a second assembly center in Washington, at Toppenish, which ultimately failed to open its gates. The chapter focuses on public health issues that illustrate the shortcomings of government planning. Sakamoto assembled a Nisei cohort to work with the army in administering the assembly center as the Nikkei community began to unload possessions and businesses in preparation for the people's exile. Chapter 5 provides an account of the processes by which the Seattle and Pierce County Nikkei were removed from their homes and placed into an assembly center that had not been completed. An advance crew from Seattle was surprised to learn that Nikkei from Alaska had arrived a day earlier. Chapter 6 details the settling in period at Camp Harmony as seven thousand Nikkei from Seattle and rural areas surrounding Tacoma converged over a two-week period and learned to endure communal living of eating, sleeping, and just getting through the day.

Chapters 7, 8, and 9 complete the saga of Camp Harmony's brief existence, which was occupied from April 27 to September 12, 1942. These chapters reveal the drear of camp life as seen through the lives of its inhabitants. A few people left for agricultural work or volunteered for work parties, but most remained until the center closed. These months were rife with conflict, less between captives and captors, more between the inmates themselves, with Sakamoto a lightning rod at the center. The story ends with a trip on re-commissioned, dilapidated rail passenger cars to the relocation center at Minidoka, in south-central Idaho.

1

Prewar Japantown

The eve of World War II found Seattle's skyline dominated by the 462-foot-high Smith Tower, built by the typewriter tycoon who eventually made Smith-Corona a household name. In 1941, with Seattle now eight decades old, this twenty-seven-year-old behemoth remained the tallest building west of the Rocky Mountains.[1]

It rose above Second Avenue at the northern edge of Seattle's original pioneer settlement. The tower's quoin faced Yesler Way, known as Mill Street when Henry Yesler skidded logs from the verdant hills above his sawmill at the edge of Elliott Bay. As the city grew, its business district moved north into cleared forestland rather than toward marshy tidelands that prevailed to the south. By the turn of the twentieth century, following an explosion of growth and affluence lasting two decades and resulting in new railroads and the markets they created, the city's residential districts migrated toward the east and north to hilly elevations whose vistas provided distance from the working masses. The Skid Road area became abandoned; its housing stock slowly deteriorated. Situated by now at the city's fringe, this area soon attracted economically marginalized itinerant laborers. It is also where Seattle's Asian minority ethnic groups—Chinese, followed by Japanese, and later, Filipino—took root.

Despite urbanization, for the most part Seattle and the Pacific Northwest was dominated by an extractive economy of seasonal fishing and logging and mining industries, which lasted far into the twentieth century. Like much of the American West, this region did not possess the essential infrastructure required to absorb workers on a permanent basis. This created a significant migratory population made up largely of single males, both whites and persons of color, who settled in the Skid Road area.[2]

During the World War I era, the "great migration" of African Americans out of the South never reached the West Coast. As a result, Seattle's minority population became predominantly Asian. And for many, Seattle served as a regional turnstile—on one hand a major port of entry from Asia, on the other a gateway to Alaska and its fishing industry, to the agricultural regions of both western and eastern Washington, and to markets beyond the Rockies. Seattle became vital to Asian Americans because it offered the resources and development of an urban setting within a largely rural context, as well as the availability of low-end jobs. Seattle also evolved into a refuge from virulent discrimination.[3]

Asian immigrants were relative newcomers to the Pacific Northwest. Chinese arrived in the 1870s to work in canneries and in the mines, and by 1884 helped bring the Northern Pacific Railroad to the West.[4] Because of their low economic status, cultural affinities, and general exclusion by the dominant whites who made up 96 percent of Seattle's population, the city's minority racial groups gradually began to occupy the area south of Yesler Way. From a window on an upper floor of the Smith Tower a prewar observer could look out over this entire area. Seattle's chief demographer Calvin F. Schmid designated the boundaries of the Jackson Street–Chinatown district as extending from the waterfront below First Avenue eastward to 23rd Avenue. North to south the district spanned seven blocks from Yesler Way to Dearborn Street. Within these two square miles lived the vast majority of Seattle's ten thousand Japanese, Chinese, and Filipinos. A small segment of Seattle's African American population also lived and worked along part of the upper Jackson Street corridor.[5]

Of the city's population of 368,302 in 1940 the total minority population stood at 14,201, or about 4 percent.[6] About half were Japanese nationals and Japanese Americans, and with their relatively large numbers filling parts of the Jackson Street–Chinatown district it soon became known as Japantown, or to many of its inhabitants, *nihonmachi.*[7]

The densest concentration of Japanese lay within the blocks immediately south of Yesler Way, on Main and Jackson streets, then eastward roughly from Fifth Avenue before thinning out at 23rd Avenue. Centered near Fifth and Sixth avenues, the main Japanese business district remained significantly unchanged for twenty years, between 1920 and 1940, after the community realized the height of its growth. However, during this two-decade period

the residential area slowly moved outward then up toward First Hill before turning southward across 12th Avenue in the direction of Beacon Hill.
This gradual departure, typical of many immigrant groups, resulted from
an improved standard of living within the community caused by the greater
adaptability of the first generation to Western life and the increased presence
of the Nisei generation. With this scattering eastward the Japanese came to
live in closer proximity to Sephardic and Ashkenazic Jews, Italians, African Americans, and other working-class immigrant and second-generation
whites residing in the area.

Most Japanese cultural, social, and financial institutions could be found
inside the boundaries defining the Jackson Street–Chinatown district. A visitor who walked up Jackson then back down Main Street would encounter
Japanese-owned or -operated hotels, groceries, laundries, barbershops, cafes
and restaurants, drugstores, variety stores, floral shops, and bookstores. A
wide spectrum of professionals—physicians, dentists, architects, translators,
real estate agents, insurance agents, and lawyers—worked in the area as well.
Three branches of banks in Japan provided business loans and safe havens for
hard-earned savings. The community's own movie theater, the Atlas, on Maynard Street, and the Nippon Kan hall, at Washington and Maynard streets,
offered traditional entertainment for homesick and nostalgic immigrants,
American-style entertainment for Nisei youth, and cultural events of interest
to the entire Nikkei community. Close by, at 14th Avenue and Weller Street,
the Japanese Language School for second-generation learners helped assure
immigrant elders their children would not lose sight of their cultural roots.
Availability of all these cultural amenities meant a non-English-speaking
Japanese immigrant rarely had to leave *nihonmachi*.[8]

In February 1942, 262 of Seattle's hotels and apartment houses operated
under Japanese management. Most of them catering to the laboring class, they
offered few amenities and corresponding low rents. With the war in Europe
two and a half years old, and the United States rushing material support to
its Allies through its 1940 Lend-Lease policy, defense workers continued to
pour into Seattle and the district. Flophouses finally filled to capacity, and
rent receipts reached new highs. Most rental operations remained small,
family-run establishments, with hotels averaging sixty-six rooms and apartments twenty-four units.[9]

Seizo Itoi's decrepit Carrollton Hotel on Main Street knew its best days during the Alaska gold rush. This sixty-room two-story walk-up became home
to "sea-hardened mariners, shipyard workers, airplane workers, fruit pickers

and factory workers," as well as to the five-member Itoi family, who occupied three rooms with their windows facing south onto Main Street. This hotel was the prewar setting for the most-read published Nisei memoir to date.[10]

Japanese also operated fifty-three restaurants, representing 10 percent of the city's total.[11] Modest in size and menu offerings, those located near the waterfront catered to defense workers and itinerants, providing American meals at reasonable prices. One area resident recalled how a full meal in a Japanese restaurant, including dessert and salad, might cost 25 cents.[12]

Nearly half of Seattle's Japanese income earners operated independent, small businesses.[13] In 1932, after twenty years of selling wares in a ground floor storefront rental on Weller Street, Sanzo Murakami moved his Higo Company 5¢ to $1 Store (later Higo 10¢ Store) to a new two-story brick building built to his specifications on the north side of Jackson Street near the heart of the business district. The store name derived from his birthplace in Japan, where he had been raised. More than a variety store offering kitchenware and general merchandise, it served as a magnet for fellow immigrants from Kumamoto prefecture. The family-run business appealed to both Japanese and Western tastes and helped draw Seattle's white residents into the area.[14]

Nearby on Weller Street above Eighth Avenue the White River Dairy began its third decade of operation. Like Higo Company it became a family-owned business operated by Japanese Americans. In 1920, Eichi Sese, son of a farmer and an early immigrant from Tottori prefecture, bought into a dairy with several other immigrants. After the partners failed to succeed, they sold out to Sese, who nursed it to profitability. Located in the heart of Japantown, the processing plant pasteurized and bottled milk brought in by refrigerated trucks from Japanese dairy farmers in the White River Valley. The dairy wholesaled its products under the labels "White River Grade 'A' Milk," "Surefreeze" ice cream, and "Maid O'Clover" butter, selling to other Japanese entrepreneurs who operated restaurants and grocery stores in Japantown and throughout the city. Like Murakami's variety store, many of these establishments also catered to a Caucasian clientele.

White River Dairy incorporated (White River Dairy Products Incorporated) shortly before Sese's death in 1936. Because the family possessed good business acumen and catered to a diversified clientele, the dairy became a profitable enterprise. When the United States entered World War II in December 1941, Sese's widow and adult children carried on the business with his eldest daughter, an Issei, at the helm.[15]

In contrast, most Nikkei-run businesses operated on a smaller scale. For example, on the eve of the war pharmacist George Tokuda, a Nisei, owned and operated Johnson Drugstore in two locations. The original store, at 18th Avenue and Yesler Way on Japantown's eastern fringe, had belonged to a white druggist who, in the midst of the Depression, hired Tokuda out of the University of Washington Pharmacy School. After his death, the druggist's widow offered to sell the business outright, and with a down payment provided by his father Tokuda took over as its sole proprietor.

Because he got along well with the public the business grew, enabling Tokuda to open a second drugstore on 12th Avenue between Yesler Way and Fir Street situated closer to the center of the Japanese community. Groups of Nikkei, African Americans, and whites living or working nearby patronized his two stores.[16]

Most Nikkei-run businesses—barbershops, beauty shops, shoe repair shops, and hole-in-the-wall enterprises—operated on a smaller scale than Tokuda's pharmacy, often involving a single individual. Large or small, they provided the economic framework defining *nihonmachi* as a viable independent community.

The Nikkei community's social structure, for the most part, centered in churches able to provide spiritual sustenance for the afflicted while serving as a social center for the immigrant generation and their American-born children. By 1942 approximately 25 percent of the seven thousand Japanese living in Seattle identified themselves as Christians attending one of the seven active Nikkei ethnic Christian churches (see table 1). Begun at the turn of the century as missions for early immigrants, these churches evolved into institutions serving both the Issei and Nisei generations.

Non-Japanese ministers who had served as missionaries in Asia led several of the congregations. Everett Thompson of the Japanese Methodist Church spoke fluent Japanese. After working with the Japanese minority colonial population in Manchuria, Father Leopold Tibesar became the priest for Seattle's Maryknoll mission in 1935, ministering to several hundred parishioners in the Seattle area and often preaching in Japanese.

Deaconess Margaret Peppers of the Episcopal St. Peters Japanese mission in Seattle and its sister mission in White River, like Tibesar, had served as a missionary (in the Philippines). Reverend Emery Andrews, minister of the largest Japanese congregation, the Japanese Baptist Church, held no prior missionary experience in Asia, yet after taking over pastoral duties in 1929 quickly built a devoted following among the Nisei.[17]

Approximately the same number of Seattle's Nikkei held affiliations with the city's Nichiren and Shinshu Buddhist sects. Razed in 1940 to make way for a public housing project, the original Seattle Shinshu Buddhist Temple

Table 1. Nikkei Congregations in Seattle, 1941

Church	Year Established	Japanese Minister	Caucasian Minister	Address
Japanese Baptist	1899	Shozo Hashimoto	Emery Andrews	901 E. Spruce St.
Shinshu Buddhist	1901	Tatsuya Ichikawa, Hideo Eiyu Terao		305 17th Ave. S.
Japanese Methodist	1904	Yaseburo Tsuda	Everett Thompson	1300 Washington St.
St. Peters Japanese	1906	Daisuke	Margaret Peppers	1610 King St.
Episcopal Mission	?	Kitagawa		
Japanese Presbyterian	1907	S. Kodaera		166 17th Ave.
Japanese Congregational	1907	?		522 9th Ave. S.
Nichiran Buddhist	1916	Kanjitsu Iijima		316 Maynard Ave.
Our Lady Queen of Martyrs	1925	—	Leopold H. Tibesar	1610 E. Jefferson St.
Konko-Kyo Shinkokai	1928	Rikimatsu Hideshima		1042 Weller St.
Konko-Kyo	1928	Rikimatsu Hideshima		1427 S. Main St.
Japanese Holiness Church	1935	?		2035 ½ King St.
Tenrikyo Elliott Church	?	Yuki Takashino(?)		1437 Donovan St.
Tenrikyo South Seattle	?	Yuki Takashino(?)		1713 Main St.

Source: Polks Seattle City Directory, 1941, 1942.

on Main Street would soon be rebuilt several blocks away and dedicated in October 1941. However, the timing of construction proved unfortunate for the congregation and the temple's architect, Allen Kichio Arai, whose career would not rebound following his wartime incarceration.[18]

Although the Japanese community centered primarily within the marginal areas of the city south of Yesler Way, a small proportion of residents dispersed throughout the city in areas unencumbered by restrictive covenants preventing home ownership by minorities. That Japanese could be found living within most of Seattle's geographic areas may have surprised some Seattle residents in April and May 1942, when the army issued civilian exclusion orders to cover every square foot of the city's real estate. Nevertheless, this dispersal proved thin, for fewer than 150 Nikkei lived in neighborhoods located between Lake Union and the north city line, an area making up one-fourth of the city's land mass. Similarly, two hundred Nikkei resided between Jefferson Park and the south city line, reflecting the slow advance of more well-to-do families out toward Beacon Hill. This left nearly six thousand Nikkei to reside inside the city's crowded hourglass center.[19]

Japantown belonged only in part to the Nikkei because *nihonmachi* was not an ethnically homogeneous area at its center or margins. While Japanese-owned businesses, institutions, and residences dominated block after block, smaller pockets of Chinese, Filipino, and African Americans also lived and assembled within the area. Ethnic enrollments in the area's public schools revealed this residential overlapping among many groups.

Growing up on Japantown's eastern fringe, Jim Akutsu attended Central School grammar school with an enrollment of approximately 20 percent Japanese Americans. He recalled direct contact with non-Japanese immigrant classmates: "We [Nisei] were all second generation. First-generation Russian, first-generation German, first-generation Italians. We used to fight each other, as a group. If I go from home to Central School I cross the German and the Irish; if they have something against us, that was it."[20]

The Chinese, whose arrival in Seattle preceded that of the first Japanese by nearly a generation, fell victim to economic hard times following construction of railroads in the West. Scapegoated, they faced expulsion as well as subsequent restrictive immigration policies established in hopes more jobs for Americans would ensue. This gave rise to a predominantly male Chinese population. In 1940, Chinese males comprised 78 percent of Seattle's 1,781 residents compared to 54 percent males in the Japanese community. Emergence of a family-based society would not begin to occur until after 1943, when U.S. immigration policy once again permitted Chinese women immigrants to enter the country in small numbers.[21]

Nevertheless, the Seattle Chinese exhibited a robust presence concentrated on King and Weller streets, around Seventh Avenue. However, in contrast to the Japanese who had preempted cheap restaurants, a Chinese specialty elsewhere, the preponderance of males discouraged Chinese merchants from establishing businesses catering to families. Thus, many merchants turned to quasi-legal or illegal activities aimed at Chinese laborers that in time would lure a citywide clientele into the district. Japanese-owned gambling operations such as the Toyo Club in combination with brothels employing Japanese prostitutes made Chinatown's reputation one of illicit entertainment that flaunted middle-class values. Chinese-owned pool halls, brothels, nightclubs, and gambling dens dotted the streets throughout the Jackson Street–Chinatown district with a handful of more traditional businesses, such as restaurants and dye works (laundries) interspersed throughout.

Numbering 1,392 in the 1940 census, the Filipino community also contributed to the Jackson Street–Chinatown district ethnic milieu. The local monthly, *Philippine Advocate,* described how Seattle's "Little Manila" sat at King Street, Maynard, Jackson, and Sixth Avenue, a small rectangle of habitation whose center of gravity lay one block south of the main part of Chinatown.[22] According to demographer Calvin Schmid, writing in 1944: "This section is . . . characterized by cheap hotels and rooming houses, restaurants, gambling 'joints,' night clubs, brothels, and an assortment of retail stores."[23]

Immigration of Filipino labor to the United States began after the turn of the twentieth century, with most arrivals seeking agricultural work in California. The only East Asians who could come legally after the Immigration Act of 1924 barred all other Asians, their numbers were limited to fifty per year after 1934. As World War II approached, the population of this largely transient male-dominated (87 percent) Filipino community continued to fluctuate with the seasons in response to the shifting need for labor in Alaska canneries or on Japanese-operated truck farms in western Washington. During the winter, immigrants stayed in Seattle, working in hotels or restaurants or as domestic servants. Too small and unstable a community to play a prominent role in shaping the character of the district, it linked to the Philippine Islands' colonial past, one where few of its citizens ever acquired independent business expertise. This resulted in most immigrants becoming consumers rather than shopkeepers.

The absence of women inhibited the growth of the Filipino community, as it did for the Chinese. In the years leading up to the war, only a few Filipinos owned or operated businesses in the district. Exceptions catered primarily to migratory workers, through labor contracting, cafes like the Rizal Club and Manila Cafe, and the Manila dance hall. Until 1941, a small-scale importing firm, the Philippine & Eastern Trading Company, rented space in the nearby Terminal Sales Building.[24]

Most year-round Filipino residents secured employment as hospital orderlies, maintenance workers, hotel cooks, dishwashers, or domestics within the service sector and competed with African American and Japanese workers for this low-paying work.[25]

In 1940, African Americans made up the second largest minority group in Seattle after the Japanese, numbering 3,789. The majority lived in the Madison Street district, a family-oriented residential area that expanded into the Cherry Street area after 1930. A second less stable settlement resided on upper Jackson Street around 12th Avenue. Dubbed the "cross-town" district, it ran across the city's center from the Madison Street district to the waterfront. Demographer Calvin F. Schmid described it as "an area of transition characterized by a high incidence of social and physical deterioration and inhabited mainly by single men."[26] This stretch of dilapidated housing heading eastward up Jackson Street above 12th Avenue also became home to Jewish, Italian, and Irish ethnic groups.[27]

Like the Chinese, African Americans brought their own mystique to the Jackson Street–Chinatown district as Seattleites headed to Chinatown to experience the jazz. Owned or operated by African Americans, most of the clubs there hired African American musicians.

Throughout the Depression years many nightclubs and cabarets in the district opened, closed, re-opened, or changed location. Patrons danced or tapped their feet to combos passing through venues like the Ubangi, a black-owned upstairs cabaret at Seventh Avenue just off Jackson Street. The short-lived 416 Club appeared on Maynard Street adjacent to the Atlas Theater, and the Basin Street Club opened in 1940 in the basement of the Bush Hotel. Others, such as The Big Apple on King Street, The Congo Club on the north side of Jackson Street between Fifth and Sixth avenues, and the Black & Tan cabaret on Jackson Street at 12th Avenue in cross-town, attracted transient African American jazz artists as establishments came and went.[28]

African Americans did not operate all the clubs. Charlie Louie, who owned the Chinese Gardens at Seventh Avenue near King Street, was well known among jazz aficionados. At his place women dressed up and men wore ties.

Japanese businessmen also took in Seattle's jazz scene. Mannosuke Shirai-shi, owner of the Tokiwa Hotel at 655½ Jackson Street, served as president of the Japanese Association of North America/Seattle Japanese Chamber of Commerce in 1940. The building also housed the Tokyo Cafe. Both establishments became favorites of black musicians who, for a few dollars a week, found a comfortable place to lie over.[29]

In addition to finding cheap hotel rooms and inexpensive food, during economic hard times musicians and other minorities could acquire welcome relief from the omnipresent discrimination throughout the larger community; Japantown, Chinatown, Little Manila, and cross-town were all oases of tolerance and acceptance.

With its numbers, inherent stability as a family-oriented society, and entrepreneurial emphasis, the Japanese community's impact on the area became profound. Influential as they came to be in the Jackson Street–Chinatown area, their impact in western Washington in relation to agriculture may have been greater. Japanese farmers tilling parcels of less than forty acres harvested produce they then wholesaled to markets east of the Cascade range and to local venues, including Seattle's Pike Place Market above the waterfront one mile north of *nihonmachi*. In addition, Japanese growers who owned or leased fifty of Seattle's eighty greenhouses provided the majority of the region's bedding plants, flowers, and potted plants.[30]

In 1941, Japanese growers in western Washington marketed produce valued in excess of $3 million ($21.5 million in 2008 dollars). Throughout the growing season nearly 2,300 alien and citizen farmers disked, planted, hoed, and harvested two dozen crops on their more than 9,000 acres. Over half the revenue came from lettuce, peas, celery, and strawberries. One-third of the total yield they shipped out of the area in refrigerated rail cars.[31]

Local white consumers came to rely on Japanese-grown produce brought to the Pike Place Market, which opened in 1907. Trucking their produce from the outlying areas of Bainbridge Island, Bellevue, Bothell, Kent Valley, White River Valley, and Puyallup Valley, Japanese vendors dominated the market. At any given time they occupied 60 to 80 percent of the "wet" stalls, selling lettuce, peas, cauliflower, spinach, celery, beans, corn, carrots, and strawberries, their primary crops. Signs communicating prices in artful *sumi* ink script and vegetables stacked symmetrically became hallmarks of Nikkei vendors, a tradition that survives to the present.

Japanese growers in Pierce County's Puyallup Valley contributed nearly one-third of western Washington's produce, worth over $1 million. And the Japanese controlled 95 percent of the tilled acreage around Puyallup, Sumner, Orting, Buckley, and Eatonville, owning or leasing 2,800 acres on 114 farms. Of the entire Nikkei population residing in Pierce County outside the Tacoma city limits, more than half involved themselves in agriculture.

By 1940, two-thirds of Puyallup Valley's 548 Nikkei farmers were Nisei; here, as in rural areas of western Washington and within Japanese communities throughout the West Coast, the second generation was emerging and beginning to come of age.[32]

However, even as the Nisei were beginning to mature at the turn of the decade, the immigrant generation continued to dominate the Nikkei community organizationally and economically. The Issei, having brought to America the attitudes and values that influenced them in Japan, passed these attributes on to their children. The family institution from which the Nisei emerged was characterized by subordination of the individual to a central authority and to the family as a whole, with the father at the head. Social guidance patterns, based on customary modes of behavior imported from Japan, continued to be reinforced by the Japanese Language School, attended by many Seattle school-aged Nisei after the public school day had ended.

The economic life of Seattle's *nihonmachi* continued to be dominated by the small shops, trades, and professional positions held by the Issei. Even among the hundred or so Nisei-owned businesses in Seattle's Nikkei community, start-up costs for many of these second-generation enterprises were paid by loans or outright gifts from parents.

Politically, the Nisei were slow to gain the necessary skills to exert independence, in part because their parents, barred from the political process and many with a language barrier between them and their maturing children, could provide little guidance. With leadership in the newly organized Japanese American Citizens League lacking political experience and adequate financial resources, the national organization remained relatively ineffective, with local chapters functioning primarily as organizers of social events.

As the Issei continued their hold on the community's economic and cultural institutions, the oldest among them were approaching retirement age, enabling the natural transfer of power to the next generation to begin. Traditional modes of behavior instilled in the Nisei during their upbringing were gradually loosening their hold as they came under competition with Western values emanating from the dominant culture in Seattle.

But on the eve of the war most of the city's Nisei remained socially isolated from the larger community outside Japantown. While retaining partial obedience to the traditional Japanese culture of their parents, they were also making their way in a world of Western traditions marked by individualism that they learned in the public schools and Christian churches to which they were drawn.[33]

In the 1940 national census, the Nisei accounted for 64 percent of the total Japanese population living in the four western states of the United States. Washington State contained 61 percent, up from the 50 percent recorded in 1930, with three-fourths of its Nisei nineteen years or younger and the vast majority of public school age, far too young to assume leadership roles in their communities.[34]

However, over 2,200 individuals, one-quarter of Washington Nisei, were now in their 20s and employed or attending colleges and universities. The oldest Nisei, children of immigrants who had arrived at the turn of the century, had reached 40 years of age with 1,100 over age 25.

Thus, by 1940, Seattle Nisei owned or operated 100 businesses, a few of them in the professions.[35] Attorneys Clarence Arai (age 41), Thomas Masuda (37), Kenji Ito (33), and Bill Mimbu (30) practiced in the district where optometrist Duncan Tsuneishi (32) had opened his office. Architect Allen Kichio Arai (41) designed the new Buddhist temple on Main Street, and Julius Fujihira (23), recently graduated from the University of Washington, took over his father's electrical contracting business. On Third Avenue, Lincoln Beppu (30) ran the family's Togo Fishing Tackle Store, and on Jackson Street George Kashiwagi (34) managed his family's men's furnishing and tailor shop. Nearby, Dick Setsuda (33), owner of Pacific Beer Distributors, promoted his beer, wine, and soft drink business: "Exclusive Oriental Distributors."[36]

Before the onset of the war, West Coast Printing, the *Japanese American Courier,* and Jackson Florists were three additional Nisei businesses in Seattle's Japantown. Other smaller Nisei businesses also enjoyed a presence in the district: Tokyo Cafe, Jackson Ice Creamery, numerous grocery stores, barbershops, beauty shops, and myriad storefront establishments.

In the coming decade, Seattle's Nisei would have in the natural course of events assumed leadership of the Japanese community reaching maturity just as the majority of Issei began to retire. The community valued education. In the twelve years before World War II, twenty-seven U.S.-born Japanese valedictorians or salutatorians distinguished themselves at Seattle's nine high schools, while the University of Washington graduated twenty-four Japanese Americans elected to the scholastic honorary society, Phi Beta Kappa. May 1942 found four more elected to Phi Beta Kappa and an additional twelve listed on other university honor societies. These honorees would receive notification of their awards while incarcerated behind barbed wire fences and guarded by soldiers with machine guns.[37]

But a good education provided no guarantee of Nisei employment during or after the Depression years because employment discrimination ruled the larger community. Often college graduates had to settle for work in family-owned businesses, impacting the education many would pursue. While degrees in law, medicine, accounting, or other professional careers assured employment within a Japanese community, some parents encouraged their sons to choose engineering. While chances of employment in the United States remained slim, they still believed a position in Japan could be found.

Knowing this, as a freshman at the University of Washington in 1933 Bill Hosokawa became an engineering student. Unable to handle the rigorous mathematics requirements, however, he switched to journalism. An instance from his junior year illustrates the pervasive discrimination Japanese Americans experienced outside their ethnic community. During Christmas and spring breaks Hosokawa's journalism classmates divided into teams assigned to work with professional newspaper staffs throughout the state. The twenty-one-year old Hosokawa could not participate; his professor told him, "We don't think the publishers would welcome having you there," and went on to discourage Hosokawa from continuing his studies.

Shortly after switching to a journalism major, Hosokawa made his way to the *Japanese American Courier* office, the first completely English-language newspaper in the United States devoted to Nikkei interests, and asked editor James Y. Sakamoto for a job. Sakamoto badly needed help but could offer no salary. By helping several times a week Hosokawa developed journalistic skills. He left the *Courier* in his junior year to work full-time at the *University of Washington Daily.*

In less than a decade, as the United States entered the Pacific War against Japan, Hosokawa's early bond formed with Sakamoto would serve to reunite them even though Hosokawa had been absent from the community for nearly four years working as a journalist in Asia.[38]

By the time Hosokawa arrived at the editor's office, Sakamoto, an influential leader of the Nisei in Seattle, had performed a guiding role in helping to establish the younger generation's independence and authority. Known as "Jimmie," at thirty-nine James Y. Sakamoto had distinguished himself within and without the Japanese community, and few perceived him with indifference.[39] Opinionated, and having dabbled in formal education after high school, Sakamoto had created widespread local political, and professional connections throughout the city. Believing patriotism and ethnic cohesion provided keys to counteract longstanding racial hostility toward the Nikkei, Sakamoto considered himself a voice for the Nisei and principal liaison between the Japanese and white communities.

Sakamoto was born in Seattle in 1903 and grew up in Rainier Valley. He attended Franklin High School in the early 1920s, lettering in football and baseball. Eager to prove himself, the hot-tempered teenager aggressively tangled with students from other schools, including Franklin's rival, Broadway High. After a Japanese newspaper described his son as a "young gang ruffian," Jimmie's father sent him east to live with the boy's older sister. While in New Jersey, Jimmie spent two uninspired years attending classes at Princeton. However, as an English editor of New York's *Japanese American News* he discovered journalism as a possible career.

During this juncture Sakamoto took up prize fighting, preferring it to judo. His athleticism led him to the professional ranks where, as a 120–pound pugilist, he took on bantamweight, featherweight, and junior lightweight contestants. In the meantime he married, and his wife gave birth to a daughter. His fortune changed when, in December 1927, undefended blows in the ring against a heavier opponent caused detached retinas in both eyes. His wife died soon after; by age twenty-five, Sakamoto, a widower, was going blind.

This led to Jimmie returning to Seattle while his daughter remained in the East to be raised by her maternal grandparents. Following his arrival Sakamoto found Seattle's sports-minded Nisei youth in disarray over an ongoing rivalry between two popular baseball teams. In the 1920s, sports provided a crucial social outlet for the younger generation; Jimmie interpreted this festering situation as a lack of Nisei leadership and guidance. Older, more mature than most other Nisei, and with experience in sports, Sakamoto felt himself qualified in assuming this leadership role.

Envisioning an all-English-language newspaper as a vehicle for the second generation's voice, he set about to guide them toward this end. Jimmie's father, who worked as a hotel operator, advanced start-up funds for the *Japanese American Courier,* first published on January 1, 1928. This from Sakamoto's first editorial: "The time has . . . arrived when the American born Japanese must take his rightful place in the life of the community and discharge his obligations and duties that were inherited by him as a natural born American citizen."[40]

From this forum Sakamoto called for a citizen league to unify and stimulate greater political action among voting-age Nisei as a group. He pushed for resurrecting the Seattle Progressive Citizens League, an earlier group organized in 1921 with the assistance of Issei to counter anti-Japanese legislation. This rebirth became a reality early in 1928 as the League reorganized with attorney Clarence Arai serving as president and George Ishihara as vice president.[41]

Two years later, several regional organizations, including the new Seattle group, set up a loose federation in the Pacific coast states with Arai as national president. Meeting in Seattle, they formed the Japanese American Citizens League (JACL), and from 1936 to 1938 Sakamoto served as the League's second elected president.[42]

Through the *Courier* Sakamoto espoused his conservative political and social beliefs. International and national news, trade, and later, foreign military action filled its front pages. From the editorial page he urged good citizenship and loyalty to America. Most Nisei, still in high school and too young to care about front-page concerns, turned to the sports page. Sakamoto's newspaper sponsored the year-round sports leagues that evolved into Courier Leagues and promoted his philosophy of personal Americanism.

Sakamoto believed that though they were loyal American citizens, Nisei should recognize Japan as the source of their cultural heritage. Therefore, they should be acquainted with it, and the *Courier* devoted extensive coverage to Japanese culture. Straddling both cultures, as one of the oldest Nisei in the community Sakamoto embodied a strict moral code and conveyed respect for the emperor and his ancestors. This may have informed his tenacity in teaching patriotism to the Nisei as well as his fervent promotion of consensus over individuality.

Sakamoto was an apologist for Japanese aggression in Asia. For a decade he defended Japan's position as a small island nation with few resources located in a region dominated for centuries by the West. He believed one should trust the government. His views appealed to many: conservative Nisei professionals, college students still forming their ideas, white scholars familiar with the Japanese in America, and politicians and elected officials he knew outside the Japanese community. Sakamoto asserted that racial hostility could be reduced through loyalty, hard work, acquiescence, and retention of strong cultural ties to the Japanese community. He opposed workers organizing to gain higher wages and improved working conditions because it would inevitably upset existing relations between Japanese and Caucasian workers. Prudent, he advised waiting for a natural evolution and cautioned workers to be grateful during the hard economic times at hand and not draw attention to themselves as the international situation worsened.

* * *

On the eve of the country's war with Japan, Germany, and Italy, Seattle's Nikkei community, not yet fifty years old, had come into its own. It had long since passed through a frontier period where working men hoped to find their fortune in America and return to Japan and into a "settling period" following the relative prosperity provided by World War I. The business community expanded; families evolved. The district with its cacophony of ethnicity and atmosphere of tolerance provided goods and services to the immediate community as well as to patrons throughout the city who found it exotic. Japanese farmers supplied a significant source of the produce for local and regional markets as the community matured to where its second generation began to flex its muscle in the Nikkei workplace.

And the new generation had a leader in Jimmie Sakamoto. But the war would nearly destroy this community and many of its institutions. Japantown as it existed in 1941 would never regain its former status in the Jackson Street–Chinatown district. Issei leadership dissolved, forcing fledgling Nisei to fill the vacuum.

2

War Comes to Japantown

On Sunday December 7, 1941, at 7:55 a.m., 40 torpedo bombers, 1,750–pound torpedoes strapped to the belly of each plane, dropped out of Honolulu's clear blue sky to initiate sea-level runs on warships moored at Ford Island's Battleship Row in Pearl Harbor. At 7:58 a.m., a navy radioman transmitted a frantic message in plain English "AIR RAID, PEARL HARBOR, THIS IS NO DRILL." Moments later, 100 high-level bombers and dive bombers followed suit with accurate payloads, as 45 Zero fighters bore down on air fields to cripple any airborne response. An hour later, a second wave of 170 bombers and fighters delivered ordnance to finish the devastation.

By 10:00 a.m. the attack ended, leaving 2,403 Americans dead, 1,178 wounded, 165 planes destroyed, and 18 vessels sunk or heavily damaged. Five battleships lay on the harbor's shallow bottom, including the *Arizona*, whose 1,100 sailors remain entombed. The ship burned for 2 days.[1]

Two time zones away, Seattle residents wiped sleep from their eyes, finished the morning headlines, and enjoyed unseasonable temperatures expected to reach into the fifties. The headline, "F.R. Sends Hirohito Note," revealed President Franklin D. Roosevelt's eleventh-hour attempt to avert war in the Pacific, reminder of a distant world in turmoil, far away from this pleasant sun-filled morning.[2]

In Japantown, twenty-eight-year-old Mark Sese looked forward to announcing his wedding engagement to family and friends at a Chinese restaurant. Bill Hosokawa raked leaves at his father's house, while Shosuke Sasaki and other Issei friends converged on the golf links at Jefferson Park above Japantown.[3] Having finished church services, Sharon Tanagi and two girlfriends headed uptown for a matinee.[4] And as usual, Jim Akutsu could be found playing ice hockey with his Caucasian buddies at a nearby arena.[5]

Around noon sketchy details begin to come over Seattle airwaves as radio announcers interrupted regular programming to report a sneak attack at a location in the Pacific unfamiliar to most listeners on the mainland. As Tanagi recalled fifty-three years later, the three moviegoers learned of the attack when an announcement appeared on the screen: "'We are at war; Japan attacked Pearl Harbor.' It really startled me. Talk about an adrenaline rush. The lights went on and we just felt everyone was staring at us. Whether they were or not, we became very uncomfortable and we all split for home."[6]

Hosokawa, who had recently returned to Seattle from Asia where he had worked as a journalist, received a phone call from his friend Jack Maki; together they wondered what would be ahead for Japanese Americans and their immigrant elders.[7] When golfer Sasaki returned home, his frantic mother blurted out the news.

Hearing the announcement at the ice rink, friends of Akutsu who had enlisted in the National Guard after high school skated over to him and said, "Okay, we'll take care of the Japs, you take care of the girls." Akutsu, an accomplished athlete, had been refused entry into the Guard for having flat feet, and even after half a century remembered this moment with bitterness.[8]

Earlier in the month Shigeto Ishikawa and his fellow thespians put on a stage show at the Nippon-Kan Hall; they then took it on the road to Portland. As they prepared the stage set the news intruded; after immediately striking the set, they headed for home: "On the way home, some of the people brought their cars down and took their family home. We went on a bus. At Chehalis they were so excited they stopped us there and we had to stay in jail overnight." After their release the next morning, they hurried north without incident.[9]

Weeks passed before the devastating details of Pearl Harbor became public. Yet before the end of December 7, Japan had formally declared war on the United States. With a single dissenting vote Congress responded in kind the next day. But the conflict had landed on Seattle Japantown's doorstep before war could be declared.

Late in the afternoon of December 7, FBI agents moved through the community assisted by Seattle police officers confiscating cameras, shortwave radios, firearms, personal papers, and other belongings. They collared then hauled Issei men to the immigration station on Airport Way not far from Japantown. Earlier, Attorney General Francis Biddle verbally issued a blanket warrant authorizing arrest of any enemy alien who might pose a national security risk or whose name appeared on a so-called ABC list. FBI director J. Edgar Hoover then teletyped instructions to the heads of his fifty-six field offices throughout the United States and its territories: "Immediately take into custody all Japanese who have been classified in A, B, and C categories in material previously transmitted to you . . . Persons taken into custody should be turned over to nearest representative of Immigration and Naturalization Service [INS]."[10]

The next day President Roosevelt established authority for Biddle's blanket warrants when he signed a proclamation declaring "an invasion has been perpetuated upon the territory of the United States by the Empire of Japan," and all resident Japanese nationals over the age of fourteen in the United States and its possessions are "liable to restraint or to give security, or to remove and depart from the United States." This proclamation, based on existing U.S. statutes, finalized Roosevelt's iron grip over all resident Japanese nationals age fourteen and older.[11]

Since their identities and affiliations were already known these could not be construed as random arrests. Furthermore, FBI agents possessed 3 x 5 cards containing data on each apprehended individual. As early as September 1940 intelligence groups produced a three-tiered classification of proscribed Japanese organizations. The degree an organization was believed to be under direct control of the Japanese government determined its assignment to a category of A, B, or C. Over the course of the next sixteen months, as their perceived threat to the nation became evident, other individual organizations joined this list. Membership in one or more of these groups was deemed dangerous and construed as guilt by association. Concurrently, the FBI quietly built dossiers on individual Japanese nationals, establishing more than two thousand personal files by 1941.[12] The so-called ABC list encompassed groups and individuals perceived by intelligence groups as dangerous and who required intense scrutiny, "potentially dangerous" people who had not yet been thoroughly investigated, and individuals suspected of pro-Japan views. Included on the list were Shinto and Buddhist priests, farmers, produce distributors, influential businessmen, fishermen with knowledge of coastal waters, Japanese-language teachers, martial arts instructors, Japanese-language newspaper editors, community servants, and even travel agents. Over time, tips provided by members of the Nikkei community or other intelligence sources helped agents add new names to the list.[13]

Early arrests focused on individuals affiliated with organizations having close political and cultural ties to Japan. When the FBI shut down the Japanese Consulate in Seattle's downtown Central Building, it confiscated intact many diplomatic papers. Consul Yuki Sato, protected by diplomatic immunity, had been confined under police guard to his home in an affluent Queen Anne Hill neighborhood. On December 30 he departed with his family to be detained with other Japanese consular officials at a luxurious hotel in West Virginia leased by the State Department until their eventual repatriation in June 1942.

The Japanese Language School on Weller Street abruptly shut its doors. On Monday, December 8, while attending classes in public schools eight hundred Japanese American students learned that classes at the language school would not be held that afternoon. Yoriaki Nakagawa, the school's principal for fifteen years, was arrested at his home on December 7. Kichiyo, his wife and a teacher at the school, and fifteen affiliated teachers were spared.[14]

Two proscribed organizations, the Seattle Japanese Association of North America and the Japanese Chamber of Commerce sharing office space on Maynard Street were shut down. Later, FBI agents scoured confiscated records to assist in arresting other Japanese in the community.

After the Issei editors of Seattle's two Japanese-language newspapers, *Great Northern Daily News* and *North American Times,* were arrested, their presses fell silent for the duration of the war. This left the Nisei-owned and -edited *Japanese American Courier* as the Nikkei community's sole voice.

Arrests continued for days, and in the end arrest patterns revealed few if any distinctions between those on the A, B, and C lists.

On December 7 agents came for Heiji (Henry) Okuda at his home. Held in high esteem in the Nikkei community as a business and community leader, as an early arrival to Seattle he helped provide immigrant Japanese labor to railroad companies through his Oriental Trading Company. Later he operated a fishing tackle business as well as the Oriental Express Company, which hauled merchandise for trading companies doing business on the waterfront. Okuda's visibility led to his holding leadership positions within the community, including the *kendo* society, whose reputation extended from Vancouver, British Columbia, to San Diego. People sought his advice on marital match making, and frequently escorted visiting delegations from Japan. Fully aware of Okuda's status, the FBI wasted little time arresting this "A" list subject.[15]

Iwao Matsushita, another community leader and an intellectual fluent in English, was also a teacher and artist. In Japan he taught English grammar to high school students and arrived in Seattle in 1919 hoping to perfect his English-language skills and study Western literature. Once he had acquired sufficient intellectual resources to share with his students in his homeland he planned to return to Japan. However, the University of Washington refused

Matsushita entry because he had overestimated his English-language skills. He subsequently sought employment to support himself and his wife, Hanaye. In time he was hired on by Mitsui and Company, a major Tokyo-based trading firm delighted to employ a college-educated immigrant. Eventually Matsushita found his way to the University of Washington, as a teacher not a student. In 1927, he introduced the first Japanese-language course into the curriculum. Matsushita's pursuits included photography and writing haiku. His varied connections and high visibility would bring the FBI to his door on the evening of December 7.[16]

Although Issei men possessing high profiles within the community may have feared for their freedom, not all aroused sufficient suspicion leading to their arrest. Kameki Inouye, a fifty-six-year-old clothier who arrived in the Pacific Northwest in 1910 to work in sawmills in rural western Washington, experienced a previous injury that ended his ability to undertake heavy work. After he and his wife, Toku, arrived in Seattle, both immigrants from Kochi prefecture, she worked as a vendor at the Pike Place Market, while Kameki, having learned to use a needle and sewing machine, bought up men's used clothes to re-tailor for cost-conscious customers. In time he purchased new clothes, and the couple opened a men's furnishing store on Sixth Avenue south, just north of Yesler Way. Following the attack on Pearl Harbor, the FBI visited Komeki's work site and home on Lane Street. In the absence of any incriminating evidence against him, he remained free. Komeki, Toku, and three of their four children stayed together throughout most of the war.[17]

Other Issei, certain they were on arrest lists, packed overnight bags with toiletries and a change of clothes. Koi Tanagi, owner of Tanagi Grocery Store on Jackson Street, had been a soldier during the Russo-Japanese War and later contributed money to a veterans group known as the *Hinumana-kai*. He felt this doomed him, but he was spared until his arrest the following February when a second roundup of enemy aliens took place.[18] Seizo Itoi's wife prepared her husband's suitcase, but either the details of his past associations never surfaced or were not of interest to the FBI because the knock on the his door never came.[19]

By the evening of December 9, 116 Seattle resident Japanese nationals had been placed behind bars at the INS immigration station; by the twenty-fourth, 13 more joined them.[20] Arrests of Japanese nationals occurred up and down the West Coast. By December 13, they numbered 353 in Los Angeles and San Diego, 102 in San Francisco. By mid-February 1942, the number had escalated to 2,311 and by November, to 5,334.[21]

Not only the immigrant generation would come under arrest. Mark Sese proceeded with the plan to announce his engagement at the Chinese restaurant; the evening's event became subdued with long faces and poor appetites, and the party broke up early. Shigeko Uno, in attendance at the party, recalled what happened next: "When we were coming down the stairs from the upstairs restaurant the FBI were at the door. They had already taken in Mr. Takahashi. His company sold scrap iron to Japan. That was the reason for picking him up and one of his workers, Ed Ozawa. They had been eating upstairs. They had gone down the stairs just before we went down, and the FBI took them."[22]

Business partners Takahashi and Ozawa would be arraigned by a federal grand jury for conspiring to export war materiels to Japan in violation of the Trading with the Enemies Act. At issue were two dismantled steel storage tanks believed to have been falsely declared, then shipped to China. First taken to the immigration station, the pair then joined the Issei detainees who arrived in increasing numbers. Neither of them able to post the required $25,000 bond, the next day the two men were transferred to the King County jail, there to wait out their subsequent trials the following spring.[23]

Arrested around the same time in other parts of Japantown, Nisei attorneys Thomas Masuda and Kenji Ito were charged with acting as agents of Japan. Like Takahashi and Ozawa, neither of them could post bond, and no Issei came to the rescue because their own bank accounts had been frozen. Like most other Nisei, they could not muster a $25,000 bond and therefore headed under guard to the King County jail.

Ito's and Masuda's cases demonstrate the government's fervor in prosecuting cases against Japanese Americans. Handed down in late January 1942, the grand jury indictment cited twenty-five events against Ito, twelve against Masuda.

Ito, then thirty-one and a prominent figure in Seattle's Nikkei community before the war, had graduated from the University of Washington Law School in 1935. A skilled debater, following his admission to the Washington state bar in 1936 he and a law school classmate took part in an eleven-month world debate tour sponsored by their alma mater, visiting China and Japan from December 1936 to April 1937. Upon returning to Seattle, Ito frequently debated and lectured throughout the state on Sino-Japanese relations. Since locating debaters on the side of China was easy, he often took Japan's position, focusing his debates and speeches on international issues relating to tariffs and commercial relations with Japan as well as conditions within the two countries. This activity led to Ito's arrest and indictment for acting illegally as an agent of Japan and possessing documents (copies of his speeches) in violation of the U.S. penal code.[24]

Charged with acting as an agent of Japan without first notifying the State Department, counts against Masuda included filing reports with the Japanese consulate in Seattle relating to public reaction to phases of the Sino-Japanese War. Both Ito and Masuda were eventually acquitted.[25]

The physical elimination of Issei leaders from the scene further crippled Seattle's Nikkei community in the days and weeks after Pearl Harbor, already reeling from the freezing of Issei assets and closure of U.S. branches of Japanese banks by the Treasury Department. This coincided with suspension of activity in all Issei-owned businesses. The barring of U.S. citizens from carrying out financial transactions with Japanese nationals slowed down dispersal of produce on the West Coast.

Having earned a college degree in social work in 1934, Nobuko Suzuki had experience working for the Welfare Department during Seattle's prewar years. With people in the Nikkei community losing their jobs or having no access to their savings and in need of immediate help, Suzuki sought out agencies that might provide temporary relief. She recalls: "It was through the Community Chest and the Family Society that we would have to have some help. I did get there and visited several families who did need help and some provision. The majority should have been through the Japanese Chamber of Commerce who took care of things like that. But all they did was give rice and soy sauce. Well, that was helpful, too, but money was another thing they needed to get the rest of their groceries. In that way I was able to help get provisions to some of the families that needed them the most."[26]

Recognizing the growing financial problems in the Nikkei community, the government soon lifted the economic ban and allowed Japanese growers who produced, marketed, and distributed agricultural products to resume operations.[27] Concomitantly, authorization of bank withdrawals equaling $100 per month enabled families to cover their day-to-day expenses. Restrictions were lifted on financial transactions by Japanese nationals who had lived continuously in the United States since June 1940. Withdrawal limits increased to $1,000 per month. This financial blockade, however brief, brought misery to those directly affected by it.[28]

Problems impacting daily life extended to the second generation, for in the confusion Nisei bank accounts were also being frozen. Their Japanese names and faces often prevented them from using public transportation; ticket clerks for rail, bus, and ferry lines scrutinized Nisei, and for at least two weeks denied many of them passage. The Black Ball Line, offering ferry service across Puget Sound to Bainbridge Island and Bremerton, refused passage to both generations until ferry executives issued orders permitting crossings to those Nisei able to document their U.S. citizenship. Distinctions between the two generations and their everyday problems blurred until they could be sorted out over time.[29]

For White River Dairy operators Treasury Department restrictions proved to be an annoyance. When the corporation began, the oldest Sese daughter, a Japanese national, oversaw day-to-day operations. Therefore, the FBI, ignorant of the legal structure informing the family corporation, seized the dairy's financial records then shut down the business. The problem was exacerbated by their attorney, Thomas Masuda, being in jail and unable to assist. Once documents could be produced to clarify the firm's status as a family corporation rather than one operated by an Issei, their records were returned, and the business continued to function until incarceration began the following spring.[30]

Uptown at the Pike Place Market Japanese vendors felt the war's impact soon after Pearl Harbor. Following an established policy, the Market issued licenses only to U.S. citizens. Since most Nikkei vendors were Issei, valid business permits appeared in their children's names. This caused a problem for Joe Desimone, who had recently purchased the main arcades of the Pike Place Market, declaring on December 9: "I am going to the Federal Bureau of Investigation today. If they tell me to fire the Japs I have working for me I'll fire them all, not only the ones in the stalls, but the ones in the wholesale houses and on the farms, too."[31]

Desimone never carried out his threat; his vendors' licenses were legal. Even so, problems at the Market escalated for the Japanese. A week after the attack in Hawaii, a fire at the nearby Sanitary Market caused extensive damage to the building and seriously disrupted businesses inside. Although its origin remained undetermined, rumors of arson spread as fingers pointed toward Japan's perceived sympathizers. The mood among Caucasian vendors turned ugly as anti-Japanese sentiment spread. Japanese vendors sported "I am an American" pins to no avail, and as Caucasian clientele fell away sales plummeted. Insurance companies ranked Japanese drivers in high-risk categories before canceling their policies. As a result, some farmers chose to stay home rather than hazard a highway accident. Others would drive stealthily into the Market in uninsured trucks.[32]

After the Japanese merchants departed, market managers claimed business activity increased at the new "All American Farmers' Row" because Caucasian patrons preferred buying from Caucasian vendors, a ruse that equated to pure face saving.[33] From 1939 to 1943 vendors' licenses issued by the Pike Place Market dropped in numbers from 515 to 196. But as the war intensified and the ranks of servicemen increased, demand for food supplies mushroomed. Army contracts for wholesale produce began competing with the Market for share: prices rose while variety diminished. Wholesalers sold all they had produced. It followed that Japanese farmers who would eventually be evacuated did not share the region's new agricultural prosperity. Unrealized profits aside, soon they would worry whether or not to plant next season's crops.[34]

Early arrests received publicity that demonstrated a government in charge. Seattle's press urged its citizens to behave with restraint, reminding readers most Nikkei living in the city were American-born and possessed an attendant loyalty. The *Seattle Post-Intelligencer* editors asserted: "This country needs all its true friends. And loyalty is not to be determined by the slant of an eyelid or the color of the skin."[35]

Political leaders joined in. Seattle Mayor Earl Milliken urged tolerance toward American-born and –educated Japanese whom "we don't want to cut . . . adrift from us in this crisis."[36] Representative John M. Coffee (D-Wash.), a longtime opponent to appeasement of Japanese military aggression and advocate of an embargo on war materiel to Japan, called attention to the plight of residents of Japanese ancestry and said from the floor of the House of Representatives: "It is my fervent hope and prayer that residents of the United States of Japanese extraction will not be made the victims of pogroms directed by self-proclaimed patriots and by hysterical self-anointed heroes . . . Let us not make a mockery of the Bill of Rights by mistreating these folks. Let us rather regard them with understanding, remembering they are the victims of a Japanese war machine, with the making of the international policies of which they had nothing to do."[37]

These assurances may have brought calm to Japantown temporarily, but were offset by the community's fear and confusion stemming from 10 percent of Seattle's Issei being behind bars at the immigration station. They were the majority of the intelligentsia and financial leaders, and served as the community's moral conscience. Those who remained free possessed minimal leadership capacity and, in all likelihood, felt reluctant to risk visibility for fear of their own arrests. This left a community without a strong or experienced voice to guide it and therefore unable to function normally. In the wake of these arrests the inevitable vacuum sucked vitality from the community.

Out of necessity, Nisei without experience as leaders and unaccustomed to looking after their elders tried to fill the void. Writing in the January 1, 1942 issue of the *Japanese American Courier*, S. Frank Miyamoto articulated the problem: "Heretofore, the Nisei have been dependent on more or less degree upon the Issei for economic as well as moral leadership. The sweeping restrictions placed upon the economic functions of the Issei, however, have produced a considerable reversal of position."[38]

Clarence Arai, "mayor of Main Street" and 1941 president-elect of the local chapter of the Japanese American Citizens League (JACL), tentatively mobilized a community response to this national emergency. However, un-folding events may have rendered him ineffectual. In this time of community paralysis Jimmie Sakamoto responded with a "Geez, we gotta do something" attitude as he began to organize.

Because his disability tethered him to his desk at the *Courier* office on Main Street, also serving as JACL headquarters, people came to Sakamoto. Many of the Nisei who arrived at his door already were in the workplace as business owners or managers, and many belonged to the JACL. Others, according to Bill Hosokawa, were "guys that would come in several times a week to shoot the breeze with Jimmie."[39] Those called on to mobilize a community response numbered among Sakamoto's friends and close associates—people he knew personally. This nucleus formed the Emergency Defense Council (EDC), organized on December 12 "to express our loyalty by deeds not words." Later this cadre provided the core of "Evacuee Administration Headquarters" at the Puyallup Assembly Center.

Sakamoto called together an initial group of Nisei to develop plans for what would become the EDC effectively under the local chapter of the JACL, similar to defense committees being set up simultaneously in Los Angeles

Jimmie Sakamoto (with sunglasses) at JACL headquarters on April 23, 1942, with members of the Emergency Defense Council. Left to right: William Mimbu, Richard Setsuda, George Ishihara, Tom Kanno, Sakamoto, Lieutenant Colonel Paul B. Malone, Bill Hosokawa. (*Seattle Post-Intelligencer*)

and San Francisco. It sought to cooperate with federal and civic defense agencies. Few doubted Jimmie should head up the group or have others take their marching orders from him. No other Nisei had secured similar visibility in the community; Sakamoto possessed the necessary political energy and contacts inside and outside Japantown to make it happen.[40]

However, other Nisei within the Seattle community holding a semblance of leadership qualifications demonstrated their capability. Attorneys Thomas Masuda and Kenji Ito may have been as qualified as Clarence Arai or more so, but under federal indictment both remained behind bars.

On December 12, after first talking informally with other Nisei and finding no challenge to his leadership, Sakamoto called for an organizational meeting at the *Courier* office. Local area JACL members attended; out of school and working, eventually they assumed positions of responsibility within the EDC. At this first meeting committees were roughed out and leadership roles assigned, but no vote cast. General Chairman Sakamoto, age 39, headed the group. Nisei attorney Clarence Arai, age 41, led the "special committee" to work directly with the FBI, while his wife Yone, age 36, took charge of Red Cross work. Takeo Nogaki, age 33, chaired the welfare committee to aid families falling victim to Treasury Department edicts or hard hit by the breadwinner's loss of a job. Ichiro Motosaka guided a campaign to sell war bonds and stamps.

Forty-two year-old George Ishihara presided over the civilian defense committee, which organized of auxiliary police and firemen, air raid wardens, medical services, and transport and evacuation plans.[41]

Toshio Hoshide, jeweler and 1941 president of the Seattle Progressive Citizens' League, served as the fiscal agent until replaced in mid-January by thirty-three-year-old beer distributor Richard Setsuda. Julius Fujihira, personnel chief of the EDC, organized a drive to register every man, woman, and child in the Seattle Nikkei community to assist in locating them later on. At age twenty-three, Fujihira, younger than most of his EDC peers, but with a baccalaureate degree, worked as an electrician and owned the Japanese-American Electric Company next door to JACL headquarters. Fujihira proved that youth and inexperience among Nisei volunteers did not prevent them from serving in leadership roles in the EDC.

Bill Hosokawa, a twenty-seven-year-old unemployed journalist living with his parents, attended the initial meeting. Sakamoto recalled this former student journalist as an unpaid "intern" at the *Courier*. He welcomed Hosokawa to the inner circle despite his four-year absence from the community and lapsed JACL membership. Based upon their prior association and his full-time availability, Sakamoto appointed Hosokawa "executive secretary" of the new EDC, a position created to handle publicity of the Council's work. He would interact with the Nikkei and Seattle communities at large on Sakamoto's behalf and work with the welfare committee to help Nikkei in need, especially those Issei hardest hit by federal government restrictions after war had been declared. With businesses closed, bank withdrawals limited to $100 per family, and physical mobility restricted to five miles from one's home, some families were unable to pay rent or travel to work. Hosokawa and other EDC members helped them answer the question asked every day: "What can I do?"[42]

On December 15 two committee heads, EDC chairman Sakamoto and spokesman Hosokawa, visited Mayor Earl Millikin's office to lay out the group's plans. During their thirty-minute meeting the mayor commented: "I know just where you Japanese Americans stand, and I'm back of you 100 percent."[43] He assured them everything within his power would be done to prevent unfair discrimination against Seattle's small Japanese business enterprises.

The next evening when three hundred enthusiastic Nisei met at the Maryknoll school, two hundred more volunteers registered for committee work, most signing on with the Red Cross committee seeking to collect its share of Seattle/King County's goal of $300,000.[44]

An Americanism Rally to be held on December 22 at the newly dedicated Buddhist temple would be EDC's first large-scale event. The meeting, organized with a dual aim to pledge the community's loyalty to the country and seek more volunteers for the EDC committees, the nearly 1,500 Issei and Nisei attendees overflowed into an adjacent gymnasium. After hearing a resolution written by the EDC pledging to fight the old country and maintain allegiance to the United States, attendees passed it by acclamation: "Resolved that we Americans of Japanese ancestry and the members of our parent generation here assembled affirm our allegiance and loyalty to the United States of America and pledge our efforts toward a victorious prosecution of the war by extending unstinting cooperation to the President of the United States and the duly constituted agencies."[45] This resolution spelled out areas of cooperation, including volunteering for military service, eradicating subversive activities, participating in the civil defense and Red Cross programs, and purchasing national defense bonds and stamps.[46]

Over the next several days, volunteers throughout the community collected over 1,300 additional signatures to the loyalty document. On Christmas morning the Council forwarded the resolution to President Roosevelt with an attached cover letter signed by Sakamoto.[47]

Mayor Millikin, meeting with EDC representatives earlier in the week, proudly noted the absence of violence by whites toward Japanese in Seattle. But he warned that if the war continued indefinitely, the United States could "find its tolerance growing thin and continued good relations may depend not only upon your loyalty, but your discretion."[48] Millikin's own patience soon ran out as subsequent remarks made during a late February congressional hearing in Seattle would bear out.

At the rally Sakamoto's statements may have alarmed community members with sights on the future, for he insisted the Nikkei community must repudiate any member exhibiting disloyal behavior toward the United States: "We have organized an intelligence service of our own. Its members are not known even to me. But we intend to protect the country and ourselves by reporting any un-American activity to the proper authorities."[49]

"Proper authorities" translated to the FBI and implied spying on the Issei generation. In other West Coast cities, including Los Angeles, JACL leaders called for similar counterespionage efforts within their Nikkei communities.[50] Recently declassified archival FBI documents reveal that cooperation with the FBI by chairman Clarence Arai as well as others predated the bombing of Pearl Harbor. Both FBI and Office of Naval Intelligence (ONI) records suggest recruiting Nisei informants to spy on their elders began as early as 1939. FBI director J. Edgar Hoover, trusting Nisei loyalty, enlisted a few voluntary informants to report on suspicious Issei activities. ONI credited the JACL informants' perspicacity in pinpointing nearly every agent with a capacity for mischief.[51]

Sakamoto, members of the intelligence committee—"not known even to me"—and other informants remained unaware their efforts had harmed innocent people like Iwao Matsushita. Information about him passed on by three informers contained a kernel of truth but, overall, misinformed FBI agents. This contributed to a two-year internment living apart from his ailing wife.[52] Such rumor, innuendo, hearsay, or information leaked in spite likely led to similar consequences for others.

In the meantime, Seattle's Japanese American community banded together to work. From EDC's onset until the end of January 1942 after West Coast politicians and other public figures had called for the removal of Nikkei from the region, Japantown residents contributed $7,300 to a "Buy a Boeing Bomber" campaign, donated over $1,300 to local Red Cross headquarters, and purchased unspecified amounts of defense bonds and stamps. Working at home, women sewed and knitted garments for the Red Cross and wrapped surgical dressings that were turned over to Fort Lewis and Fort Lawton. Each wrap and stitch demonstrated the community's loyalty to America even as the nation turned increasingly hostile toward them.

While the political community generally lauded Nikkei efforts, ones acknowledged in newspapers, Seattle's citizenry continued to withhold widespread support. Nikkei business activity dropped precipitously during a period when the EDC registered names of 150 newly unemployed workers. By late January, the conflicted reaction to the community had turned irrevocably negative.

At the end of January 1942, Seattle began voicing its opinion on both sides in regard to the Nikkei, most of it appearing in the *Seattle Post-Intelligencer*. This occurred after a California representative suggested the removal of all Nikkei from the West Coast following release of a commission report revealing the causes of the Pearl Harbor disaster. From December 7, 1941, through January 18, 1942, the *Seattle Post-Intelligencer* published four letters to the editor on the subject of Seattle's Japanese community, followed by a three-week period beginning January 19 in which fifteen letters appeared written under the Voice of the People banner. Beyond that, when removal to the Puyallup Assembly Center got underway, through the end of April 1942 the editor published forty-six additional letters.

On January 21, 1942, Congressman Leland M. Ford (R-Calif.), citing the "seriousness of the Japanese situation on the West Coast," publicly advocated removal of all Japanese, American-born and alien, to concentration camps. He argued native-born Japanese might be no more loyal than the foreign-born. The Associated Press story became front-page news in the *Seattle Times*; its bold banner read: "Seize all West Coast Japs, Solon Demands."[53] Employing illogical thinking in defense of his position, Ford acknowledged many loyal Japanese currently serving in the armed forces would willingly sacrifice their lives in the country's defense. Therefore, it was not asking too much for other Japanese to make their own sacrifice by permitting themselves to be placed in concentration camps for the duration.[54]

EDC chairman Sakamoto quickly responded with an open letter to Ford published in the *Seattle Post-Intelligencer*. He reminded him how as American citizens Nisei stood together with the nation defending and sacrificing, some in the armed services with their lives.[55] The nation's interests would be better served through participating in the fight rather than in becoming the government's charges. Sakamoto wrote: "We realize that most suspicion naturally falls upon the foreign-born. We are cooperating actively with the authorities to uncover all subversive activity in our midst, and if need be we are ready to stand as protective custodians for our parent generation to guard against danger to the United States arising from them."[56]

Had Ford been alone in criticizing the Japanese American presence on the West Coast little might have resulted from his call. Instead, his statements marked the beginning. Two days later, on January 23, an increasingly ominous threat to Nikkei communities on the West Coast emerged in the Roberts Commission report on Pearl Harbor.

Chaired by Supreme Court Justice Owen J. Roberts and sent to Hawaii by President Roosevelt, the commission first investigated then determined causes of Japan's December 7 attack. They, like Secretary of the Navy Frank Knox a week after the attack, concluded Hawaii's military commanders inadequately prepared the islands' defense, leveled responsibility on a Japanese American fifth column, and partially blamed its spies in and outside the consulate: "There were, prior to December 7, 1941, Japanese spies on the island of Oahu. Some were Japanese consular agents and others were persons having no open relations with the Japanese foreign service. These spies collected and, through various channels transmitted, information to the Japanese Empire respecting the military and naval establishments and dispositions on the island."[57]

Despite the lack of any corroborating evidence this statement nevertheless, backed by the authority of a Supreme Court justice, ultimately served to cast a shadow over every Japanese American.[58]

Two weeks later, Representative Ford and fellow members of the Committee on Alien Nationality and Sabotage met during February 5–13, 1942, to consider extending special control measures to U.S. citizens of Japanese ancestry. Organized by Senator Hiram Johnson (R-Calif.) who in 1924 spearheaded the drive to federally legislate Japanese exclusion, the caucus, chaired by Washington Senator Monrad C. Wallgren (D-Wash.) and comprised of senators and representatives from the three western states, unanimously recommended the following: "The immediate evacuation of all persons of Japanese lineage and all others, aliens and citizens alike, whose presence shall be deemed dangerous or inimical to the safety of the defense of the United States from all strategic areas."

Representative John Coffee (D-Wash.), one of three moderating voices on the committee, had argued successfully for an evacuation to be limited to strategic areas and not the entire three states and Territory of Alaska included in an earlier draft.[59]

In the aftermath of Ford's public statements, the fifth column "finding of fact" from the Roberts Commission report, and the recommendations of the

Wallgren Committee, Seattle residents spoke out through letters to the *Seattle Post-Intelligencer* under an ongoing heading, "Japanese Problem." Because the editor published opinions on both sides of the issue, opinion evenly divided for and against the Nikkei likely reflected his professional decision to present evenhanded views.

Those who advocated Representative Ford's position perceived treachery among "footloose Japs [who] could do plenty of damage," and were convinced the ultimate loyalty of Japanese Americans lay with Emperor Hirohito. One writer, certain that Japanese forces would not bomb their own people, advocated Japanese in the United States be herded into defense industry areas to protect the industry from air bombings. Others expressed suspicion toward these American-born only one generation removed from a culture of Oriental customs and barbarity. Some Japanese pilots shot down at Pearl Harbor, went the claim, had been American-born. Writers opposed to Nikkei remaining on the West Coast made minimal distinctions between Japanese military aggressors and Japanese Americans. One wrote: "I think that these little yellow Aryans should be moved out of the West Coast timber belt before the forest fire season opens."

Writers in support of Seattle's Nikkei typically referred to direct association with the Japanese community through their work or neighborhoods; some asserted the American-born had the same rights under the Constitution as any other U.S. citizen.[60]

The *Post-Intelligencer* editorial board entered the discussion on February 7, citing the "Japanese problem" as a Gordian knot, a difficult if not impossible puzzle to solve. Part of the Japanese population is loyal: some are enemy sympathizers. It should be the job of the Japanese to help ferret out enemies in their midst because the FBI cannot do it alone. They would elaborate: "Loyalty isn't a matter that can be demonstrated solely by purchase of Defense Bonds or even by Red Cross subscriptions . . . The real test of the degree of loyalty within the Japanese community, we believe, is to be found in the extent to which its members cooperate with the authorities in efforts to locate and round up the enemies of this country . . . The government is trying to untie the [Gordian] knot and should welcome the assistance of the Japanese community in this effort. If the knot cannot be untied it will have to be cut."[61] In the eyes of the board the Nikkei community appeared both problem and solution.

Joining the fray was columnist Walter Lippmann who, in his nationally syndicated column, wrote that the absence of sabotage proved Japanese Americans were only waiting until they could strike with greatest effect.[62]

Two weeks later, the *Seattle Post-Intelligencer* published an opinion stating in part: "If it is decided that native born Japanese and German and Italian refugees loyal to the United States, are to be included in any removal order affecting the definitely 'enemy alien' groups, they should realize that it is done in their own best interest and look upon it as part of their contribution to the national defense."[63] This final editorial appeared February 21, two days after President Roosevelt signed Executive Order 9066 authorizing his military commanders to create military exclusion zones and remove anyone from them. His order ended the freedom of those West Coast Nikkei who remained in the forbidden areas of the Western Defense Command (WDC) and led to the incarceration of 120,000 Japanese aliens and Japanese American citizens. Even though the February 19 order did not specify Nikkei by name, the press, with the guidance of military public relations officers, informed the public the Japanese were the targeted group and would be removed.[64]

The eviction began on March 30 when 257 residents of Bainbridge Island, Washington, boarded a cross-sound ferry to Seattle under military guards and climbed into rail passenger cars for a long train journey to the Manzanar Reception Center in eastern California's Owens Valley. This exodus occurred one month before the Puyallup Assembly Center opened. Two months later, west of the Cascade range in Washington State's Pacific Northwest free living residents of Japanese ancestry were nowhere to be found.[65]

3

Preparing for Exile

On Saturday February 28, 1942, John H. Tolan (R-Calif.), chairman of a House of Representatives select committee investigating national defense migration, opened hearings at the County-City Building in Seattle to take testimony concerning future evacuation of Japanese Americans from the West Coast. After chairing similar hearings in San Francisco and Portland, the four-man Tolan Committee spent two days in Seattle before moving on to Los Angeles.

With Executive Order 9066 having appeared a week earlier, expulsion became a virtual certainty. This meant the hearings would be remembered primarily for the public opinion reflected by Caucasian and Japanese Americans who sat before it. By the time Tolan and his colleagues reached Seattle, the overwhelming majority of Caucasian witnesses, made up of public and private citizens, had spoken in favor of removing all Japanese aliens and their American-born children from the West Coast.[1]

Washington Governor Arthur B. Langlie (R), the Seattle hearings' first witness, assured committee members his state agencies would cooperate with any action planned by the army. However, because irrigation canals, dams, and facilities utilized for production of war materiels dotted the region, he went on to argue against relocation of Japanese into the state's inland areas east of the Cascade range. At the same time he observed a relative lack of malice and "intense jitteryness" throughout the state that otherwise might lead to social breakdown. "Up to the present time, our people have kept their feet on the ground very well."[2]

Seattle Mayor Earl Millikin (Nonpartisan) declared his constituency's overwhelming support of a forced evacuation because individuals feared another Pearl Harbor might occur in their midst. His earlier support of Seattle's Japanese appeared to waver when he stated that even though the "Japanese citizens' league" might put a stop to any subversive activities, in reality the Japanese could not be counted on to inform against their own. "There is no doubt about those 8,000 Japanese, that 7,900 probably are above question, but the other 100 would burn this town down and let the Japanese planes come in and bring on something that would dwarf Pearl Harbor."[3]

Washington State Attorney General Smith Troy (D) advocated expedient removal of both aliens and the citizen Japanese, but underscored Governor Langlie's concern in regard to including eastern Washington among the possible relocation sites. He continued by saying: "Then after close scrutiny and investigation, those useful and loyal citizen Japanese could be, through some licensing form, or some other method, brought back into the territory here where we could use them."[4]

Among politicians providing testimony, only Tacoma Mayor Harry P. Cain (R) opposed a wholesale evacuation. He insisted guilt related to the individual; local authorities could differentiate between the loyal and disloyal: "I think, within reason, it can be done; but it is going to place upon the person who makes that decision a lot of work. I think that a man's background, regardless of who he is, very generally has much to do with what he is going to do. If born in this country; if a Christian; if employed side by side with others who fill that same classification, for years; if educated in our schools; if a producer now and in the past; if maintained in a position of production—I should think that person could be construed to be a loyal American citizen."[5]

Over the two days thirty-one citizens presented oral testimony, including Emergency Defense Council chairman Jimmie Sakamoto. These citizens' interests arced across political, business, religious, and social spectra. An additional twenty written statements appeared as exhibits in the published testimony. While most individuals spoke or wrote in opposition to Japanese remaining in the region, supporters of the Japanese presence proved to be vocal and organized. Floyd Schmoe, spokesman for the American Friends Service Committee (AFSC), reminded the committee that Nisei were the product of local public schools as well as citizens by virtue of their birth and training. Furthermore: "Justice cannot be done by branding all men, who by accident of their birth, come from countries now at war with America, as enemy aliens."[6] Other religious leaders, most with direct links to Seattle's Japanese community, represented the Northwest Oriental Evangelist Society, Japanese Methodist Church, and Seattle Council of Churches. They stepped forward and spoke out against a mass evacuation rooted in racial prejudice; some offered alternative solutions.

University of Washington faculty, administrators, and students generally opposed a mass removal. All knew Nisei students directly, either in the classroom or through campus activities, and appealed to justice and fairness, declaring Nisei students on campus to be "above all, Americans." Professor Jessie F. Steiner, chairman of the sociology department and former missionary in Japan, conceded to plans for removing enemy aliens away from defense plants and other strategic sites. "But when this plan of evacuation is enlarged to include citizens as well as aliens on the ground that American-born Japanese are inherently disloyal to this country, we are starting in motion a dangerous mass movement growing out of war hysteria and differing little from the treatment of minorities by the totalitarian governments in Europe and Asia."[7]

A senior University of Washington student urged the committee "to consider if we can even remotely demand or expect that these American citizens will remain loyal if instead of tolerance, we give them intolerance, mass hysteria and blanket condemnation? Can we ask them to believe in democracy if democracy does not believe in them?"[8]

Representatives from patriotic groups, labor and agricultural organizations, and business interests countered with pro-evacuation testimony and written statements. At the extreme, virulent testimony opposing the Japanese came from publisher Miller Freeman, longtime opponent of Japanese immigration. Freeman offered no distinction between the alien and citizen Japanese. In a prepared statement citing his version of the historical record of Japanese colonization in the United States, he asserted the Japanese presence had come about through "fraud, deception, and collusion" with the assistance of "pro-Japanese elements in this country." Allegiance, regardless of birthright, belonged to the emperor.[9] Freeman's unyielding testimony overshadowed statements by more moderate witnesses who shared his belief that the Japanese should be expelled.

In the afternoon session on the first day of the hearings another uncompromising anti-Japanese opinion came forth. Into the written record the committee entered a statement submitted by Mrs. Dale J. Marble, president of the Seattle Council of Parent-Teacher Associations(PTAs): "We, the executive committee of the Seattle Council of Parent-Teacher Associations, are in favor of direct action by the Government toward the evacuation from this State of all aliens, and the American-born children of all aliens, whose home governments are at war with the United States, as a protective measure for all children."[10]

This followed the previous evening's action taken by the Seattle school board in accepting the mass resignation of twenty-three Nisei female office clerks from area public elementary schools. Opposed to having Japanese American girls work in the elementary schools, prior to Executive Order 9066 PTA members had initiated a complaint with the school district. Meeting their objectives with success the night before may have led Mrs. Marble to suggest protection of Seattle's school children required not only the removal of these young clerks, but banishment of all residents of Japanese ancestry throughout the state.

As the 1941–42 school year began, former Nisei students held over one-third of the Seattle area elementary schools' clerical staff positions. Twenty-three young women typed, filed, and performed other secretarial duties in citywide principals' offices at the prevailing rate of 40 cents per hour.[11]

During the first week of February 1942, three weeks prior to promulgation of Executive Order 9066, the Seattle School District received a formal complaint from a four-member committee representing the council of the PTA that focused on American-born Japanese girls who worked in Seattle public schools. Claiming to represent parents of students at the Gatewood School in West Seattle, they expressed concern for the safety of the school's students in the event of a war-related emergency. Tapping into allegations that many clerks possessed dual citizenship, they feared the worst should Nisei girls continue working in or near school cafeterias or practice deliberate negligence in first-aid work. They should not be permitted to answer telephones because, "After all, in the event of a raid on the city, they [Nisei clerks] would be the ones to take any calls intended to put schools on the alert."[12]

After their original complaint failed, on February 22 the Gatewood School mothers demonstrated in front of the school, soliciting signatures for a petition demanding the school board dismiss the office girls. Despite her being "efficient and capable in her duties," they targeted the part-time employee at the Gatewood School.[13] The gathering of 250 signatures emboldened them; they threatened to take their petition to the governor or FBI. Should they be unsuccessful at higher levels, they threatened to remove their children from the school.

Superintendent of Seattle schools Samuel Fleming and his staff, unable to resist these mounting pressures, became caught in a legal bind that left them unable to fire a U.S. citizen under such circumstances. But school district officials saw a way out if they could force the clerks' mass resignation. Fleming went to Japantown and laid out the problem before Jimmie Sakamoto in an attempt to engage his assistance. Sakamoto responded by calling a meeting of the clerks at the *Courier* office to discuss the situation and plan a course of action.[14] The school clerks arrived at his Main Street office on February

24. Documentation shedding light on what took place at this meeting has yet to appear, but its outcome became clear the following day when the clerks submitted a letter to the school district offering their immediate mass resignation. The young women explained their rationale as follows: "We take this step to prove our loyalty to the schools and to the United Sates by not becoming a contributing factor to dissension and disunity when national unity in spirit and deed is vitally necessary to the defense and complete victory for America . . . We hope the welfare of the schools will be served by our action in resigning from the positions we now occupy."[15]

Although the statement's language reflects unanimity, this decision was rooted in acrimony. Sakamoto's intention was never to negotiate with the clerks but to inform them that their patriotic duty demanded immediate resignation. Some protested his order, including Sally Shiminaka, one of the office secretaries. "Some of us said, we're all products of the Seattle School system. They have our records. They know we went through the school system. Why would they see us with any suspicion? Well, we are at war and to show we are good citizens we must resign. This is being good citizens by resigning, in effect. This is what he said. Some of us were under protest. We were almost coerced into signing. Either that or be fired."[16]

Subsequently the school board voted to accept their resignations, their decision possibly influenced by Executive Order 9066's appearance a week earlier, dooming the Japanese community to removal en masse from the area. Afterward board members would issue a statement commending the clerks' fine spirit "in offering their resignations [that] testifies to their high regard for their responsibility as American citizens."[17]

Sakamoto carried the day. Though unpopular with school clerks and others within the Nikkei community, his position remained congruent with long-held beliefs that maintenance of a low profile within the larger community and utterance via consensus rather than individual expression provided necessary keys to reducing discrimination against Japanese Americans. This incident, however, indicates how his philosophy lacked unilateral acceptance. In the weeks and months ahead his worldview would be put to the test.[18]

In the meantime, other Nisei local and state employees received termination notices, including twenty-three at the University of Washington.[19]

*   *   *

As the drama of the school clerks unfolded, the impact of Executive Order 9066 continued to radiate. On February 22 the FBI instigated a new wave of arrests among community residents, immediately netting 102 lower-echelon

Seattle area Japanese nationals who had been added to the list since December. Most had remained unknown to intelligence agencies because their activities and associations had not raised suspicion sufficient to warrant arrest. Information gleaned from translated documents seized during the first roundup offered fresh information to provoke suspicions. Although FBI director J. Edgar Hoover opposed this second roundup as undermining the legitimacy of his earlier sweep through Japanese communities throughout the country in the weeks after Pearl Harbor, these follow-up spot raids may have helped give the impression the FBI was still in charge.[20]

Kazuko (aka Kakuzo) Kawakami, who was taken into custody on February 22, 1942, had arrived in the United States in 1900 at the age of twenty-three and four years later entered into a partnership with another immigrant Japanese. Together they purchased and operated the Tacoma Hotel on Jackson Street in the heart of Japantown. By 1942, Kawakami and his wife, Fuku, had four adult children; one served in the army at Camp Roberts, California.

Kawakami, who heretofore had escaped arrest, had against him three incriminating marks that led to his apprehension—first, the arrest and subsequent internment of his business partner on December 8, 1941; second, the appearance of his name on a seized membership list of the *Sokoku Kai*, a proscribed organization; and third, records found in his possession of the Jackson *Kinzu Chuchiku Kumiai*, a quasi credit union, or "rotating credit association." This group involved sixty-four local members who pooled money to loan to its members, a group Kawakami was believed to head up.[21]

Membership in proscribed organizations provided sufficient grounds for apprehension and detention. Kawakami's affiliation remained unknown to the FBI until translation of the group's membership list. Prior to February 1942, the FBI appears to have compiled no dossier on him, and his business association with a detainee aroused little suspicion.

Following a brief detention at the Immigrant and Naturalization Service (INS) immigration station, Kawakami was shipped to the Fort Missoula detention station to await a loyalty hearing before the Alien Enemy Hearing Board for Western Washington. Interrogation at his hearing on April 8, 1942, revealed his association with *Shokoku Kai* involved a six-year subscription to *Shokoku* Magazine he had purchased to accommodate the seller. As a businessman he belonged to the Seattle Japanese Chamber of Commerce, but did not actively participate in the organization's activities. Finally, the board seemed unimpressed by his leadership role in a credit union that appeared to bear no direct ties to Japan.

That neither his daughter, employed by the Social Security Board at Seattle's U.S. courthouse, nor his son who served in the army possessed dual citizenship also reflected favorably on Kawakami. In concluding this Presbyterian Christian posed no threat to the United States, the hearing board recommended his release. U.S. Attorney Charles Dennis agreed; Attorney General Biddle signed the order on June 3, 1942.[22]

However, Kawakami's freedom was short lived. With Nikkei banished from the West Coast by authority of Executive Order 9066, on that same day he was escorted to the Puyallup Assembly Center by INS guards to join Fuku and two of their children, Toshio and Yukiko, who had arrived there a month earlier.[23]

On December 8, 1941, Koi Tanagi's upstairs neighbor was detained because of his leadership role in the Nikkei community and active affiliation with the proscribed Japanese Chamber of Commerce. Tanagi, certain of impending arrest, remained free until spot raids resumed in February.

Beginning in 1919, with his wife, Fuyo, he operated Tanagi Grocery Store at 653 King Street, thirteen years after first arriving in the United States. Tanagi had served in the Russo-Japanese War and contributed to a Japanese foreign wars veterans group, *Hinumana-kai*. Despite a continuous twenty-three-year residence in the United States, ongoing ties to the homeland resulted in his detention and ultimate internment. Tanagi's family endured two years of separation.[24]

The total number of Seattle Issei arrests during the second wave remains unclear. However, on March 19, 150 detainees who had lived for weeks behind bars at the Seattle immigration station left King Street Station on a train bound for Fort Missoula.[25] By March 31, the number at the immigration station stabilized at eighteen, suggesting the second wave of raids lasted approximately three weeks.[26]

Spot raids occurred in other Japanese communities on the West Coast, evidenced by increases in the numbers of detainees at Fort Missoula, Fort Lincoln, and, after March 13, 1942, within a new INS barbed wire facility for Japanese detainees located outside Santa Fe, New Mexico.[27]

As they witnessed their immigrant elders being hauled into detention, some Nikkei made plans to leave their communities voluntarily. Although Executive Order 9066 had not been specific as to the individuals or groups subject to removal, statements by often anonymous officials made clear to most Japanese Americans that the government's focus centered on Japanese from the West Coast states. In a February 20 memorandum to the chief of staff summarizing developments on the control of alien enemies and other subversive persons on the Pacific coast, Major General Allen W. Gullion, provost marshal and an architect of Executive Order 9066, explained the aim of the plan of his subordinate, Lieutenant General John L. DeWitt: "To provide progressively for exclusion of all Japanese, initially only around the more critical areas, making full use of whatever voluntary exodus that private impetus and recognized relief agencies can stimulate."[28]

Soon DeWitt put his plan into action. On March 2, 1942, the commander of 4th Army and the Western Defense Command issued Public Proclamation No. 1 setting forth the geographic boundaries of two military areas, Military Area No. 1 and No. 2, to extend throughout Washington, Oregon, California, and Arizona. With this proclamation the army staked out its authority over ingress, egress, and who could remain in these areas. Army planners initially divided Military Area No. 1 into twenty-two basic units, each one creating a community of Japanese to be moved together to the same assembly center, and later to the same relocation center. As demographers tabulated data from the Census Bureau they carefully studied each area's structure and characteristics, further refining the units into 108 geographic areas. These boundaries formed the basis of civilian exclusion orders to allow for an efficient military operation.

In both areas the proclamation established ninety-nine special zones, including Zone A-1, a strip of geography approximately fifty miles wide running the length of the coast from the Canadian to the Mexican border, and along the Mexican border through Arizona, zones coinciding with areas previously designated by the Justice Department.[29]

In Washington a line demarcating the two military areas roughly followed the channel carved by the Columbia River from the 49th Parallel designating the Canadian border south to the Oregon border. West of this natural boundary the area included all but 549 of the state's 14,565 Nikkei residents.[30]

Since no separate restrictions existed for Japanese Americans living and working within its borders, the fact of the fifty-mile-wide prohibited strip paralleling the Pacific coast within Military Area No. 1 had little impact on this population. Most of the ninety-eight other special zones were located in areas of low population density as well. However, Proclamation No. 1 brought the actual intent of Executive Order 9066 into intense focus for Nikkei living in the affected areas, as they came to realize that large-scale eviction was undeniable. For the first time the order specified "persons" as "any Japanese, German, or Italian alien" or "any person of Japanese ancestry."

The army initially encouraged voluntary migration into Military Area No. 2 for anyone first completing Change of Residence Report Cards. Forms mailed to the provost marshal of the Western Defense Command (WDC) enabled the army to maintain a count of individuals remaining in Military Area No. 1.

Unwilling to accept the fate of those who still resided in the coastal regions, many individuals hurriedly planned to migrate out of the area. A few packed up and moved inland. However, until March 11 no special section existed within General Headquarters to monitor and support the voluntary migration program. Without the Wartime Civil Control Administration (WCCA) yet in place to handle civil affairs, General DeWitt chose to address this problem personally, and as a result the program was slow to gain momentum. After March 11, as the WCCA began to provide supervision, control, and assistance of voluntary migration out of Military Area No. 1, numbers gradually increased. The WCCA disseminated information in relation to employment and living facilities and established field offices for families and individuals with definite resettlement plans in forty-eight cities.[31]

On March 16, General DeWitt issued Public Proclamation No. 2, charting four additional military areas that encompassed Idaho, Montana, Nevada, and Utah.[32] These two proclamations covered the entire WDC with special exclusion zones added to establish perimeters around dams, bridges, power stations, and other strategic sites to protect the nation from sabotage. The newly established Military Areas Nos. 3 through 6 added five thousand Nikkei residents to its census. DeWitt's intention became clear—rid the WDC of its entire Japanese population. He ultimately failed to achieve his aim only because superiors at the War Department intervened.

By the time the second proclamation came into effect, two new agencies of Headquarters WDC existed to plan and execute the forced evacuation. March 10, 1942 brought establishment of the Civil Affairs Division (CAD), the planning agency responsible for the "formulation of policies, plans, and directives" pertaining to "control and exclusion of civilians," followed the next day by the WCCA. Colonel Karl R. Bendetsen, on General DeWitt's staff since December, became head of CAD and directed the WCCA, reporting directly to DeWitt. He was a prime architect of the program to remove the Nikkei from the West Coast.[33]

Bendetsen, from Aberdeen, Washington, and a practicing attorney in his hometown, accepted a commission in the Judge Advocate General's Corps with the rank of captain in 1940. As head of the Aliens Division of the Provost Marshal General, he served as liaison between the War Department and WDC in regard to planning for the mass removal of Japanese Americans and became the logical choice to head the CAD and WCCA.[34]

Pressure on the Nikkei communities increased on March 24 with implementation of Dewitt's first restrictive Proclamation No. 3. It imposed an 8:00 p.m. to 6:00 a.m. curfew throughout Military Area No. 1, impacting enemy aliens and all persons of Japanese ancestry as well as restricting them to a five-mile radius surrounding their homes. These new limitations motivated Japanese Americans with sufficient resources to quickly pack up and leave.

Yet circumstances would prevent many Nikkei from exiting the military area. The limited assets of Issei who headed most households hampered their ability to finance departures, and the possibility of employment opportunities and housing options in the new areas remained uncertain. As a growing hostility toward the Japanese spread eastward, the absence of friendly contacts or potential sponsors to assist in their relocation made the prospect of moving there difficult. A migration that would require starting over, in the end fewer than 5,000 of the 107,000 Nikkei who lived within Military Area No. 1 successfully carried out the move and avoided incarceration. Many who tried returned when rampant hostility they encountered inland overwhelmed the desire to remain free. An official government history provides details: "Those who tried to cross into the interior States ran into all kinds of trouble. Some were turned back by armed posses at the border of Nevada; others were clapped into jail and held overnight by panicky local peace officers; nearly all had difficulty in buying gasoline; many were greeted by 'No Japs Wanted' signs on the main streets of interior communities; and a few were threatened, or felt that they were threatened, with possibilities of mob violence."[35]

On March 27, 1942, General DeWitt halted further voluntary migration after concluding Japanese Americans posed too serious a threat to remain on the West Coast. That day he issued Proclamation No. 4, ordering a freeze on "all alien Japanese and persons of Japanese ancestry who are within the limits of Military Area No. 1" and desiring to leave that area "for any purpose." The result was a rush to post offices to complete change of address forms. State and local officials as well as the populace of interior regions supported DeWitt's stance.

Because most Japanese Americans migrated in family groups, heads of families often left early to locate employment or establish residence, with wives and children following later. This meant that families in transition could reunite after the March 30 deadline passed.

At least 499 Washingtonians exited the state's Military Area No. 1 during the voluntary migration period, representing approximately 10 percent (499/4,889) of the total number leaving the four-state region. Of those migrating out of western Washington, 208 ventured no farther than Spokane, whose prewar Japanese community numbered 362. Nikkei who moved into the agricultural areas of Idaho and beyond claimed the meager opportunities that may have existed in the midst of the growing hostility.[36]

*   *   *

At the outbreak of war with Japan, Seiko Miyagawa, a single, twenty-two-year-old employee of the Tokyo Cafe on Seattle's Jackson Street, served ham and eggs to her predominantly African American clientele. In the wake of Executive Order 9066 Seiko understood the changes facing Nisei. Vowing to avoid participating in any mass eviction, she said she would attend Spokane's Christian Youth Council Conference to be held in March, and then stay in Spokane for the duration of the war. Fearing for family members who remained behind, Seiko's father supported his daughter's plan to avoid incarceration even though it meant separating the family.[37]

Upon arriving in Spokane, Miyagawa found employment opportunities sparse even with the assistance of an employment agency. Given the uproar on the coast, few employers hired Japanese Americans. The wife of a sympathetic local attorney needing a cook and domestic help finally offered Miyagawa room, board, and a salary of $9 per month, amounting to little more than spending money and one-third less than the earnings of a clerk incarcerated in an assembly center. Even so, because the job provided shelter out of harm's way she accepted. Future kindness extended throughout her employment reinforced Miyagawa's initial positive impression of her new employer.

Most Spokane Nikkei watched with increasing alarm as newcomers trickled into their midst; they feared a large-scale influx of Nikkei would jeopardize their precarious standing within the conservative Spokane community.[38] Already numerous exclusion zones in eastern Washington had barred all Japanese, as calls throughout the state of Washington for removal of all Japanese increased. This meant many local Nikkei would resist refugees from west of the Cascades, particularly in the downtown area, where an increased presence of Japanese might heighten attention from an already skitterish populace.

Cordial relations between Miyagawa and her host family assured ongoing work, secure employment to insulate her from the growing friction. As expulsion from Military Area No. 1 drew near, the couple offered her their summer home in nearby Liberty Lake, permitting Miyagawa's family to leave Seattle before the voluntary migration period ended.

This experience with her Spokane family would prove an exception to the discrimination against new arrivals emanating from the local residents, including Nikkei. After settling in, Seiko's father applied unsuccessfully for a municipal lease permit to run a downtown hotel. After appealing the decision to the city council, he failed again. One councilman justified his vote: "We don't want any more Jap money in the businesses in downtown Spokane."

During the war fears expressed by Spokane's prewar Nikkei population never materialized despite a substantial increase in their numbers. Unlike in California, Washington's Military Area No. 2 never became an exclusion zone, meaning any Nikkei entering the area before or during the voluntary migration period remained safe from incarceration.

The inability of Nikkei living east of the Cascade range to assist those fleeing western Washington extended into Idaho. Mae Takahashi, a twenty-seven-year-old mother of two children, her youngest born immediately after the bombing of Pearl Harbor, worked with her husband at the North Coast Import Store, owned by a local Japanese businessman. Takahashi's parents and two brothers farmed outside Caldwell, Idaho. This fortuitous connection enabled members from both sides of the family to move in the face of eventual economic hardship; nine family members journeyed to Idaho, joining the two households.[39]

The farm could not provide an extended family's wages, so the new arrivals eked out a living for room and board. Like their Spokane counterparts, Caldwell area Nikkei feared too many new arrivals coming into the area would expose their small community and result in problems for them all. In addition, Idaho's Governor Chase Clark, an outspoken opponent of the Japanese, believed, as did General DeWitt, that separating the loyal from the disloyal would be an impossible task.

Fearing a backlash, Idaho's Japanese American Citizens League (JACL) groups met in Caldwell to pass a resolution "pledging all members of the league in Idaho to discourage all evacuee relatives, friends, and others from coming into Idaho." Pocatello JACL president Paul Okamura underscored the resolution by writing Governor Clark, asking him to "make a distinction between coast evacuee Japanese Americans and those of us who reside in Idaho permanently." As yet no reply from Clark has been found.[40]

These actions may have discouraged some Nikkei from seeking safe haven in the area. Ironically, Idaho farmers would soon pursue every available Nikkei they could possibly hire, as farm labor shortages had increased throughout the high desert country. Japanese American seasonal leave workers from the Minidoka Relocation Center later harvested 20 percent of the state's 1942 sugar beet crop.[41]

In Seattle, as the voluntary migration program moved forward Jimmie Sakamoto became increasingly aware of resistance felt by citizens within the inland states. As early as February 28 in oral testimony before the Tolan Committee he expressed concern over social and economic problems faced by Nikkei who attempted to move inland.[42] But soon his attention turned toward the encroaching involuntary evacuation and incarceration.

On March 23, 1942, after reading about the impending removal of the Bainbridge Island Nikkei community, Sakamoto wrote to General DeWitt describing a resettlement project designed to relocate the entire Japanese community to central Washington's farming country near Moses Lake. He suggested the 270 island residents headed to the Manzanar Reception Center be included in the venture. They would be permitted to live with their Seattle relatives and friends pending a decision on the resettlement plan.[43]

Sakamoto's ambitious vision for Moses Lake involved creating a permanent irrigation project and what he termed a "model city" within the vast Columbia River Basin's 1,250,000 irrigable acres. To bring water into the area an irrigation project currently under consideration for implementation by the government in 1943 or 1944 would employ the men to build irrigation ditches under Works Progress Administration (WPA) supervision. Planting would follow. Factories invited to take advantage of the area's labor supply or ones built and outfitted by the army to produce uniforms and other wearing apparel needed by the army would employ women and older men. Sakamoto cited the Seattle Glove Factory as a role model. Since more than a hundred well-trained Japanese women employed by the glove factory would provide ideal workers, plant owners agreed to relocate.[44]

To determine his plan's feasibility Sakamoto sent architect Frank Toribara to report on the Columbia Basin's site and its soil conditions, available water supply, and existing utilities. While reporting favorably on his trip to the sagebrush country, he also cautioned that the start-up costs would add up and possibly equate to $15,000 per section (640 acres) of farmland.[45]

Moses Lake's community responded favorably to a scaled-down version of the plan. Mayor Eric Peterson and representatives of the Columbia Basin Co-operative Growers, anxious to embark on an agricultural project, proposed inviting 30 Japanese families to sharecrop 1,200 acres of potatoes, carrots, and onions. Planting needed to occur within the next several weeks, and farm representatives promised additional irrigated acreage later on. Pleading the case to Milton Eisenhower, who had come over from the Agriculture Department to become the first War Relocation Authority (WRA) director on April 9, 1942, the group advised him that at least "90% of the people are in favor of having Japanese come into the community and farm the land." Earlier, the county agricultural agent had worked out a scheme hoping to utilize members of the Bainbridge Island Japanese community before their banishment to California. This aspect now was moot, but implementing the original version required only official approval.[46]

All efforts to carry out Sakamoto's course of action had been thwarted, and the willingness of Moses Lake residents to embrace the Japanese did not represent the attitude of most rural communities throughout the western states. Although DeWitt was not responding to public opinion, his freezing order of March 27 reflected the hostility most communities felt toward Nikkei moving inward. Furthermore, to realize the plan would require an army waiver impossible to obtain.

Unfortunately, Sakamoto's plan came at the time the WRA was just beginning to organize. Director Eisenhower soon introduced a strategy to move volunteers into the farming areas clamoring to access this sudden labor pool. Though an idea like the Moses Lake project must have intrigued Eisenhower, his emergent organization lacking concrete plans and opposition by the states' governors made such a plan exceedingly unlikely. He could only provide reassurance.

Another seven weeks passed before the first seasonal farm workers left the Portland Assembly Center for eastern Oregon.[47] By now the army had evacuated Sakamoto and the rest of the Seattle Japanese to the Puyallup Assembly Center, ensuring the plan's demise.

The Catholic Maryknoll Fathers set forth concurrent proposals for moving smaller groups of Japanese Americans out of the military area. The first plan sought to evacuate parents and their children attending Seattle's Maryknoll School on East Jefferson Street into Maryknoll parishes in the Midwest and East. This would involve four hundred individuals with Father Leopold Tibesar, their pastor for six years, accompanying them. However, by mid-March, negative sentiment in cities housing these parishes curtailed the move, and plans were dropped.[48]

At the same time, Bishop Walsh, national head of the Maryknoll community, issued orders to both Father Hugh Lavery, head of the Los Angeles church, and Father Tibesar to accompany Japanese families to St. Louis, where a new community would be established. Volunteers from any religious affiliation were welcome to accompany the priests to this strongly Catholic community.[49] As a Catholic, Sakamoto exhibited a strong interest. Hopes for such a move survived into early April, when details of a settlement proposal provided by the West Plains Chamber of Commerce appeared in a newspaper serving the fertile Ozark Mountains of south-central Missouri, located within reach of St. Louis and Kansas City. By then, with the army's plans to evict the Nikkei from the West Coast well underway and voluntary migration ended following the issuance of Proclamation No. 4, this plan went into the dustbin to join the others.

* * *

Currently in the planning stages, the orderly military evacuation process would become an immense undertaking. On March 2, 1942, Proclamation No. 1 set the stage for an operation unprecedented in the nation's history. The first major logistical problem involved locating a hundred thousand residents of Japanese ancestry, a job for the Bureau of the Census. It fortuitously had completed the 1940 census with "Japanese" included as one of the items in the "race" data field. Therefore, an essential component in planning became the Statistical Division, one of seven divisions within WCCA and the only one headed by a civilian, Dr. Calvert L. Dedrick.

At the behest of the provost marshal, Major General Allen W. Gullion, Dedrick, chief of the Statistical Research Division at the Bureau of the Census, arrived in San Francisco on February 27, anticipating a two-week duty assignment designed to help in preparing forms and procedures for the registration of enemy aliens on the West Coast. General DeWitt's decision to purge the West Coast of Japanese Americans extended his tour of duty to more than a year. His expertise would influence all aspects of planning. Working out of an office in the Whitcomb Hotel under the direct supervision of Colonel Bendetsen, Dedrick became the Bureau's West Coast representative and received full authority to act on behalf of the Bureau.[50]

Primary duties involved assisting military authorities with planning and implementing the forced evacuation, first to assembly centers and subsequently to WRA centers. Anticipating the immensity of this job, the new Statistical Division head recruited University of Washington Professor of Sociology Calvin F. Schmid, a noted demographer, as his assistant during the months of planning. Schmid, an expert in local and state demography and pioneer in development of graphical displays of empirical data, had full responsibility for the cartographic unit. This group's primary objective was to generate the necessary maps detailing boundaries of geographic units that compartmentalized each Japanese community in the military areas. Many maps eventually appeared in the published civilian exclusion orders.

Schmid's role in defining geographic boundaries contained within the subsequent 108 civilian exclusion orders helping to operationalize the Nikkei removal may have been limited, for overall responsibility in defining the estimated size of an area fell to Dedrick, who later wrote an unpublished report focusing on the accuracy of his estimates.[51]

By the time Dedrick reached San Francisco, considerable headway had been made in locating the Japanese population on the West Coast and elsewhere. Most demographics known to DeWitt's staff had been compiled and disseminated in the two weeks following Pearl Harbor. Quick general tabulations from raw data on Japanese Americans existed because of their relatively small numbers living on the West Coast; a single sort of punch card data could be made on the special category on race, which specified "Japanese." By December 11, the Census Bureau had disseminated numerous unpublished tabulations on Japanese Americans in the United States, its territories, and its possessions, including sex and citizenship status for selected U.S. cities at the county level in Washington, Oregon, and California, and at the state level in Utah, Nevada, Idaho, Montana, and Arizona.[52] This may explain why press releases in the days after the United States entered the war contained specific details on the presence of Japanese Americans.

These reports offered limited value when it came to shaping plans for placing Nikkei in the assembly centers because they could not specify the locations of Japanese within large population centers in Los Angeles, San Francisco, and Seattle, where nearly half of them resided. Only processed data from minor civil divisions (towns, townships, villages, and city wards) and large urban areas (census tracts involving populations in the four thousand to eight thousand range) made field operations possible at the local level within urban and rural areas.

Until World War II, confidentiality requirements constrained the Census Bureau from disseminating data revealing an individual's identity. This was based on wording in the Census Act of 1929: "In no case shall information furnished under the authority of this Act be used to the detriment of the person or persons to whom such information relates."[53] To overcome this "detriment clause" language, suspending the confidentiality provision of the Census Act became part of the Second War Powers Act of 1942, enacted in March 1942.[54]

Much of the data analysis requested by the army had been completed by Dedrick and the Bureau; by the time Congress enacted the Second War Powers Act, it was in the hands of WCCA. In fact, tabulations from the 1940 census relating to the 281 Japanese then living on Bainbridge Island as well as a map detailing the island's minor civil division boundaries had both been turned over to the WCCA on March 21, 1942. Three days later, Civilian Exclusion Order No. 1 appeared in public places on the island announcing the exclusion, effective March 30.

The Bureau had been requested to provide census data on enumeration districts, enabling evacuation planners to determine how many Japanese lived within individual city blocks.[55] Whether the Bureau disclosed data revealing the names and addresses of Japanese from enumeration lists still remains conjecture. However, with the eventual banishment of all Nikkei living in

Military Area No. 1 and the California section of Military Area No. 2, such micro data may not, in most cases, have been necessary.[56]

Census data on the Bainbridge Island Japanese community provided to WCCA planners formed the basis of the first Civilian Exclusion Order (CEO No. 1). That the Bainbridge Island group was removed first is no coincidence, for the army intended to purge areas in the order of their relative military importance. The island and its farming community bordered the channel leading directly southward to the Puget Sound Naval Shipyard at Bremerton. The next four CEOs blanketed vicinities surrounding other military installations and port facilities in San Diego County, San Pedro, and Long Beach, as well as most dock areas plus San Francisco's waterfront.[57] The Boeing Aircraft Company, lines of communication, and power supply feeding it passed through areas heavily populated by Nikkei, making western Washington an early focus for WCCA planners.

Similar in content and identical in format, the 108 exclusion orders issued by the WCCA employed census data on all Nikkei living within Military Area No. 1 and the California portion of Military Area No. 2. Orders were crafted to include an average of approximately 1,000 individuals, equaling 250 families. Actual orders ranged in numbers from a low of 45 in southwest Oregon's rural counties (CEO No. 87) to a high of 3,877 in the Sacramento area (CEO No. 52). These orders impacted a total of 109,650 individuals, of whom 91,401 eventually were transferred directly from their homes into 16 assembly centers and 11,711 to 3 relocation centers placed in operation in May and July.[58] The last two orders, CEO No. 107 and CEO No. 108, dated July 22, 1942, covered portions of California's Military Area No. 2 and led to completion of the expulsion operation.[59]

Moving communities intact helped maintain morale and preserve existing local institutions, such as church congregations and social hierarchies, as well as other networks crucial to order and cohesion. While this goal could not be uniformly achieved, that virtually Seattle's entire Nikkei population went to the Puyallup Assembly Center offers convincing evidence this had been the plan.

Dedrick's staff prepared 16 CEOs encompassing the distribution of Nikkei throughout Washington, 7 of which included the 7,300 eventually entering the Puyallup Assembly Center from King and Pierce counties (see table 2).

On April 24 large notices appeared inside Seattle's affected locations. Taped and stapled to telephone poles, shop windows, and other visible spots with heavy foot traffic, large bold headers on each notice, INSTRUCTIONS/TO ALL PERSONS OF/JAPANESE/ANCESTRY, could be read from across the street.

Boundaries of the first two exclusion orders, CEO No. 17 and CEO No. 18, included roughly the western half of Seattle from the north city to the south city line; 1,952 Nikkei lived inside those municipal boundaries.

Each CEO poster provided the text describing geographic boundaries within the order excluding "all persons of Japanese ancestry, both alien and non-alien." The term *non-alien* conveniently hid the fact that the exclusion also involved U.S. citizens. During specific hours one responsible member reported under orders to register the family at a designated civil control station. Failure to comply met with defined penalties. In addition to large format posters, pamphlet-sized versions went out through the mail.

The locations of the six civil control stations in Seattle set up to process the city's resident Nikkei may be found in table 2. A seventh station, located in Puyallup, handled the Pierce County Nikkei also destined for the Puyallup Assembly Center.

Nine days later, on May 3, posters providing details for two new exclusion orders (CEO No. 36 and CEO No. 37) appeared on city streets affecting Nikkei living within the specified boundaries. By now those targeted by the first two exclusion orders were incarcerated. Zones encompassed in the May 3 orders included areas bounded on the north and south by Yesler Way and

Table 2. Total Persons Taken to Puyallup Assembly Center through May 31, 1942

Civilian Exclusion Order No.	Date of CEO	Dates of Evacuation	Total Number Evacuated*	Principal County	Civil Control Station
17	April 24	April 28–May 1	1,182	King	2100 Second Avenue, Seattle
18	April 24	April 30–May 1	770	King	1319 Rainier Avenue, Seattle
36	May 3	May 8–May 9	918	King	Japanese Chamber of Commerce, 316 Maynard Avenue, Seattle
37	May 3	May 8–May 9	1,149	King	Buddhist Temple 1427 Main Street, Seattle
40	May 5	May 10–May 11	1,392	King	Washington Hall, 14th Avenue & East Fir Street, Seattle
57	May 10	May 12–May 16	836	King	Christian Youth Center 2203 East Madison Street, Seattle
58	10-May	May 12–May 16	1,052	Pierce	City Hall Auditorium, South Meridian Street, Puyallup

* In addition, 249 arrived from other areas of Washington and Oregon (18), from Justice Department camps (80), and from Alaska (151).

Source: Civilian Exclusion Orders, Calvin F. Schmid papers.

Dearborn Street, and west to east by 5th and 23rd avenues. These boundaries defined a smaller locale than either of the first two orders, yet within it lay Japantown's heart occupied by 2,067 residents soon to become exiles.

Final exclusion orders issued on May 5 (CEO No. 40) and May 10 (CEO No. 57) covered Seattle's remaining sections, including its eastern extents from Yesler Way to the north city line and east to the Lake Washington shore. On May 10 1,053 rural Pierce County residents received instructions on their exclusion (CEO No. 58), completing the series of seven orders affecting 7,300 residents of Japanese ancestry from Seattle (6,247) and Pierce County (1,053).

This number represents little over half the Nikkei living in Washington's Military Area No. 1 who eventually were incarcerated. Seven additional exclusion orders blanketed the remainder of western Washington, including Tacoma and rural areas extending from Canada's border to the Columbia River. The largest concentration of Nikkei in Military Area No. 1 east of the Cascade Mountains, totaling 1,156 people, lived in the Yakima area.

With its maximum capacity set at 8,000, the Puyallup Assembly Center proved too small to accommodate all Washington Nikkei living in Military Area No. 1. This meant removal of the Yakima community to the North Portland Assembly Center, and of the 3,497 living west of the mountains in Tacoma proper and rural areas, to the Pinedale Assembly Center in Fresno. By June 30, Washington's Military Area No. 1's 13,000 residents of Japanese ancestry had been entirely removed.[60]

As spring returned to the lowlands of Puget Sound and to the Pacific Northwest, Japanese Americans who witnessed the army's March 30 dress rehearsal on Bainbridge Island began to consider their own future exile, a stark reality entering into everyone's mind.

4

Puyallup Assembly Center

In September 1941, over 310,000 fairgoers walked through turnstiles on their way to the Western Washington Fairgrounds to enjoy the Puget Sound region's annual weeklong event in the center of Puyallup. Up from a quarter million the year before, attendance reflected ongoing and widespread interest on the part of residents in Tacoma, Seattle, and the rural communities throughout western Washington. At the turn of the decade, the Puyallup Fair had come to signal autumn's arrival. Crowds who flocked to the fertile Puyallup Valley attended grandstand shows with live entertainment and enjoyed livestock exhibitions, as well as competitive fruit and vegetable displays. And they rode the carnival's forty-five-foot-high Ferris wheel and wooden roller coaster permanently installed in 1935.

It began as a farm fair on a vacant lot in October 1900, but when the Valley Fair Association moved to a new venue it evolved into a ten-acre plot. By now the town of Puyallup, situated in a fertile river valley whose waters from Mount Rainier's northern slopes emptied into Puget Sound, was a quarter century old and its surrounding area was being developed into small-farm operations.

A racetrack in the middle of town formed the permanent fairground's nucleus, and its popularity quickly grew. Acquisition of additional acreage in the 1920s and 1930s led to completion of permanent livestock pavilions, horse stables, exhibition halls, and a six thousand-seat grandstand whose arc spanned one-third the distance around the racetrack and parade ground.

By the 1930s, the fair had received national recognition from political dignitaries. In 1932, while campaigning for the presidency Franklin D. Roosevelt, governor of New York, addressed thirty thousand people who had congregated on the grounds. A decade later, an executive order he signed as president resulted in a five-year suspension of this popular weeklong event.

Encircled by Puyallup with its population of 7,500, in 1940 the fairgrounds site covered 43 acres of lawn-covered fairways, parade grounds, and 41 permanent buildings on the grounds. Along the northern and eastern boundaries lay 3 open parking lots, the largest with spaces for 7,500 automobiles, one of the most expansive lots in the Pacific Northwest.[1]

This public facility's available infrastructure and open space would attract army surveyors in the spring of 1942 as they searched western Washington for locations to warehouse large groups of Japanese "enemy aliens" and "non-aliens."

As debates over eviction of Japanese from the West Coast heated up, on February 5, 1942, Major General Jay L. Benedict, from his post at Fort Douglas, Utah, telegraphed Washington Governor Arthur B. Langlie requesting he initiate a survey to determine feasible state, county, and municipal facilities for "evacuated enemy aliens and their families." Benedict offered as suggestions prison farms, state parks, migratory farm camps, fairgrounds, "pauper farms," and similar installations with existing shelter and sanitary facilities. Langlie conducted the survey without drawing the public's attention.[2]

Langlie passed his results on to the general, itemizing the most promising sites. The short list included Longacres Racetrack near Renton south of Seattle, the Western Washington Fairgrounds at Puyallup, and on the eastern side of the Cascade range, Golden Hop Yard at Toppenish, near Yakima.

With similar surveys conducted simultaneously throughout Oregon and California, the army established a portfolio of potential locations from which eventual assembly center sites could be chosen. This list was compiled even before news of Executive Order 9066 reached the public.

The daunting task of removing and sheltering a hundred thousand men, women, and children awaited the army. Diseases and epidemics had to be prevented, the sick cared for, daily meals prepared for the multitudes, and activities organized to avert disintegration of morale and quell possible insurrection. The question loomed where to warehouse this many people until completion of permanent encampments in the country's interior.

A potential assembly center site had to possess preexisting facilities for housing and community services, as sufficient time to build them from the ground up did not exist. Each location required preexisting electrical power, lighting, adequate water supply, and sanitary facilities for at least five thousand people. Centers had to be situated in close proximity to the communities being evacuated; routes for transporting evacuees out of their homes would be required, and each enclosure would need sufficient open spaces to provide recreational activities for the inmates.[3]

Before selecting a final plan Wartime Civil Control Administration (WCCA) officials considered at least two options for housing evacuees—the first, to employ existing abandoned shelters built by the Civilian Conservation Corps (CCC)as early as 1933. This idea proved unworkable because most sites occupied insufficient space to accommodate more than two hundred individuals. Nor were they conducive to housing the youngest or oldest members of an imprisoned population. The same number of staff would be required to operate, supply, and guard cohorts of two hundred or two thousand individuals.[4]

The second option involved utilizing more spacious shelters situated on military installations, locales better suited to guarding inmates and enforcing regimented living. A prior agreement between the Justice and War Departments had created a plan for moving German, Italian, and Japanese resident enemy aliens detained in Immigration and Naturalization Service (INS) camps onto military reservations for permanent internment. Enlarging the scale might be a possibility. However, existing theater of operation shelters to house middle-aged and elderly men could not be adapted to accommodate women and children. In addition, required real estate and necessary resources were also increasingly scarce as new divisions of troops had to be organized for combat. Abandonment of this plan proved wise in light of a large influx of German and Italian POWs from the North Africa Campaign into U.S. military installations that began in late 1942.[5]

Because these options proved unworkable, in early March 1942 WCCA planners decided to appropriate existing public facilities in or near city limits and near the exclusion zones to be purged. WCCA surveyors visited sites from their lists that included fairgrounds, livestock pavilions, and racetracks located throughout Washington, Oregon, and California.

Of at least nineteen sites receiving serious consideration, fifteen became temporary holding pens the army euphemistically designated "assembly centers." A sixteenth, at Manzanar (Manzanar Reception Center), was built from scratch and eventually turned over to the War Relocation Authority (WRA) for use as a relocation center. The sixteen assembly center sites included thirteen locations in California, and one each in Arizona, Oregon, and Washington.

By the first week of April 1942, the army had identified three sites in Washington State for potential development in time for transfers slated to begin in mid-month. Longacres seemed a logical site since a few weeks earlier the Santa Anita racetrack at Arcadia had been selected as an assembly center for evacuees from Southern California. And soon the Tanforan racetrack at San Bruno, near San Francisco, would be converted into an assembly center.

Selection of the Longacres site would bring cancellation of the June 27 through Labor Day season and certain disappointment to horse racing enthusiasts.[6] But the site's existing infrastructure presented multiple problems; except for the grandstand and horse stables, few structures were in place to house Seattle's seven thousand Nikkei men, women, and children. Perceiving the relatively small population of Japanese in the Pacific Northwest insufficient to warrant two operations in western Washington, the WCCA quickly eliminated Longacres from the list without entering into lease negotiations with racetrack representatives. Puyallup's Western Washington Fairgrounds provided a more promising alternative.[7]

Arriving at the fairgrounds' site, army surveyors found its permanent buildings in good repair and upgraded power, water, and sanitation utilities in place. They noted 43 acres of admissions grounds could accommodate 3,000 inmates while 34 acres of adjacent parking lots possessed sufficient capacity to house 5,000 more. The appeal of these three peripheral expanses of flat land overrode inevitable problems arising from separation of the lots from each other and the main fairgrounds by intervening open public spaces. This challenge would be met later.

The army surveyor team visited the Golden Hop Yard at Toppenish, a third potential site to incarcerate the Nikkei community living around Yakima. They found a small housing compound surrounded by acreage devoted to hops, agreeing it could be transformed into a center to accommodate 1,200 people, the approximate number of Japanese Americans residing between the Cascade range and Columbia River located at the eastern boundary of Washington's Military Area No. 1.[8]

Satisfied these sites could meet the army's needs, leases were drawn up with representatives of the two sites containing provisions for renovation and new construction to begin immediately. At Puyallup A. E. Bartel, secretary and manager of the Fair Association, signed a renewable lease specifying an annual rent of $15,063. Included in the agreement were the fairgrounds and 41 of the 45 existing buildings, plus the 3 surrounding parking lots. Leases subsequently negotiated with private landowners unaffiliated with the Fair Association added five acres, thereby pushing the largest parking lot's boundary farther to the east.[9] Following completion of the lease agreements, on March 29, 1942, Bartel assured the public the annual fair would take place on time in September 1942. In fact, the fairgrounds did not reopen to the public until 1946.[10]

The Toppenish lease included a clause requiring the army to vacate the grounds prior to hop picking season. Landowners wanted to avoid a potential crop loss estimated at $1 million; their timeline allowed an occupancy of no more than three months.[11]

On March 28, 1942, the district engineer at the U.S. Army Corps of Engineers office in Seattle received his order from General DeWitt: "Provide accommodations for 8,000 Japanese evacuees with necessary sanitary and messing facilities at Puyallup fair grounds and adjacent 34–acre parking lots. Completion date: April 15, 1942. MUST."[12] DeWitt sent a similar order to the district engineer in the Toppenish area, giving the U.S. Army Corps of Engineers seventeen days to plan, budget, purchase materials, hire labor, and construct necessary barracks and other structures, a project requiring five million board feet of lumber.

Following site grading and other preparations over the weekend, a hundred carpenters began construction at the Puyallup site on Monday morning, March 30. Hammering started even before draftsmen had sketched a general layout of the buildings. The Tacoma Building Trades and U.S. Employment Service recruited carpenters and laborers for the open shop construction project; work cards in hand and eager for work, men reported to the army personnel office in Seattle for dispatch to a project that would generate several weeks of wages.[13] Within a week, 1,085 men with hammers, saws, pipe wrenches, and wire cutters in their hands worked 8–hour shifts, 24 hours a day. Construction proceeded rapidly despite spring mud and huge lumber piles that provided obstacles to automobiles maneuvering throughout the construction site. Supervisors soon resorted to horses to transport them through the project.[14]

Family barracks arose atop mud sills set directly on the expanse of each converted parking lot. Floorboards rested a few inches above the soil, every building constructed twenty feet wide and varying in length, with eight-foot-high inner walls dividing the long structures into multiple family compartments.[15]

Areas of new construction on the former parking lots, now identified as Areas A, B, and C, had been built for autonomy with their own set of mess halls, latrines, showers, and laundry facilities. Area A, the largest and designed to hold 3,000 inhabitants, had 6 mess halls with concrete floors and dimensions of 40 x 100 feet; this permitted 500 people to be fed at a single sitting. Three warehouses served the mess halls. Two laundries, 18 latrines, each with 12 water-flushed toilets and 6 shower areas, completed the plan. The 100–foot-wide firebreak that divided Area A into halves permitted a recreation area named Pitcher Field after one of the center administrators. Two watchtowers faced each other on opposite perimeter walls. Areas B and C, proportionally smaller and designed to hold 1,100 and 900 inmates, respectively, lacked adequate open spaces for significant recreational use within the barbed wire confines.

On the site of the fairgrounds proper, existing structures and irregular location of open spaces required construction of 20–foot-wide barracks of varying lengths. Housing units arose as 3 separate clusters. The elliptical parade ground held 24 rectangular barrack units; they ranged in length from 20 x 24 to 20 x 281 feet. Workers also converted open space beneath the existing grandstand into 105 individual cell-like "apartments."

Allotting 50 square feet per person as planned, the new assembly center was capable of holding just over 8,000 individuals.[16]

A view from the grandstand in Area D of living quarters located on the parade field. Some barracks of Area A may be seen at the top left. (National Archives)

Theater-of-operation architecture informed assembly center construction. However, instead of employing standard gable construction, each apartment had a single window cut into the eight-foot back wall, while a windowless doorway on the ten-foot front wall opened out to face another barrack. The eight-foot-high interior walls were thus unable to reach the roofline, leaving multiple triangular openings that funneled sound from one end of the barracks building to the other. Tarpaper laid down on roofs was absent from the perimeters' walls, which remained exposed. Although electrical wiring ran the length of every barrack, each apartment had only a single light socket hanging from the ceiling. Common shiplap covered the floors, preventing contact with the ground underneath. On top of these overlapping boards, in each living space sat a wood stove fueled by wood scraps from the construction and firewood brought in from outside.

Many inmates who later described their accommodations recalled them as unfit for families, "nothing more than a shed on a chicken ranch."[17]

Built behind the grandstand an "E"-shaped hundred-bed hospital arose to serve the medical needs of the population anticipated to be eight thousand. Existing buildings would be used as community halls, office space for Caucasian and Japanese American office workers, and mess halls. Eight-foot, ten-strand barbed wire fences surrounded the converted fairground, as did strategically placed watchtowers equipped with flood and spotlights. The fences surrounding each of the four areas would indelibly impress many of the inmates more than their "rabbit hutch" apartments.[18]

At midnight on April 15, resident engineer Otto R. Lunn announced completion of major construction. Three days later, a color guard from nearby Fort Lewis hoisted the American flag within the assembly center grounds as a field artillery band played the national anthem.[19]

Army public relations officers began referring to the Puyallup Assembly Center as "Camp Harmony" as early as April 23, with the first Nikkei arrival still four days away. The euphemism remains in use to the present day.[20]

Meanwhile, construction at the Toppenish site proceeded with considerable difficulty, its inherent problems evident from previous viewpoints offered by outsiders as well as the army. During the first week of April American Friends Service Committee (AFSC) volunteer Floyd Schmoe visited the site, observing: "Tiny huts—dirty floors—no windows—dust, dirt, filth. Nice new barracks for the soldiers who are to guard the internees. Conditions far worse than Puyallup."[21]

Construction continued. However, by the end of April, the camp had not yet seen its first inductee. On a follow-up visit Schmoe reported soldiers to be the only occupants. Because sentries refused him entry he could not examine the buildings closely. Those he'd seen had been painted dark red with gray windows and doorframes. As yet no barbed wire, but he reported a newly constructed combination water tank and watchtower clearly visible and new bathhouses and mess hall. Considerable improvements had been made since his first visit, "if anything a little better than Puyallup."[22]

Although Schmoe's visual inspection, undertaken from a distance, suggests emergence of adequate facilities for the Yakima area Japanese, from the army's perspective construction proceeded poorly. By April 25, 1942, two days before the first arrivals from Alaska entered the Puyallup Assembly Center, structural deficiencies at the Toppenish site still prevented occupancy. The fourteen double pit (two seat) latrines used at the hop farm had been condemned, requiring replacement. Fire protection equipment, critical in eastern Washington's dry climate, was inadequate, with only ten extinguishers available for a camp devoid of barrels and buckets. Water pressure in existing wells could not support a two-inch hose. Because the heating system had been declared dangerous, workers removed all sheet metal stoves. The site lacked sufficient space for organized outdoor recreational activities, being surrounded by mature hop-producing acreage. Finally, tests of available water sources from the immediate area and a new well developed on the site were yet to be completed.

Yet even with these obstacles, considerable effort had gone into development of the site. The mess hall, equipped with stoves, oven ranges, and griddle tops, as well as adequate hot water and refrigeration, stood ready to serve five hundred people at a sitting. A new twenty-six-bed infirmary with separate ward had been completed for isolating patients with contagious or infectious diseases. New construction of five buildings and upgrade of ten existing structures intended to house a single military police company also stood finished. All buildings were hooked up to newly installed gravity-to-gravel septic tanks.[23]

With minimal land available to construct additional housing units, on-site army inspectors recommended adding second stories onto each cabin to increase total capacity to 460, with 3 people occupying each unit. But time was running out.

Construction problems had their solutions, but they would delay occupancy into May. This created a schedule that conflicted with the lease stipulation to vacate the property before start of hop harvest. WCCA planners therefore terminated the project.

The decision to abandon the Toppenish project enabled installations rushed into place to meet DeWitt's deadline—kitchen equipment, medical units, and other infrastructure, to be quickly disassembled and transported to the Puyallup Assembly Center and the Tule Lake Relocation Center then under construction in northern California. The 1,200 Nikkei residing in the Yakima area were reassigned to the Portland Assembly Center.[24]

* * *

As construction progressed at the two sites Lieutenant Colonel Paul B. Malone, acting provost marshal for the states of Washington and Oregon, and members of his staff visited Jimmie Sakamoto at the Seattle Progressive Citizens' League office on Main Street to discuss a plan for self-government at the Puyallup Assembly Center. More than fifty years later, Bill Hosokawa recalled how the army arrived at Sakamoto's office without knowing how to proceed or how to organize the Seattle community's move to Puyallup. Sakamoto offered the Emergency Defense Council's (EDC) services to Malone, suggesting confusion could be avoided with an organized group in place to run the center and assist the army.[25]

Eager to cooperate with evacuation, by now a foregone conclusion, Sakamoto saw himself as the one to guide his community into captivity. "It is up to us to cooperate with the government loyally and cheerfully," he said earlier to members of the Japanese American Citizens League (JACL) at a national gathering in San Francisco.[26] Over the course of the next few weeks he and his group organized what became known as "Evacuee Administration Headquarters." Malone suggested this administration be set up along military lines, with general headquarters having four sections: personnel (G-1); information (G-2); operations (G-3); and supply (G-4). Each area would have its own assistant director to assemble section staffs according to each area's needs.

Malone and Sakamoto arranged for the headquarters staff to assume responsibility for planning and setting policy for the entire center. The unique physical layout, with its four housing areas separated from each other by city streets, would result in administration of all four areas being carried out centrally.

Next, Sakamoto sat down with his lieutenants Bill Hosokawa, Dick Setsuda, George Ishihara, Bill Mimbu, and Tom Kanno, all from the earlier EDC, to fill the needed slots. Following the earlier staffing pattern of the EDC, those receiving assignments would be Sakamoto's friends and acquaintances, who would build a staff based on prior trust and long-term relationships. EDC members constituted the vast majority, with additional JACL people completing his staff.

Bill Hosokawa advised the national secretary of JACL on May 7, 1942, that the Japanese community had supported JACL-backed leadership in Seattle since the first week of the war because of the EDC's successful response to the national emergency. "We were fortunate to have good key men who worked with the problem since the first week of the war, and it was a simple matter for them to swing over into the evacuation phase."[27]

These "good key men" would provide the core of the "Japanese administration," a staff of thirty-five who filled supervisory positions in the four "G" sections. Sakamoto and his closest advisors hand-picked most subordinates while still in Seattle awaiting their removal to Puyallup. All but three being Seattle residents known to Sakamoto and his group, other Nisei in the same age group found themselves outsiders. They grumbled that Jimmie had given the best jobs to his friends and left them out. This created friction in the community; Sakamoto responded by identifying certain people outside the committee whom he knew were competent and willing to serve; Auburn resident Thomas Iseri, JACL chairman of the Northwest District JACL Council; Satoru "Lefty" Sasaki, from Orting, president of the Puyallup Valley JACL; and Dick Naito, from the Kent Valley, also an active JACL member. Nevertheless, since the Pierce County contingent at Camp Harmony constituted over 14 percent of the population, assignment of these three left the rural group underrepresented in community affairs.

Appointees came from the ranks of older Nisei. Averaging 32 years of age, the headquarters group ranged from 21 to 49. Two of the three female appointees were wives of other staff members. Paymaster Kenjiro Saito, at 49 the only Issei in the headquarters group, was Sakamoto's senior by a decade.

As "chief interpreter" of the headquarters staff at Camp Harmony, Bill Hosokawa, former executive secretary of the EDC, served a similar public relations function in his new position and was Sakamoto's right-hand man. George Ishihara, chairman of the EDC's civilian defense committee, became the headquarters staff personnel supervisor, holding possibly the headquarters staff's most important position behind those of Sakamoto and Hosokawa.

Dick Setsuda, William Mimbu, Tom Kanno, Clarence Arai, Julius Fujihira, and others were holdovers from the EDC. One newcomer to the staff, Masaru (Chick) Uno, admired Sakamoto. An outstanding boxer in college, he had much in common with his friend four years his senior. Sakamoto placed Uno in charge of the recreation program.

All members of the headquarters staff had graduated from high school, with twenty-five acquiring some college education; ten others had baccalaureate or advanced college degrees. Many owned or operated businesses or had assumed leadership roles in the prewar community.[28]

According to a contemporaneous account by S. Frank Miyamoto, a young sociologist who observed and recorded the daily experience at Camp Harmony and later, Tule Lake Relocation Center, after selecting the headquarters staff, Sakamoto, Hosokawa, Ishihara, Kanno, and Setsuda filled section staff positions in the various areas with William Mimbu, Takeo Nogaki, Tom Arai, and Hiroyuki Ichihara section leader designates for Areas A, B, C, and D, respectively.[29]

Sakamoto's group clearly understood that Seattle's Nikkei would be removed by geographic area over a two- to three-week period. With Lieutenant Colonel Malone's approval, Sakamoto and his core staff remained in the community to assist the evacuation process until the last day. Located at 517 Main Street within an area to be evacuated early, the JACL office moved up the hill to the Maryknoll School at 1610 East Jefferson Street, within the geographic area designated as the last to be emptied. Throughout the eviction period the WCCA maintained a small office adjacent to JACL quarters.[30]

While mechanical aspects of the planned exile became well known throughout the Nikkei community, residents did not know when it would occur or where they would eventually be placed. Would families remain intact or be separated as occurred earlier with the FBI's arrest of community elders? Confusion reigned as the government withheld information until the last moment.

With their ultimate destination unknown, Seattle Nikkei's healthcare community worried about public health problems known to threaten large groups during extended periods of close confinement. Inoculations against typhoid, diphtheria, smallpox, and other communicable diseases often occurring in overpopulated areas such as prison camps alarmed Dr. Mitsao Paul Suzuki, one of five prewar Nikkei physicians practicing in Seattle. His wife, Nobuko (Yanigamachi) Suzuki, a social welfare worker among Japanese indigents during the Depression, worried as well. She had visited Seattle's Health and Sanitation Department and Seattle area hospitals to help Japanese-speaking clients convey their ailments to Caucasian doctors.

Up to this point the WCCA remained silent regarding plans to inoculate Nikkei residents, and since General DeWitt did not initiate contact with the U.S. Public Health Service (USPHS) until March 28, 1942, likely no plan existed.[31]

Suzuki knew that individuals who went directly to the Seattle Health and Sanitation Department north of Japantown could obtain typhoid serum at no charge. For the elderly and newborns, however, travel uptown to receive inoculations consisting of three injections spaced a week apart posed a significant barrier. In an attempt to better meet her community's need, Suzuki met with the epidemiologist responsible for administering immunizations at the health department. He assured her a sufficient vaccine supply was on hand for the entire Nikkei community, but that the community would have to administer the program using its own doctors and nurses at field stations set up in centralized gathering places. In addition, permission to release the vaccine would have to come from the office of the commissioner, Frank M. Carroll. Suzuki's subsequent meeting with Carroll resulted in his refusal to release it under any circumstances. Another alternative would have to be sought.[32]

The Association of Japanese Cannery Workers came to the rescue on April 4 when it announced free inoculations for its members at association headquarters on Main Street. Dr. Suzuki and his two nurse staff volunteered to provide the 3–part inoculations, and 200 of the 350 eligible members received the initial dose on April 9. Fearing typhoid fever might rage through an unprotected incarcerated community, the association extended sponsorship of the program community-wide by purchasing additional doses using its own funds.

On April 13 Suzuki and his staff inoculated nearly six hundred individuals who stretched into a queue along Main Street. They offered their arms, averaging nearly one every minute. Not counting others inoculated elsewhere, subsequent inoculations promised for April 20 and April 27 enabled more than eight hundred Seattle Nikkei to participate in the program by the time buses began to head southward toward the Puyallup Assembly Center.[33]

At the last minute WCCA officials announced the USPHS staff would take over the inoculation program for anyone not receiving the complete series of typhoid shots or not up to date on diphtheria or smallpox immunizations.[34]

Meanwhile, construction at the Puyallup Assembly Center neared completion. Although army engineers met DeWitt's April 15 deadline for the center's basic construction, it was not yet ready for occupancy, and the hospital would not open for weeks after the center opened. Final construction projects, proving troublesome, caught the public's eye. Floyd Schmoe's early reports on construction at Puyallup and Toppenish had discouraged those who would have to live there. Now the Fellowship of Reconciliation (FOR) became involved.

FOR, an interfaith peace organization begun in England with the outbreak of World War I, sought "to replace violence, war, racism and economic injustice with nonviolence, peace and justice."[35] Its New York–based staff's early activities became a thorn in the side of Colonel Bendetsen and the WCCA during the assembly center period.

On April 23, 1942, FOR's secretary A. J. Muste, a labor and peace activist, sent a telegram to President Roosevelt drawing his attention to the "EXCEED-

INGLY BAD" conditions at some of the assembly centers, "ESPECIALLY AT STATE FAIRGROUNDS AT PUYALLUP NEAR SEATTLE" and at the Golden Hop Farms in Toppenish, still being readied to house Nikkei from the Yakima area.[36]

The White House forwarded the telegram to the director of the WRA with copies sent to the War and Justice Departments. Bendetsen became involved. His first response requested that the army's press relations consultant, T. W. (Ted) Braun, check into the validity of the charges and find out more about the "so called 'Fellowship of Reconciliation' organization." The next day Braun reported FOR's primary activities to be in the East. However, a node of thirty to forty members reputed to have many conscientious objector students existed throughout the state, centered on the University of Washington campus. Its organizer was F. B. Farquharson, a professor of engineering.[37] His wife, Mary, then a senator in the state legislature, served as a member of FOR's national council.

On May 2 Bendetsen posted a reply to Muste on behalf of General DeWitt. Sensing little threat from the group, his message was terse: "Facilities necessary for the housing, health, and welfare of evacuees at temporary centers are being provided consistent with the urgency of the program."

This response failed to address the growing controversy over conditions at the Puyallup fairgrounds. According to a local press report on April 28, Pierce County health director Dr. Norman E. Magnuson protested the U.S. Army Corps of Engineers' poorly designed methods of sewage treatment and disposal in place at the center. This would soon become a significant public health problem for inductees scheduled to arrive by the thousands within the next two weeks. He warned that an influx of seven thousand inmates, doubling the city's population almost overnight, would cause "an extreme danger to community health."[38]

Finding himself in a public relations bind, Bendetsen, following consultation with Braun, agreed in writing that a problem indeed existed and would be resolved.

By no means the last time Bendetsen heard from the group, FOR defended the Nikkei community throughout the war to help alleviate "the government's outrageous action."[39]

*   *   *

Even before the first Civilian Exclusion Order (CEO) posters appeared, by early March, with Military Areas No. 1 and No. 2 in place, the inevitability of exile was beginning to set in. Many, if not most, *nihonmachi* residents began to consider disposing of their businesses, high-value items such as automobiles, as well as other personal but expendable possessions to obtain cash for uncertain times ahead. One's property could be disposed of through private sale or the alien property custodian with the Federal Reserve Bank (FRB) of San Francisco could assist with transfers.

With the appearance of the first exclusion orders on Seattle streets in mid-April identifying April 28 as the scheduled start date for the transfer to Puyallup, time had grown short. How to part with personal belongings— washing machines, refrigerators, automobiles, heirlooms, pets? Leases had to be broken, businesses dissolved, shelf stock dispersed.

The Murakami family lived within the geographic boundaries of CEO No. 17 and had to leave with the first major wave out of Seattle on April 30. The family decided to hold on to Higo 10¢ Store throughout the war. In the days before his family's departure Murakami boarded up his numerous display windows to protect the business from vandalism and theft. A second-floor non-Japanese tenant agreed to keep watch over the vacant store until the family's return.[40]

The Itois held a binding long-term lease on the Carrollton Hotel, whose owner allowed the family to store household belongings in the vacant rooms under his watchful eye.[41]

Until days before evacuation the White River Dairy venture remained profitable due to its owners' good business sense and the Treasury Department relinquishing its hold on the accounting books after December 7, 1941. But as family shareholders awaited their departure, no trustworthy individual or corporation could be found to manage the business in their absence. With mothballing the building not feasible, the corporation put the business up for sale. The Alpine Dairy purchased it at fair market value as the Caucasian-owned operation sought to expand operations during the war.[42]

For George Tokuda, who had recently opened his second drugstore in Japantown, the impending evacuation came at a bad time. He closed this store, consolidating merchandise into his original business, where he also stored fixtures from the new store. With the future uncertain he asked a Caucasian neighbor to maintain the business. While at the Puyallup Assembly Center, however, Tokuda received less than $100 from the caretaker. When a trusted friend told him of his nearly empty store, the betrayal finally surfaced. Denied a one-day leave from the center to resolve the problem, he had no choice but to employ an attorney to help sell off the fixtures and what remained of the merchandise, all at a loss. When former Nikkei residents began returning to Seattle in January 1945, the man who purchased the remains of Tokuda's business placed a "No Japs" sign in the window.[43]

By 1942, in addition to owning their home on Alder Street and shoe store and shoe repair shop in Japantown, the Akutsu family had also accumulated several rental properties. With their father detained by the Justice Department, arranging long-term leases fell to Jim and his brother Gene. Although Jim had experience in real estate, he needed help locating quality tenants and someone to look over the properties and collect rents in the family's absence. Help came from John Wesley Dolby, acting Spanish consul and father of a high school friend who faithfully performed these services throughout the war as an act of friendship. Jim and Dolby's son, battery mates on the diamond, had been longtime friends at Broadway High School. Summers they trekked across the Olympic Mountains and backpacked in the Cascades. Jim, a frequent guest in the Dolby home, had become a favorite of the family.[44]

But Dolby could not protect the Akutsu shoe businesses. Long managed by other Issei with primarily a Japanese clientele, no one remained to take over the business or provide a customer base. An evacuation sale in the Business Opportunities section listed the New Golden shoe store at 650 Jackson Street. No takers appeared.

Koi Tanagi's wife, son, and daughter kept their grocery store going from February to April, but as evacuation drew near sold stock at a discount and ate from the remaining rice and canned goods. Comparing her family's situation to that of others in the community, Tanagi's daughter, Sharon Aburano, recalls: "I thought we were more fortunate than others because we could still eat. The shelves were all full with canned goods. We had rice, and we used to make bean sprouts around the corner, in Canton Alley, where we had a place rented that was humid."[45]

Their store taken over by the owner of the building, the Tanagis closed their doors. "We just left the place."

Soon after Proclamation No. 1 appeared, Business Opportunities columns in want ads section of local newspapers carried two- and three-line classified advertisements identifying Japanese-owned businesses for sale. Scattered throughout the daily column with increasing frequency, they began to compete with other business opportunities offered at sacrifice by those with an illness or other life-altering situation or by draft-age men called into the service:

> JAPANESE evacuation necessitates immediate sale 55–room brick hotel. Best linens, furnishings: steam heat, steady tenants. Main 8670, after 5:30.
>
> EVACUEE OFFERS LEASE and FURNITURE in OUTSTANDING Seattle downtown hotel. Mr. Best. SE. 2161. 212 Lloyd Bldg.
>
> Groc. & Beer License (4 rms. & bath. Low rent.) Excellent location; doing $40 dly. $1,000. Sacrifice. Evacuee. 2608 Judkins.

Cafe. $500 cash takes all. Estab. 19 yrs. Low rent. Evacuation sale. 78 Stewart.

1/2 Price. Hotels & Apts. All sizes. Evacuation sales. E. Fujitomi, 517 1/2 Jackson.

HOTEL 62 rms. Downtown. 2 yr. Lease. Evacuees. 168 Main.

Beauty shop, Living rms. possible. Near New Yesler Terrace. Evacuee. Sac. 112–12th Ave.

HOTEL and grocery for sale. Forced to sell due to evacuation. Cash or terms. Seneca 9741. 1908 Seventh.

Some Nikkei business owners preferred professional brokers to handle their sales. One firm brokered multiple Japanese businesses, offering a "fine opportunity to take over an ESTABLISHED BUSINESS at a FRACTION of its VALUE." In a single ad it listed five barbershops, six dry cleaning shops, three grocery stores, and a florist shop, all fully equipped. Some Nikkei hotel and apartment operators sought out well-known real estate agents such as Henry Broderick, West & Wheeler, and John Davis & Co., in hopes of attracting new owners or lease holders who possessed increased capital. Advertising under a large font heading, "Alien Hotels and Apartments," Ed C. Metzger also offered "a few select hotels and apartments for sale or lease."

In another instance, twenty-five Nikkei business owners jointly composed a single want ad listing stores being offered accompanied by their *nihonmachi* addresses. "Full information can be obtained from Japanese owners at the respective addresses."[46]

Leases and occasionally outright sale of hotels and apartment houses ranging from 20 to 120 rooms appeared on the market. One ad appearing in the adjacent Business Opportunities Wanted section sought a "bargain" Japanese hotel or apartment house. Its cost could have been saved had the advertiser walked up Jackson Street and through Japantown, where available hotels and apartment houses existed everywhere.

Faced with a choice of abandoning their automobiles or storing them at their own expense only to rust, owners placed ads to help generate desperately needed cash. Although automobiles remained in high demand by the civilian population throughout the evacuation period, identifying oneself as an evacuee would all but guarantee less cash for a seller with potential buyers prepared to wait it out. Most ads lacked an asking price because everyone realized the forced evacuation was inevitable:

> 1936 DESOTO sedan. Attached overdrive, gas-saver transmissions; four new tires. Evacuation forces sale. Phone East 2178 after 8 p.m.

EVACUEES' CARS, TRUCKS Big Sacrifice. Japanese Interpreting Service. Eliott 1555.[47]

Fewer want ads appeared for household appliances, furniture, and other bulky items to be left behind. Secondhand dealers moved through the community offering low prices for items that suddenly glutted the market, leaving little need to advertise. Take-it-or-leave-it offers were taken on mangles, stoves, refrigerators, furniture, carpets, dishware, and other belongings quickly converted to cash. On rare occasions anger flared in response to a low offer for valuable heirlooms, sending potential buyers fleeing.[48]

Resisting low offers, many Nikkei property owners turned for assistance to the FRB of San Francisco. Upon learning of "numerous sacrifice sales" by Japanese to secondhand dealers and real estate profiteers, on February 23 and 28 the Tolan Committee cabled the secretary of war to recommend appointment of an alien property custodian.[49] On March 11 the FRB of San Francisco became the government-appointed property custodian for both alien and U.S-born Japanese. Four days later, the Farm Security Administration (FSA) assumed responsibility for helping farmers obtain fair disposition of their crops and land, leaving the FRB to handle personal, nonagricultural properties from branch offices in Los Angeles, Portland, and Seattle. Later, satellite offices overseen by the WCCA opened in rural areas of the West Coast, including eight in Washington.[50]

The alien property custodian functioned as "contact man" aiding in the transfer of evacuee property or leases, including hotels, farms, and other major holdings, and assisting evacuees who chose to retain their properties and needed responsible trustees, renters, or solid operating arrangements. Agents acted upon grant of power of attorney by property owners or by assuming the power to act in absence of authorization.[51] If possible FRB officials encouraged Nikkei to make their own deals without sacrificing value and, in the event they were unable to avoid gouging, cheating, or outright fraud by unscrupulous buyers, to then contact the FRB. R. T. Symmes, representing the FRB's Seattle branch, stated: "I am sure that we shall prevent, so far as humanly possible, forced sales by which the evacuees might suffer severe financial losses that are neither contemplated nor desired by the government."[52]

The WCCA, through the FRB, began to define how Japanese automobile owners should dispose of their cars. As with other properties, agents encouraged private sales, an exception being 1942 models required to be sold to new car dealers now begging for stock, automakers having converted production to war materiel. A second was to store or sell their cars through the FRB. Private automobiles driven to the Puyallup Assembly Center had to be pre-registered with the FRB at the WCCA's civil control stations and upon arrival turned over for final disposition. Sale to the army at Blue Book wholesale value presented a third option. Whatever choice car owners exercised turned to gain for new car dealers, the public, or government and to loss for the seller who because of circumstances possessed no leverage with which to bargain. Deals made through the FRB helped some owners avoid being fleeced altogether.[53]

Problems resulting from the impending evacuation often became more complex for farm operators than for those who ran hotels or other urban businesses. Long-term leases had to be transferred, expensive farm machinery disposed of or stored by sympathetic neighbors. Growers had to decide whether or not to plant crops for the 1942 season.[54]

To invest in planting without guarantee they would reap the harvest or have an adequate mechanism in place to ensure equity in the crops seemed foolish by any standard. In addition, the evacuation's uncertainties curtailed credit by lenders based on crop mortgage. Two of the region's three banks had already suspended credit, and growers without available cash could not purchase seed or fertilizers.[55]

Nikkei farmers wanted to stall until their future looked more certain. By March 5, many farmers in the White and Puyallup valleys had stopped planting, returning fertilizers and other farm supplies for rebates to fund travel and subsistence.[56] Aware of this, the army pressured farmers to remain on the land. On March 10, 1942, the day of the Civil Affairs Division's creation, Tom C. Clark, liaison between the Justice Department and WCCA, equated continued crop production with a measure of loyalty: "There can be no doubt that all persons who wish to show their loyalty to this country should continue farming operations to the fullest extent."[57] Three days later, Clark elevated crop neglect or damage to an act of sabotage.[58]

For many Japanese growers still holding on to farms in King and Pierce counties, the issue of loyalty was reduced to dollars and cents. By then, according to Floyd Oles, manager of the Washington Produce Shippers Association, a cooperative group engaged in marketing fresh produce grown in western Washington to markets outside the region, "It is quite useless even to discuss the possibility of having others farm these lands at this late date at least as to 1942 crops."[59]

Even with government threats, given lack of credit and the uncertain future, Nikkei farmers could no longer be counted on to maintain their acreage in full production. In order to salvage any part of the growing season, transfers of leases to new tenants or an outright sale of land to new owners became essential and needed to be accomplished quickly. Cauliflower plants ready for transplanting and hothouse lettuce plants had to be moved outdoors by the end of March. This brought the FSA in to aid in the transfer of croplands.

By April 2, the FSA registered enough Caucasian and Filipino farmers to take over about one-third of the Nikkei farms in western Washington.[60] Progress on transfers moved slowly since truck farming on small acreage was alien to most white farmers; appeals went out to part-time and retired farm families with experience in small-scale farming.[61]

Persistent rumors that Nikkei would be allowed to remain on the land to harvest their crops further hampered transfers. Efforts by Oles and others who encouraged General DeWitt to allow Issei farmers to remain through harvest season while "under whatever safeguards the Army and the Department of Justice found to be adequate" were ignored.[62] Even though the FSA advised in early April that "there is absolutely no policy planned for permitting them to remain until the harvest," rumors persisted into mid-month.[63] By then a new rumor had declared a rolling evacuation under study by the army would first remove urban Nikkei, with rural areas evacuated after the harvest.[64]

By April 17, 1942, 60 percent of farmland operated by West Coast Japanese and Japanese Americans had been transferred to other operators. Washington's figure was 58.7 percent.[65] Fewer than one-half of King County's 150 Nikkei farms were now in Caucasian or Filipino hands. Transfers continued to lag throughout April, causing Charles A. Agers, field agent for the FSA in Seattle, to send forth another patriotic appeal: "Food is as important as guns in our national war effort. Qualified farmers can buy, lease, or manage the land through any fair transaction, which they can make with the former owners. All sizes of holdings are available. There are many varieties of crops. The government needs the farmers' help. They can help win the war and at the same time make a sound farm investment."[66]

Any eleventh-hour hopes of Nikkei farmers who still remained on the land disappeared on May 5 with the appearance of CEO No. 39, ordering evacuation of the first group of King County Nikkei from important farmlands southeast of Seattle, including the White, Green, and Snoqualmie valleys. The next day fifty-four additional farm operators registered with the FSA. In the end, only the public appearance of evacuation orders moved the majority of Japanese growers in western Washington to grant power of attorney to the FSA, thus enabling it to dispose of their acreage.[67]

One former Puyallup Valley resident testifying before the Commission on Wartime Relocation and Internment of Civilians in 1981 recalled efforts of the Issei truck farmers in his area who continued farming up to the last minute: "By the middle of May, when the valley folks were sent to the assembly center, the telephone peas were waist high and strung, the pole beans were staked, early radishes and green onions were ready for the market, strawberries were starting to ripen and the lettuce had been transplanted. Not much is known how the crops fared in the harvest nor what prices were obtained, but the Issei farmers went into camp with their heads held high, knowing that they had done everything that was possible to help our nation face its first summer of World War II."[68]

Dick Nishi, another prewar farmer testifying before the Commission, offered an opposing view: "We were forced to continue farming with no financial gain because the government stated that any neglect on our part would be considered an act of sabotage."[69]

Many King and Pierce county Nikkei heading for the Puyallup Assembly Center must have felt like outcasts abandoned by the democracy and Constitution they believed would protect them. The populace in the inland states had refused them entry even though Nikkei possessed vital skills required to advance the war effort. Their patriotism rejected, their president signed the order banishing them from the West Coast. Although subdued in their opposition to the presence of the Nikkei in their midst compared to other regions in the country, Seattle residents, for the most part, appeared indifferent to their losses.

5

Exile

General DeWitt's Public Proclamation No. 3 established curfew and travel restrictions. Effective March 27, it impacted Japanese, German, and Italian aliens, and "all other persons of Japanese ancestry" within Military Area No. 1, as well as Military Areas Nos. 2–6 throughout the entire Western Defense Command (WDC) established earlier in Public Proclamation No. 2.[1] (See table 3.) This augmented the attorney general's February 4 curfew order for enemy aliens and added restrictions, which included U.S. citizen Japanese. Now Seattle's seven thousand Nikkei and all resident Japanese throughout the West had to be "within their place of residence" between 8:00 p.m. and 6:00 a.m. Furthermore: "At all other times all such persons shall be only at their place of residence or employment or traveling between those places or within a distance of not more than five miles from their place of residence."[2]

With travel outside the city now off limits, families were cut off from one another except for telephone and mail contact. Farmers hauling produce to the Pike Place Market could be stopped for any reason while Nikkei living in Seattle's distant reaches had to plan their travel to avoid being out past curfew and violating the five-mile travel ban.

The curfew order affected campus life. Live-at-home Nisei students could no longer study at the University of Washington's Suzzallo Library in the evening or linger with friends and classmates without arranging for accommodations on or near the campus. Freshman Kenji Okuda, a commuter from Beacon Hill, found a spare bed at Eagleson Hall, the off-campus student YMCA where he was an active member.[3] Others doubled up in cramped apartments occupied by fellow Nisei students or Caucasian friends. Or they

Table 3. Western Defense Command Proclamations Governing the Forced Evacuation Process

Proclamation No.	Date	Provisions
Public Proclamation No. 1	March 2	Establishes Military Areas Nos. 1 and 2
Public Proclamation No. 2	March 16	Establishes Military Areas Nos. 3, 4, 5, and 6 covering the remainder of the Western Defense Command
Public Proclamation No. 3	March 24	Establishes an 8:00 p.m.–6:00 a.m. curfew and a five-mile travel restriction throughout the six military areas of the Western Defense Command
Public Proclamation No. 4	March 27	Prohibits voluntary migration out of Military Area No. 1 after March 29
Public Proclamation No. 5	March 30	Extends exemptions from exclusion for certain alien enemies, and the blind

Source: Daniels, *The Decision to Relocate the Japanese Americans*, documents section.

simply complied with the order and left campus early. Yet even with nearby accommodations, when study mates sounded the warning, Nisei students hurried home from the library to be off the streets by 8:00 p.m. The forty-nine students who bunked at the nearby Japanese Students' Club made a beeline to their shelters before the campus bells struck eight.

Twenty-four-year-old Gordon Hirabayashi lived at the YMCA's twelve-man dormitory and earned his bed by maintaining the furnace. With his Nisei cohorts he made his way to the empty dorm well ahead of the others who drifted in after the library closed.

Hirabayashi entered the University of Washington for the 1937 fall term as a mathematics major. To help defray college expenses he worked as a "schoolboy" in the home of a doctor, cleaning the house and maintaining the yard. For two years he attended classes during fall and winter terms, then returned to the family's Thomas farm during planting, growing, and harvesting seasons.

Hirabayashi's academic interests would turn to the social sciences during his junior year when he became active in the student YMCA. In 1940, as a delegate to a national meeting in New York, he came under the influence of leaders of the pacifist Fellowship of Reconciliation (FOR). His pacifist beliefs were informed by his Christian parents whose principles and spirituality, not unlike that of the Quakers who reject military service and war, accompanied them to the United States. While at the university he discovered the University Quaker Meeting and attended regularly. Upon his return from New York to Seattle and following passage of the peacetime conscription law, he successfully registered as a conscientious objector; in the latter part of 1941 he became a member of the Society of Friends.[4]

The curfew order took effect as Hirabayashi finished the first quarter of his senior year. After a week of dashing to his dormitory barely in time to beat the curfew, he suddenly stopped this behavior. Believing curfews to be irreconcilable with the U.S. Constitution, he began to ignore the curfew order. Shortly, he also ignored the five-mile travel restriction, choosing instead to come and go at his own discretion like any other free citizen of the United States.

Hirabayashi had not planned to make his personal stand public. However, his thinking changed when Civilian Exclusion Order (CEO) No. 57 posters appeared in the University District, ordering registration for Nikkei and their families who fell under its jurisdiction. By this time two thousand people from Seattle, Puyallup Valley, and Alaska were incarcerated at Camp Harmony.[5]

From the onset of the first exclusion order Hirabayashi and fellow student and friend twenty-one-year-old Bill Makino, who also ignored the curfew and travel ban, completed dozens of trips to the assembly center, hauling baggage as American Friends Service Committee (AFSC) volunteers. They had argued the merits of resisting their forced removal. When their own order was issued, they set about to resist it. However, when Makino realized his aging parents would have no one to look after them in camp, he bowed out, leaving Gordon on his own.

After departure of the last bus to the Puyallup Assembly Center, Hirabayashi considered roaming the streets to await arrest. But after consultation with Arthur Barnett, a thirty-five-year-old Seattle attorney and fellow Quaker, he chose to confront authorities head on. After waving goodbye to departing evacuees on May 16, Barnett, having alerted agents, accompanied Gordon to the FBI office, where the young student turned himself in. Gordon handed agents a four-page statement on his refusal to register for evacuation, arguing that "If I were to register and cooperate . . . I would be giving helpless consent to the denial of practically all of the things, which give me incentive to live. I must maintain my Christian principles. I consider it my duty to maintain the democratic standards for which this nation lives. Therefore, I must refuse this order for evacuation."[6]

Hirabayashi had expected jail, but agents escorted him instead to the civil control station at Maryknoll Mission House in an attempt to register then send him off to Camp Harmony, thereby bringing 100 percent compliance with CEO No. 57. The FBI's effort failed. Next, after transporting Hirabayashi to the King County Courthouse, agents booked him into the county jail's "federal tank," the same lock-up that earlier held attorneys Kenji Ito and Thomas Masuda during their legal ordeals with the federal government.

On May 20 bail was set at $5,000. Because posting bail would result in immediate transfer to the Puyallup Assembly Center, on principle Hirabayashi refused the opportunity. He insisted on the freedom enjoyed by any other citizen not subject to exclusion. Jailers, of course, denied his plea.

One week into his confinement Hirabayashi received a summons to the Federal Courthouse. Here Captain M. A. Ravisto, Wartime Civil Control Administration (WCCA) adjutant in Seattle, asked him to submit to registration whereupon all charges would be dropped. Once again, refusal. During this interview Hirabayashi first learned he was the only Japanese American in the country to refuse registration orders for evacuation. As a consequence of his failure to back down, he spent the next nine months behind bars at the county jail facing charges for violating exclusion and curfew orders.[7]

* * *

On March 30, 257 members of the Bainbridge Island Nikkei community arrived in Seattle via the cross-sound ferry. Buses waited at the dock to take them to a train headed southward to the Manzanar Reception Center. From the day CEO No. 1 posters first went up on the island until the group's removal this operation served as a dress rehearsal for the whole process of evicting the Nikkei from the West Coast. The operation went smoothly in large part due to the civil control station set up on the island to process the families. Similar stations existed in tandem with all 108 CEOs as a means of executing a frictionless shift from freedom to captivity.

The WCCA-supervised stations were set up in community halls, school gymnasiums, auditoriums, and other public places within Nikkei population centers. The first official notice to residents was in the posted CEO ordering "A responsible member of each family, preferably the head of the family, or the person in whose name most of the property is held, and each individual living alone, [to] report to the Civil Control Station to receive further instructions."[8]

Teams of representatives from cooperating federal agencies assigned to each civil control station would provide needed services to evacuees, the major role to be played by the Federal Security Agency serving as an umbrella agency for participating smaller government units. Charged with establishing the stations, the U.S. Employment Service also provided oversight of the operation. The Social Security board registered all evacuees and provided financial assistance and other aid to individuals in need. The U.S. Public Health Service (USPHS) conducted medical examinations designed to cull from the ranks people with medical or mental conditions assembly centers could not adequately manage.

The Federal Security Agency and Federal Reserve Board continued ongoing attempts to locate others to operate farms, help settle financial matters, and arrange for storage or sale of properties.

Five-digit identification numbers on tags to be worn by every family member and displayed on each piece of luggage were distributed at the civil control stations. The Itois of Seattle: family #10710, the Uno family: #10936. While these numbers served an organizational purpose they reduced families to anonymity.

Set up to process people under all 108 CEOs, some variation existed in practice although the civil control stations all fulfilled similar missions. The Seattle Nikkei, for example, were located only thirty miles away from their final destination compared to most other western Washington evacuees, who faced a multiple-day train journey to the Pinedale Assembly Center, near Fresno. For the Seattle group, medical examinations took place after arrival at Camp Harmony rather than before. Public health physicians assigned to Seattle civil control stations attended primarily to invalids and exceptional medical cases requiring temporary or permanent deferment from incarceration.

Recruitment of advance crews to prepare assembly centers for occupancy became a task for U.S. Employment Service representatives. Nisei volunteers were sent as a group to Camp Harmony to prepare for the two thousand people scheduled to arrive on May 2. These individuals possessed the discrete skills required to execute an efficient induction process. Among them were information supervisors, publicity officers, mess officers, foremen, and stenographic office workers. Many of them were particularly qualified. Dr. Kyo Koike, an Issei physician, was tapped to head the hospital staff because of his seniority. Setting up a workable examination protocol at the center and making ready a comprehensive inoculation program for new arrivals defined his primary tasks.[9]

The advance party of 284 Nikkei arrived at Camp Harmony on April 28 and moved into Area A, the only section of the assembly center ready for occupancy.[10] This group enjoyed certain privileges by virtue of their volunteerism and being among the earliest arrivals. Since the army had transported and delivered their household goods, this advance group had brought more in the way of possessions than allowed later groups, the majority of whom were permitted to transport only what they could carry in their arms and on their backs. In addition to setting up residence within the area's most convenient location, only they and a few hundred others were assigned cotton mattresses. Later arrivals slept on ticking filled with straw.

Upon arrival at Area A's gate the volunteer group, to its surprise, found eighty-seven Alaska Nikkei who, having docked the previous day in Seattle's

Elliott Bay under military guard, had been bussed to the assembly center. The *Seattle Post-Intelligencer* reported on April 23 that an Alaska contingent would soon be arriving at the center.[11]

In the 1890s, Japanese immigrants, predominantly single males, began arriving in Alaska, where they worked in the fishing industry and settled in the coastal regions. Because few had families to support some Japanese found employment after venturing into the northern and interior regions, including the Arctic. Marriage within the Alaska native population became common, and couples gained acceptance in both native and white Alaskan communities.[12]

After the army's March decision to expel Japanese communities from the West Coast, Alaska's Nikkei responded with worry and fear to events unfolding more than a thousand miles away. They had reason for their concerns. After December 7, 1941, Alaska was cleansed of its Japanese aliens. Now in army custody, they were first transported to Fort Lewis near Tacoma, then to Fort Sam Houston, Texas; altogether, ninety-four Alaska Issei would eventually sit out the war at the Lordsburg internment camp, in New Mexico.[13]

The remaining 126 Alaska Nikkei had to fend for themselves. Among them were 54 adult Nisei males and 72 women and children scattered throughout the territory in over 20 locations and at all points of the compass. Most worried about their thinned ranks as they lived in relative isolation, hoping to elude Executive Order 9066's long reach.[14]

What minimal security Nikkei could glean from their remote geographical locations gave way to despair on April 2, 1942, when Alaska's newspapers reported that Alaska's Japanese would share the fate of their peers living in the coastal states to the southeast. That day General Simon B. Buckner Jr., commanding general of the Alaska Defense Command, issued his own Proclamation No. 1, declaring Alaska to be a military area "which requires every possible protection against espionage and against sabotage to national defense material, national defense premises and national defense utilities," and ordering all "persons of Japanese blood whether American citizen or otherwise" excluded from the area of his command. Citing Executive Order 9066 as his authority to act, Buckner set a deadline of April 20 for all Japanese residents sixteen years of age and older to report to the military installation nearest their residence for ultimate removal to the continental United States.[15]

On April 2, 1942, Buckner sent a telegram outlining salient points of his proclamation to acting Governor E. L. Bartlett.[16] This information, immediately disseminated in newspapers throughout Alaska, appeared the same day in the *Fairbanks Daily News Miner,* which published the proclamation in its entirety.[17]

No stranger to Alaskans, Buckner had been appointed commander of the Alaska Defense Force and assigned to directly supervise expansion of its military defenses.[18] In February 1941, the War Department created the Alaska Defense Command, a subordinate command of the Fourth Army also under the newly established WDC. Brigadier General, and subsequently Major General, Simon B. Buckner Jr., son of a Confederate Army general and later a governor of Kentucky, became commanding general of the new command, answering directly to General DeWitt at the Presidio in San Francisco.

On April 20, in compliance with the order, Alaska's Japanese Americans from Fairbanks to Ketchikan and from Ekuk to Tanakee dutifully reported in person to army officials at Alaska's army outposts or registered through the mail. They then awaited instructions on their removal to a reception center in the continental United States.[19] Soon they gathered at Fort Richardson (Anchorage), Fort Raymond (Seward), Ladd Field (Fairbanks), Fort Ray (Sitka), the Juneau air field, and Annette Island landing field (Ketchikan), where they received confirmation that Puyallup's Western Washington Fairgrounds would be their first destination.

Two days earlier, on April 18, the *Anchorage Daily Times* announced the imminent expulsion of the city's ten Nikkei residents. For the first time the public became informed as to the Puyallup, Washington destination. However, this article did not speculate on the ultimate destination "at an undesignated location in inland United States." Instead it stressed the assembly centers' primary purpose being to prevent separation of families and communities.[20]

Despite this stated objective, the unusual circumstance of living in Alaska inevitably disrupted some families. Because of absent fathers in army custody at least nine families received public assistance from the Territorial Department of Public Welfare. Seven others qualified for public relief. Due to the earlier arrest and detention of his Issei father, William Kawata, age eleven, had been sent to live with family friends in Wrangell.[21] In Petersburg Amelia Kito, a twenty-two-year-old Alaska Tlingit-Japanese, eight months pregnant with her fourth child, had been separated from her husband Saburo, the sole family provider, who was also interned. She received $55 relief per month, yet needed a deferment to give birth to her child while still in familiar surroundings. The army's denial of this request put her at medical risk during the long trip south to Washington. On May 18 Kito gave birth to Harry Donald, the first baby born in captivity at Camp Harmony.[22]

Another hardship befalling Alaska's Japanese Americans was the high frequency of intermarriage between Japanese nationals and Alaska Natives. General Buckner's Proclamation No. 1, defining how a Japanese woman might be exempted from evacuation, brought mixed marriages to light. One extreme case demonstrates the scarcity of exemptions allowed by the WCCA. Henry Hope, the eighteen-year-old son of an Issei father he had never seen and an Eskimo mother who died during his infancy, had been adopted as a baby by an Athabaskan Native American woman and her Eskimo husband. Henry had never traveled below the Arctic Circle or met a Japanese person before he arrived in Fairbanks to register as a person of Japanese ancestry. He'd grown up in the hills around Wiseman, working in the winter for a mining company freighting supplies and operating a caterpillar tractor in the summer.

During a visit to the Presidio by Alaska Governor Ernest Gruening, the WCCA denied Henry's exemption request. Gruening's radiogram to Bartlett, "Western Defense Command regrets that no exemptions can be made," left Henry no choice but to comply with the exclusion order and report to Ladd Field, from where he and four other Fairbanks area Nisei departed for Camp Harmony.[23]

Two transfers occurred via army transport ships, the initial group of eighty-seven departing on April 23 and inducted at Camp Harmony on April 27, and a second contingent numbering thirty-nine that arrived at Camp Harmony on May 5.[24]

*   *   *

Sandwiched between arrivals of the two Alaska groups, nearly two thousand Seattle Nikkei traversed the thirty miles to the Puyallup Assembly Center. The vast majority traveled on public buses chartered by the army while a few dozen people with preauthorization drove privately owned vehicles. After a lull between May 8 and May 11, another 3,500 Seattle Nikkei left their homes, making their way to prearranged collecting points at Eighth Avenue and Lane Street or to a point at the north end of Jefferson Park on Beacon Hill. After two or more hours of waiting, they stepped onto the buses for the trip to Camp Harmony. After this second major transfer, only a thousand Seattle Nikkei remained behind, among them individuals living between Madison Street and the north city line (CEO No. 57) including the University of Washington. After this last removal, which spanned the next several days, the evacuation operation concluded on May 16.

They moved by the hundreds, leaving the gathering points at nine in the morning and at two in the afternoon. After dropping their passengers at the end of their morning runs, drivers retraced their routes to Seattle to repeat the process in the afternoons. Transporting 1,137 Japanese Americans on May 8 and 9 required thirty-two trips.[25]

On each appointed evacuation day, announced earlier at the civil control stations, families received instructions to arrive at their prearranged gathering area with personal belongings in hand: bedding, linens for family members, toilet articles, extra clothing, eating utensils, and essential personal effects. Amounts were limited to what could be personally carried by family members. No furniture could be carried or delivered to the assembly center. Family pets were to be left behind, most never seen again.[26]

The gathering point at Eighth Avenue and Lane Street near the heart of Japantown was located in the center of Seattle's red-light district. Adjacent to a large open expanse, it accommodated people, bundles of rope-bound belongings, buses, army personnel, army trucks, and the well wishers who saw them off. A second gathering point along the route to Puyallup on Beacon Hill was located just south of Japantown at Beacon Avenue and Columbia Way, near the north end of Jefferson Park.

Shosuke Sasaki recalled baggage lining both sides of Lane Street and evacuees standing in the drizzle waiting for the order to board the buses.

Evacuation day gathering point on Beacon Hill for transport to the Puyallup Assembly Center, April 30. A caravan of charter busses, moving vans, personal cars and trucks, and army vehicles participated in the moves in April and May 1942. (Museum of History and Industry, Seattle P-I Collection—28048)

Among them were his sister and her two infant children. The door of a brothel opened, and the madam invited the three into her parlor to wait out the rain.[27]

Tamako Inouye remembered the Lane Street departure point sat right outside the family home. "For many days we saw our friends leave from here. They would come to that corner. And we saw. They used our bathroom and everything before they left. So I was familiar with the routine before we left. The last night I remember we all slept on the floor. Whenever there was a departure we'd always try to serve coffee to the people, our friends who'd come to the house. Finally our day came. All I remember is everyone was so exhausted. Our friends came to see us off."[28]

The few families who arranged to drive their own automobiles fared better than those who traveled by bus. Some vehicles served as mini-moving vans in which heads of the family loaded and strapped possessions and oversized bundles onto roofs and oversized fenders, leaving family members to ride the buses to free up precious cargo space. These caravans snaked their way to Puyallup led by army military police vehicles.[29]

Throughout most of the two-week exodus to Camp Harmony, cloudy, cold, raw weather in Seattle, Puyallup, and the entire Puget Sound region brought misery to the entire operation.[30] On April 30, when the first major movement took place, two-thirds of an inch of rain fell in Seattle with temperatures barely reaching the mid-50s. The second day, as new Seattle arrivals joined those who arrived less than 24 hours earlier, another 0.20 inch of rain turned unpaved alleyways between long rows of freshly constructed barracks in Area A to mud and muck. Sunday, May 10, and Monday, May 11, brought a drear rain with frequent torrents and a penetrating chill. Parts of Seattle received half an inch.[31]

Drenching rain poured down on four of the seven major migration days; more than a quarter-inch of precipitation was recorded on May 15, when 689 demoralized nomads entered Camp Harmony's gates.[32] The rains, subsiding during transfer respites, returned as more Nikkei boarded buses in Seattle, got off at Puyallup, or both.

Many Seattle residents witnessed this two-week migration: some who saw them off; curiosity seekers who stood silently by; individuals who hurled epithets; and the friends, neighbors, employers, clergy, or other Nikkei soon to ride these buses within the next few days, even as they waved goodbye in the drizzling air.[33]

Some witnesses left a written record. Tom Bodine of the AFSC, present at each departure, wrote that some families had arrived at gathering points in

A street scene showing the shed-like barrack construction and mud in the alleyway from the ubiquitous rains present during the first days of incarceration. (*Seattle Post-Intelligencer*)

taxis, while others came in their own cars, with someone along to drive it away after the bus departed. In a report on the Nikkei removal written for Clarence Pickett, executive secretary of the Friends in New York, Bodine recorded a memorable scene: "One morning I watched a dark black negro fellow drive a Japanese family up in a fine new Plymouth. He helped them unload and then stood next to them on the sidewalk and in his beautiful deep throaty voice said, 'Well, ma'am, I'll be saying good bye. You know that if there's ever anything I can do for you whether it be something big or something small, I'm here to do it.' And he shook her hand and then turned to the husband and slapped him on the back: 'Goodbye now and good luck.' And then down on his hands and knees for a final farewell to the three little kids."[34]

For weeks other quiet dramas played out up and down the West Coast, from Seattle to San Diego. By the end of the evacuation period, more than ninety thousand resident Japanese Americans and their immigrant elders had been moved from their homes in the Pacific coast states and Arizona into WCCA assembly centers.[35]

∗   ∗   ∗

Public proclamations and civilian exclusion orders affecting all people of Japanese ancestry offered no language to permit exceptions for their removal from military areas on the West Coast. In practice, deferments for in-patients in hospitals and sanitaria and inmates in jails arose once the WCCA determined that temporary assembly centers would not be equipped to care for or maintain them. Some mixed racial couples received deferments later.

At best everyone who had registered at a civil control station would evacuate from their homes on the prescribed day, at the appointed times board prearranged buses, trains, or car convoys, and reach their assigned assembly centers without delays. While operations proceeded smoothly with the vast majority of evacuees following the script to the letter, exceptions invariably occurred. Most civil control station personnel issued temporary deferments on a case-by-case basis and in a small number of instances issued permanent exemptions.

The time frame for temporary deferments for these special cases lasted anywhere from a few days to weeks. The majority involved health issues, mostly contagious childhood diseases such as chickenpox and mumps. USPHS personnel carefully screened evacuees because of a threat of epidemics within large numbers of people confined to small areas such as Camp Harmony. Children determined to be too contagious for transport remained at home with a responsible caregiver until symptoms had passed; severe cases were hospitalized. Small numbers of individuals suspected of harboring the tuberculosis bacillus received orders to remain behind until laboratory test results documented them safe enough for release to assembly centers.

For example, among the 1,100 Seattle residents under the jurisdiction of CEO No. 17, twenty-five adults and children received nine-day deferments following testing for tuberculosis, with nine others involving two families quarantined for mumps.

New mothers in hospital maternity wards received permission to complete a standard ten-day postpartum period before transferring with later groups. Pregnant women in their eighth or ninth month were admitted to public hospitals at government expense except in a few cases when the family remained at home because facilities were unavailable.

Shigeko and Masaro (Chick) Uno, two of the small number of Seattle evacuees who received temporary deferment, lived within the geographic area defined by CEO No. 17. Scheduled to depart on April 30, twenty-seven-year-old Shigeko was eight months pregnant. Nearly four years earlier a Caucasian doctor had delivered her first baby. Now, in expressing his outrage to authorities that no obstetrical facilities existed at Camp Harmony, this same physician implored WCCA officials in Seattle to allow his patient to remain behind so he could deliver her baby at term while under his care. Army officials advised this would be possible only if Uno was confined in a hospital; otherwise the baby would have to be delivered at Pierce County's Tacoma General hospital by the doctor on call.

Determined to have both her babies delivered by the same doctor and willing to challenge the army in the process, Shigeko entered Seattle's Providence hospital. With labor quickly induced her daughter, Naomi, was born one month early, one day before the first major contingent of Nikkei exited Seattle for Camp Harmony. Uno recalled: "The baby was born on April 29th. Our family moved out of the home on Beacon Hill, two blocks away, on the 30th. The doctor had it so I would have my baby on the 29th so they could come over and see the new baby. Then they left."[36]

Uno remained in the hospital throughout the prescribed ten-day postpartum period. Upon her release, with Masaro and her older daughter having gone ahead to Camp Harmony, Shigeko and Naomi stayed for a day at the Japanese Women's Home, operated by the Japanese Baptist Church. Here an elderly Caucasian missionary helped change diapers. She washed and dried them in time for the May 11 departure to Camp Harmony. A truck driver formerly employed by the family's White River Dairy drove Uno and her newborn to Camp Harmony as part of the convoy accompanying the group evacuated under CEO No. 57. Upon arrival Naomi became the youngest inmate to be inducted into the Puyallup Assembly Center.[37]

Temporary deferments resulted in various administrative difficulties for WCCA officials responsible for individuals remaining behind: where they lived, how long they would remain in the exclusion zone, how to obtain proper documentation from USPHS stating worrisome health conditions had passed, and how to arrange transportation to their assigned assembly center.

Long-term deferments would prove more problematic, as they often required transfers to publicly funded institutions where patients could be confined for months or, as in some cases, permanently. Confined to six hospitals or sanitaria, nine Seattle Nikkei initially scheduled for transfer under CEO No. 40 would never set foot in Camp Harmony. Four had tuberculosis, one advanced stage heart disease, one pneumonia, and three suffered from mental illnesses requiring they be institutionalized.[38]

Permanent exemption went to some partners of mixed marriages. The army's justification for incarcerating the entire West Coast's Nikkei population centered on a belief in the impossibility of separating the loyal from the disloyal. This created a problem of what to do with non-Japanese spouses and children born of mixed-race marriages. The spouses included Caucasians, Chinese, Filipinos, African Americans, Hawaiians, and Native Americans, while some part-Japanese exiles became aware of their mixed ancestry only after the war began.[39]

As minorities among the Nikkei majority, many non-Japanese family members accompanying their families into captivity found life to be extraordinarily difficult. Others, who in staying behind thereby divided the family, experienced additional problems.[40]

The WCCA assumed non-Japanese family members to be thoroughly Americanized. Posing little threat to the nation's security they should therefore be permitted to leave the centers. This assumption led to a plan providing for the release of mixed marriage families. Revealed on July 12, 1942, the plan initially applied only to mixed marriage families with children and granted eligibility to three mixed blood groups: Japanese wife and a U.S. citizen Caucasian husband; U.S. citizen adults of mixed blood; and a Japanese husband and Caucasian wife.[41]

Families satisfying these criteria had to meet several other conditions prior to their release. Each adult member had to obtain an army Military Intelligence Division clearance and one member had to provide evidence of an offer of employment or other means of avoiding becoming a public charge. Finally, local authorities had to authorize entry into their region. As exceptions, eligible families could not reside in Colorado, Wyoming, or New Mexico even though these states did not fall within the WDC area. With such stringent conditions in place, few among this small cohort succeeded in obtaining releases within the first month of eligibility.

Within a week WCCA revised its initial plan by adding families with alien spouses from countries in support of the Allied cause. Thus a family with a Japanese wife and alien non-Japanese husband or a Japanese husband and an alien Caucasian wife could qualify to leave the assembly centers, but they too had to leave the WDC area.[42]

Later, dependent Japanese children reared by Caucasian foster-parents were added to the list as well as the Japanese wives of non-Japanese spouses serving in the U.S. Armed Forces.[43]

Nine mixed marriage families and mixed-blood individuals were exiled to the Puyallup Assembly Center. Among them one family and three adults of mixed blood became eligible for release. However, three marriages listed on WCCA records involved no children, thereby making these couples ineligible for release. A fourth marriage, on the eve of the removal to Camp Harmony, between Seattle Caucasian Lorraine Iris King and Nisei Shigenobu Fujino, was not listed.[44] The newlyweds remained at the center and in August were transferred to the Minidoka Relocation Center.

At least two mixed marriage releases took place on May 21 at the Puyallup Assembly Center. Because the mixed marriage policy was still two months away these releases may have involved non-Japanese spouses who voluntarily evacuated with the community only to find life in the barracks unbearable.[45] Eventually twenty individuals meeting the qualifications were discharged from the Puyallup Assembly Center.[46] A total of 206 mixed marriage releases took place from all assembly centers between March 21 and October 30, 1942, with all but 10 returning to locales within the military exclusion zones.[47]

Individuals receiving temporary and permanent exemption from incarceration were minuscule compared to the number of Nikkei subjected to civilian exclusion orders. In the Pacific Northwest fewer than 150 received temporary deferments for special circumstances. An additional dozen receiving permanent exemptions from incarceration never passed through Camp Harmony's gates.

*   *   *

Seattle's Japantown lost nearly seven thousand residents over a nineteen-day period in 1942 beginning April 28 and ending on May 16. What had been an independent, vibrant, noisy, organic community prior to the war became a temporary ghost town, and in early May momentarily fell to stunned silence with storefronts boarded up and litter swirling in the streets. Traffic in and out of the area dwindled. Yet, before the last bus to the Puyallup Assembly Center departed its Lane Street gathering point, the void began to fill.

On May 15, 1942, the African American newspaper *Northwest Enterprise* published a report from a survey it had conducted earlier in the year concerning the impact of an evacuation on business opportunities for the area's "race men and women." Mid-May found two grocery stores, two dry cleaning establishments, and five hotels and apartment houses now run by African American entrepreneurs. Charles W. Taylor, operator of Bremerton's Sailor's Recreation Club near the naval shipyard, had purchased the Eagle and Kiosa hotels outright. This added six more blacks to the employment rolls. Both hotels had been owned by Japanese operators, now inmates at Camp Harmony. Dave Lee, owner of C. C. Billiard Parlor, acquired two more hotels, an apartment building, and the Atlas Cafe, and hired twelve more African Americans.[48]

Other Japanese-owned small businesses turned over to African Americans with business aims in the district included the Elliot Cafe at 1209 Jackson Street, one of the most popular prewar Japanese-owned cafes in the district. Serving American meals to a racially mixed clientele, it was now run by the owner of Rose Cost Grocery and his female business partner. Fujii's Cafe on Yesler Way became the Banquet Cafe; the Tokyo Cafe at 655 Jackson Street the United Nations Tavern and Cafe. Bunshiro Tazuma's variety store at 12th and Jackson, in a block formerly dominated by Japanese businesses, became

Display windows of Higo 10¢ Store on Seattle's Jackson Street covered with wooden planks, May 1942. Former second-floor tenants were Paul Shigaya MD, S. Fukuda, DDS, and Kenji Ito Law Office. (Museum of History and Industry, Seattle P-I Collection—28069)

Kay's 10¢ store, whose new owner advertised in the *Northwest Enterprise* as being "Under New Management—100% American."[49]

In Seattle, African American gains became evident as early as February 27, 1942, a week after President Franklin D. Roosevelt signed Executive Order 9066. As Nikkei workers continued losing their jobs blacks soon gained them: Red Caps at Union Station, Western Union delivery boys, cooks, waiters, and service personnel at various social clubs. Jobs formerly held by Japanese men at the Rainier Club, College Club, and Washington Athletic Club, and domestic positions elsewhere became filled by African Americans.[50]

But advances of a few black entrepreneurs and their new hires involved only a fraction of the African American community overall. More significant progress would occur following Executive Order 8802 signed by President Roosevelt in June 1941, designed to prohibit government contractors from engaging in employment discrimination based on race, color, or national origin. Doors opened for blacks arriving in increasing numbers, mainly from the South. At the Boeing Aircraft Company and regional shipyards they helped fill the seemingly inexhaustible job openings resulting from the war.[51]

Blacks taking over Japanese businesses benefited from an influx of defense workers of all backgrounds. Hotels, lodging houses, and apartments limping along before the war at partial capacity and with marginal profits by Japanese owners now operated at full capacity and with increased rents under African

American and other non-Japanese tenancy. Had they remained, Japanese operators would have benefited from the trickle-down profits associated with the war effort.

A few African Americans upgraded their living conditions by moving into housing Japanese tenants had formerly occupied. Any such upward mobility had been difficult before the war since neighborhood restrictive covenants confined blacks to the Madison, Jackson, and Cherry Street areas. But newly arrived Caucasian workers who contributed to the wartime expansion of Seattle's population also sought housing accommodations. Except for those families fortunate enough to move into recently built Seattle Housing Authority public housing near the edge of the Jackson Street–Chinatown district, most blacks with increased incomes continued living in run-down housing because, for the most part, Japantown's housing was itself substandard.

Although blacks profited at the expense of former Japanese business operators, whites with available capital to maximize the economic opportunities that fell their way enjoyed the greatest benefits resulting from the army's forced evacuation.

*   *   *

In the meantime the moving-in period at the Puyallup Assembly Center had just begun for Nikkei from Seattle and the Puyallup Valley; most were shocked upon encountering their living quarters. Evacuee S. Frank Miyamoto, his master's thesis on Seattle's Japanese community published in 1939, recalled his own experience nearly half a century later: "It was early May 1942 that we were evacuated to the Puyallup Assembly Center. The sight of hundreds of people assembled with assorted baggage lined up to board the buses at the embarkation point, with rifle-bearing soldiers standing around as guards, is still imprinted in memory. And I can still remember the acute sense of embitterment, humiliation, resentment, anger, depression, concern, and other mixed feelings which I felt as we rode the 30 miles to the Puyallup Fairground. The miserable facilities at this assembly center compounded these feelings."[52]

Many exiles, particularly those U.S. citizens who believed their country had failed them during a period of crisis, probably shared Miyamoto's feelings. The shock of their incarceration set in after seeing the barbed wire fence, row after row of "chicken hutch" barracks, and the presence of armed sentries everywhere.[53]

Monica Itoi, then twenty-two years old, recalled her first night at Camp Harmony: "Of one thing I was sure. The wire fence was real. I no longer had the right to walk out of it. It was because I had Japanese ancestors. It was also because some people had little faith in the ideas and ideals of democracy. They said that after all these were but words and could not possibly ensure loyalty. New laws and camps were surer devices. I finally buried my face in my pillow to wipe out burning thoughts and snatch what sleep I could."[54]

The mass migration came to an end on Saturday, May 16, as the Puyallup Assembly Center recorded a population of 7,376 King and Pierce county Nikkei, 70 percent of them from Seattle, 29 percent from rural Pierce County, and a clutch of involuntary nomads from Alaska.

For the vast majority of Japanese Americans the forced removal from their homes to the confines of the Puyallup Assembly Center was a harsh transition from freedom to incarceration. The next four months of imprisoned life there would prepare them physically, and to an extent psychologically, for their three years of subsequent incarceration at the Minidoka Relocation Center in south-central Idaho's high desert country.

6

Settling In

A light drizzle began to fall, coating bare black heads with
tiny sparkling raindrops. The chow line inched forward.

—*Nisei Daughter*, 175

During the settling-in phase at Camp Harmony, a period lasting
from April 28 to May 25, the population at the center remained stable. Following the last major influx of 428 inductions from King and Pierce counties on May 16, the total reached 7,376, within 14 of the peak reached 10 days
later. During that time people with temporary deferments straggled in, those
numbers countered by transfers out to Justice Department custody, to the
Pierce County jail, and to the Pierce County Hospital. The first major departure occurred on May 26, when 196 volunteers formed an advance party
that headed to the Tule Lake Relocation Center to prepare for arrival of its
first inductees.

Families experienced chaos during their first day at Camp Harmony.
Groups of five hundred stepped off the buses and onto the assembly center
grounds, all burdened with personal belongings. They still had quarters to
find, mattresses to stuff, first meals to consume, and beds to assemble and
shove into place. Recruited from the advance group, young male volunteers
and other early arrivals helped newcomers transition into captivity. Still ex-
periencing their own varying degrees of shock, the helpers found dawn-to-
dusk physical labor assignments a diversion, at least for the short term.

Hours after they arrived in Area B and received assigned quarters, Tamako
Inouye stood with her father in a room inside a 20 x 200–foot-long barrack
devoid of furniture and piled nearly to the ceiling with straw. Assisted by
volunteers, here the pair stuffed then transported straw-filled mattress covers to the quarters where their family would stay for the next four months.[1]

A similar drama took place approximately a city block away in Area A.

Twelve-year-old Sharon Tanagi accompanied her mother to the outdoor hay field where thousands of crude sack mattresses would be created. Halfway through stuffing their family's mattresses, her mother suddenly stopped what she was doing. Sharon related to the author the next moment: "I think the thing that impacted me the most was my mother who had shown no emotion up until this time. When we were assigned our room we were then told to go to this area where they had this pile of straw and canvas bags. We were told to fill it for our mattresses. I think that was the last straw that broke her back and she started to cry. I didn't know what to do."[2] Recalling this moment more than a half-century later brought her own tears.

On May 1 a meager allotment of 175 additional cotton mattresses transported from the quartermaster depot at Fort Lewis supplemented the few already on hand. Expecting no additional mattresses, center manager Robert Turner had purchased enough straw to fill 900 pounds of mattress covers he had received on the same day, and this barely met the needs of the 1,985 evacuees quartered in the center's Area A. Absent sufficient stocks of ticking and straw, Turner advised his superiors in San Francisco that additional evacuees could not be handled.[3] In fact, the next major influx of 970 Seattleites did not occur until May 8. Two days prior Turner had only promises that fresh supplies were en route.[4]

This meant those "fortunate" enough to arrive at Camp Harmony with the advance group on April 28 and the Alaska contingent who came a day earlier would be the ones to receive the three hundred or so two-inch cotton mattresses, a mere fraction of eight thousand requisitioned units, but all that would arrive. Upon their subsequent arrival family members of the Japanese headquarters staff received mattresses put aside for them. Bill Hosokawa and his wife and son were given them upon arriving in Area D on May 15 long after the original supply had run out.[5] For those with allergies or physical maladies, hay-filled mattresses became difficult to endure, for over time chaff dust filtered through the ticking into nasal passages. Pressure points molded to outlines of hips and spines were punched and pushed out during the day.[6] Only a doctor's prescription might succeed in freeing up one of the coveted mattresses.[7]

Entering their quarters, inmates discovered army canvas cots for children and metal bed frames for adults, a single light bulb hanging from the ceiling. In the middle of the room sat a small platform for a wood burning stove, often unassembled and set off to the side. Occupants soon discerned the sheet metal wood burners had no dampers and thus allowed most of the heat to escape up the stovepipe. This would make creation of a warm living space

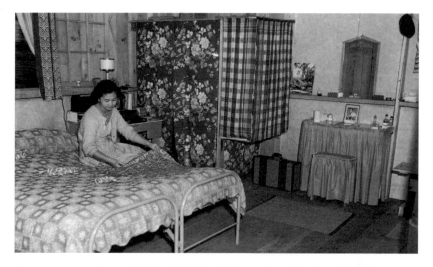

Spartan quarters made more livable with fabrics, bedding, and curtains. Note shiplap floor boards sealing the apartment against the ground located a few inches away. The floor-to-ceiling wall suggests this apartment was located at the end of a barrack. (Museum of History and Industry—86.5.6681.2)

during the region's damp springtime a chore.[8] No chairs, tables, cabinets, or privacy existed for individual family members, for such luxuries required carpenter's tools, labor, and lumber scraps and nails scrounged from the construction heaps recently left behind.

Monica Itoi recalled "two canned sausages, one lob of boiled potato, and a slab of bread"[9] as her first meal at Camp Harmony shortly after the family's late morning arrival from Seattle on May 1. Some former inmates attest to their lifelong aversion to canned Vienna sausages; Tom Bodine, however, describes a brief period in early May when even canned food was in short supply: "There hasn't been enough food to go around because there were more arrivals than were expected. Some have gone without meals several times. There has been no fresh vegetables: *no* fruit (and a large part of the population children), no fresh meat, but plenty of canned food for those who were early in line to get it."[10] Despite numerous anecdotal reports and personal histories of diets lacking fresh foods and insufficient quantity, especially among the earliest arrivals to the center, both fortunately were relatively short-lived. Later arrivals would experience monotonous food and spot shortages for a matter of days since a sufficient supply of fresh meat and produce began to reach mess hall tables by May 19.

Quantity or quality aside, getting the food to the mess hall table was problematic during the settling-in phase. In Area D, the last of the four areas to become fully occupied, until the second week of June 2,two thousand inmates made do with enough dishes and silverware for five hundred. This resulted in prolonged meal times and imposed a major strain on inexperienced volunteer mess hall workers. Breakage and hoarding of plates, bowls, and cups continued until only 350 full sets of dishware remained.[11]

Camp Harmony's four geographically separate areas filled by mid-May; first the former parking lots, beginning with Area A, then Areas B and C, and finally Area D, on the fairgrounds proper. This division created an immediate problem for inmates who wanted to move between them to visit friends and relatives, conduct center business in Area D, or attend religious services and social events outside their own areas of residence. To move from one area to the other involved passing through a gate guarded by sentries and required crossing a city street with an escort. A clumsy operation had been devised where inmates gathered at the gate to be chaperoned across by inmate monitors. This option was restricted to individuals possessing work-related or special passes or to those participating in organized events. This made crossing the street on a whim impossible.

At the outset, friends and associates of Camp Harmony's inmates who made the hour-long trip to Puyallup by car would encounter their own difficulties. Lacking special passes or designated places to meet, they congregated at the fence where visitors might signal a child playing nearby and pay him a pittance to locate the friend and announce their arrival. Every day five

Inmates lining up in the rain outside a mess hall in Area D. Some bring their own drinking cups, suggesting a scarcity of tableware. (Museum of History and Industry—86.5.6681.3)

hundred people lined up to peer into what resembled a prison camp, where the inmates looked out through the fence toward freedom lying just beyond their reach.

Because Camp Harmony's residential barracks had been built from scratch inmates were spared both the unsanitary conditions and accompanying humiliation endured by their counterparts at Tanforan, Santa Anita, and North Portland assembly centers once providing shelters to animals. However, the hundred bachelors' apartments erected beneath the grandstand in available open space lacked ventilation, and natural daylight proved to be an exception. To eliminate this deficiency and reduce other crowded conditions Turner urged his superiors to relocate promptly a thousand inmates. May 26 brought partial relief when the volunteer advance crew departed Camp Harmony for Tule Lake.[12]

Although spared the indignity of inhabiting animal stalls, people still lived in close quarters. Every inmate shared the communal reality of mess halls, latrines, and shower rooms, as well as the barracks themselves. Late at night proved to be no exception, for open spaces between the tops of eight-foot walls and sloping ten-foot ceilings created a triangular megaphone that amplified sounds ricocheting through the entire barrack. Insomniacs endured snoring, coughing, arguing, sounds of beds creaking, babies crying, adults crying; they heard whispers, loud voices, pacing, doors opening, doors slamming, and sounds of love making. As rain fell on the tarpaper roofs water trickled down low-angled slopes through cracks and onto blankets, clothes, and faces. Such miseries informed Camp Harmony's first nights.

The forced move into captivity happened abruptly with just two weeks' advance notice, which often provided insufficient time to put affairs in order—pay rents, arrange proper storage of furniture and other belongings, dispose of property, care for the sick in hospitals, and make accommodations for pets not allowed in camp. Upon boarding the buses to transport them to the Puyallup Assembly Center, Seattle residents severed many of their prewar connections—social, cultural, and commercial. In addition many Nikkei now cut off from their churches faced a test of their faith.

Few outside organizations actively ministered to the myriad needs of Camp Harmony's community. While most mainstream churches in the Puget Sound region remained silent throughout the forced evacuation period, congregations that did step up probably had significant numbers of prewar Nikkei parishioners on their membership rolls.

In addition to the Buddhist tradition that the earliest arrivals from Japan brought with them, a strong Christian tradition also persisted among Japanese from the time of their arrival in the Pacific Northwest, as evidenced by the five Japanese Protestant churches that belonged to the Seattle Council of Churches at the outbreak of the war: Baptist, Congregational, Episcopalian, Methodist, and Presbyterian. In February Reverend Harold Jensen of Seattle's First Baptist Church, representing the Council as its president, testified at the Tolan Commission hearings opposing evacuation and relocation. He confronted the congressional committee, saying that to single out the Japanese community exhibited nothing more than race prejudice.[13]

When the army evacuation became a reality, the Council offered practical support to the Japanese community. Member pastors and individual parishioners joined with ministers from Japanese churches to help ease the transition from home to assembly center by offering relief supplies, food for families in need, and space to store furniture and household goods. When moving day arrived a few white parishioners offered to drive families rather than see them subjected to the humiliation of the bus trip.[14]

The Wartime Civil Control Administration (WCCA) prevented clergy ministering to the Nikkei from living among their parishioners in the assembly center. In response, Father Leopold H. Tibesar of the Seattle Maryknoll mission's Our Lady, Queen of Martyrs parish moved to Puyallup, set up headquarters at the Puyallup rectory, and made daily visits to Camp Harmony. At the outbreak of World War II the parish, in existence since 1916, offered a single mission to provide for Japanese and Filipino Catholics. Seattle's Maryknoll School, with an enrollment of 145 Japanese American children and 15 Filipino Americans, held commencement exercises for 14 graduates of the eighth-grade class on Friday April 24, 1942, a week before they departed for Camp Harmony. Here Father Tibesar announced he would accompany his parishioners to the center. "We are leaving for a concentration camp and for a future which is decidedly uncertain."[15]

Father Tibesar became the parish priest in 1935 after serving eight years in Manchuria with the colonizing Japanese population. He preached in fluent Japanese and reached out to both generations. In August this became clear shortly before the move to Minidoka when nineteen parishioners, including James Sakamoto, his wife, children, and aging parents, received confirmation in the Catholic faith in a ceremony led by Father Tibesar.[16]

On hand to greet the May 4 arrivals from Seattle, Father Tibesar said Mass in the mess hall of Area A for these early arrivals on their first Sunday in captivity.[17]

The Protestant clergy and their representatives assisting the Japanese community shuttled back and forth from Seattle to Puyallup, helping resolve financial matters, disposing of property, liquidating business inventories, and communicating directly with family members left behind. Some evacuee families had to leave individual members in sanitaria, in area hospitals, or in jail. Because Nikkei could not return to the city, their representatives, primarily the clergy, filled in to address these matters.

Like Father Tibesar, Deaconess Margaret Peppers of the Episcopal St. Peter's Japanese Mission in Seattle and its sister mission, St. Paul's in White River, was herself no stranger to minority groups. Before arriving in Seattle in 1932, she served for ten years in the Philippines teaching Igorot people of Northern Luzon and Chinese in Manila. She ministered to the faithful along with Father Tibesar and other Christian pastors throughout the Camp Harmony period.[18]

Reverend Everett Thompson, representative to the Seattle Council of Churches and assistant pastor to Thomas Machida of the Japanese Methodist Church, conducted services at the center every Sunday. Having served as a missionary in Asia, he also spoke fluent Japanese. Popular among the youth, when he appeared at Camp Harmony attendance at his services was high. For many, Sunday services offered diversion from the ongoing boredom of camp life, for others a renewal of spirit and hope.[19]

Reverend Emery E. Andrews, also held in high esteem by many of Seattle's Japanese Americans, had been ordained in California in 1917 and went on to work within local Italian and Mexican communities. He came to Seattle to pursue sociology and education at the University of Washington. After graduation in 1929, he became pastor of Seattle's Japanese Baptist Church, ministering to the Japanese congregation there for the next thirteen years.

Andrews and his "battered Chevy van" helped retrieve personal belongings held in storage for members of his congregation now residing at Camp Harmony. Following transfer of his flock to the Minidoka Relocation Center in August, he set up residency in a nearby Twin Falls rental home, from there making more than fifty trips back and forth to Seattle on their behalf.

Using his ever present vehicle, Andrews retrieved many household items, such as chests of drawers, bassinettes, even an Underwood typewriter, all loaded up then driven the thirty miles to Puyallup. A smaller item reclaimed on behalf of one of Andrews's parishioners was a woman's "crest watch" that her husband authorized him to remove from his safe deposit box at a Seattle bank.

Other requests involved financial matters, such as taking care of unpaid bills. In one case a tenant not paying his rent resulted in the now incarcerated building owner asking Andrews "to look into it." Other inmates requested of him affidavits confirming the moral and political character of "enemy alien" elders detained by the Justice Department who were awaiting loyalty hearings that would help seal their fates as parolees or internees for the war's duration.[20]

Soon after Pearl Harbor the American Friends Service Committee (AFSC) became involved in relief work for Seattle's Japanese community and others as well. Begun in 1917 as the special service organization of the Religious Society of Friends (Quakers), the Committee assisted war victims behind Allied lines and helped rebuild villages. After World War I, the Committee helped feed the hungry masses throughout Europe; closer to home it came to the aid of a hundred thousand West Virginia coal miners out of work after the war.

In 1942, after Philadelphia headquarters recognized that Japanese communities on the West Coast would require America's largest relief effort, it opened an office at the University Friends Meeting in Seattle. It appointed Floyd Schmoe, who thereupon took a leave of absence from his duties as instructor in the University of Washington's College of Forestry to head a small staff and focus full-time on the relief effort.[21] Schmoe never resumed his academic position.

Clergy did not forget Camp Harmony inmates whose prewar homes were in the Puyallup Valley. Protestant ministers present to conduct weekly services at the center included Reverend Joseph Chester of the Puyallup Methodist Church; Dr. E. W. Setters, rector of the Puyallup Episcopal Church; and Professor J. Victor Martin of the Tacoma Japanese Methodist Church.

Although the Christian clergy conducted the majority of religious services, over a thousand Buddhists also resided in the center. The FBI, after shutting down most Buddhist churches on the West Coast shortly after December 7, 1941, took many, but not all, Issei priests into custody. Because of their "ABC list" status few were granted parole. This meant considerably fewer Buddhist priests remained to serve the incarcerated population, in contrast to their Christian counterparts. In the Pacific Northwest Reverend Gikan Nishinaga of the Tacoma Buddhist Church and Reverend Tatsuya Ichikawa of the Seattle Church were both interned in Justice Department camps, leaving Ichikawa's assistant, Reverend Hideo Eiyu Terao, and Reverend Sunya Pratt, a Caucasian, to assume major responsibility ministering to the Buddhist faithful at Camp Harmony.[22]

A British subject, Pratt arrived from England and in 1931 settled in Tacoma with her family. She took an active role in the Tacoma church under Reverend Nishinaga's predecessor, Reverend Shawshew Sakow, helping run the Sunday school program. Even though she lacked official status, her success with young people led to Pratt eventually heading the program. Her presence meant the services and classes held exclusively in Japanese before her arrival now could be conducted in Japanese and English. While she was not bilingual, Pratt imparted Buddhist teachings in simple English to those Issei with a rudimentary knowledge of English and to the Nisei with little understanding of Japanese.

Sunday school enrollments increased as study groups made up of students eager to learn more about Buddhism met during mid-week evenings. Requests for Pratt's services extended to neighboring churches in Seattle, White River, and as far away as Portland. At her first ordination from Bishop Masuyama during a special ceremony held at the Tacoma Buddhist Church, she received official recognition for her part in the growth and development of the youth group's understanding of Buddhism and active participation in the church. Here, on April 23, 1936, she received her name, "Sunya."

The Tacoma Buddhist Church closed in May 1942 following Reverend Gikan Nishinaga's arrest in December and the subsequent removal of Tacoma's Japanese community to California's Pinedale Assembly Center. WCCA officials in San Francisco permitted Reverend Pratt to continue serving Buddhist worshipers who were at Camp Harmony. She visited the center daily to teach willing teenagers and conduct a Sunday school program, and continued these activities until her congregation relocated to Minidoka in August. Inmate Reverend Terao, Reverend Ichikawa's assistant at the Seattle Buddhist Church, and Reverend Pratt conducted Sunday services in all four areas of Camp Harmony for both Japanese- and English-speaking churchgoers. Here, as elsewhere, doctrinal differences between Buddhist sects were put aside in favor of a shared, trans-sectarian Buddhism.[23]

*   *   *

The WCCA looked to the Work Progress Administration (WPA) to fill the assembly centers' civilian field personnel positions. On March 28, 1942, General DeWitt called upon Rex L. Nicholson, regional WPA supervisor, to assist with the task. His successor, Emil Sandquist, appointed on June 30, 1942, remained as chief of the Assembly Center Branch at WCCA until the program's dissolution. As WPA activities were winding down at the national level, personnel became temporarily available to the WCCA program. With the exception of internal security people recruited separately and not under assembly center managers' control, most staff employees of the assembly centers came from WPA's ranks.[24]

In the course of its 139 days of existence Camp Harmony would have two center managers. R. F. Turner oversaw its first month of operations, or "settling-in" phase, before his reassignment to San Francisco headquarters. His replacement, forty-three-year-old John J. McGovern, described as a big, good-natured, good-humored man by an anonymous writer in the *Camp Harmony Newsletter*, was married and with his two sons farmed a small acreage with hogs and cattle near Everett, north of Seattle. Like Turner a WPA administrator, McGovern continued as the center's manager until relinquishing control to Fort Lewis caretakers on September 30 and then went to headquarters in San Francisco.[25]

On loan from the WPA, administrators headed the Service, Works, Finance, and Mess and Lodging Divisions while others held subordinate positions within them. At Puyallup, government men eventually filled the center's thirty-four civil service staff positions at annual salaries ranging from $1,500 for truck drivers to $3,600 for management positions.[26]

Turner's was a brief and somewhat conflicted tenure. On April 28, 1942, WCCA headquarters ordered him to ignore "any organization of Japanese which has taken place outside of the center prior to their induction." Knowing an army officer had helped set up the Nisei-led administration, he ignored the directive. Furthermore, having resided in the Pacific Northwest, he knew Sakamoto personally and viewed him as an asset to the community.[27]

Accompanied by his family and Seattle's last wave of exiles, Sakamoto arrived at the center on Saturday May 16. With the four areas now fully occupied, according to plan he took the reins of the so-called Japanese Administration. Until May 7 only Area A had been occupied, thereby making administrative tasks relatively simple. Earlier Sakamoto appointed attorney Bill Mimbu to coordinate the early moving-in process. Now that Camp Harmony was filled to capacity, a more centralized coordination was called for that extended beyond Area A. Personnel supervisor George Ishihara became temporary chairman on May 13 pending chief supervisor Jimmy Sakamoto's arrival the following Saturday. In the meantime area councils had come into being headed by directors appointed to initiate the administrative machinery required to handle inevitable problems the waves of new inductees would soon create.

In the second issue of the *Camp Harmony News-Letter*, published on May 7, editor Richard Takeuchi discussed this move in relation to self-government promised to center residents, urging residents' complete cooperation: "That this camp should be allowed to retain local autonomous government and the greatest measure of freedom allowable under the circumstances is entirely dependent upon each individual within this camp . . . so that the army will not be forced to take over the administration of Camp Harmony."[28]

The Nisei appointees heading each area reported to the central administration headquartered in Area D. Assistants to area directors received assignments in keeping with individual area needs. During the settling-in phase major tasks included helping new arrivals move into their quarters and setting up the mess halls to prepare and serve food, clean tables, wash dishes, scrub pots, and then prepare for the next meal.

As work parties assembled to assist the new arrivals, clerks recruited from the advance party went to work in the administration office and area warehouses.

By May 6, the 2,027 inductees at Camp Harmony had nearly filled Area A. The next groups, arriving on May 11 and 12, filled the remainder of Area A and most of Area B, with Area C and Area D becoming fully occupied by the end of the day on May 16.

* * *

As a general policy the U.S. Public Health Service (USPHS) and WCCA agreed that prevention of communicable disease must be made a high priority during the evacuation period and in the centers. Health care would be provided without cost. The USPHS, "within the limitations of the authority granted and funds made available," equipped, staffed, and operated medical care facilities and paid for medical care outside the centers while county health departments oversaw provision of public health services within them.

If building, equipping, and supplying medical care facilities became the American taxpayers' responsibility, actual health care provided within the centers fell to inmate professionals. On the eve of the war 87 Issei and U.S.-born doctors (47 U.S.-born), 137 nurses (110 U.S.-born), 105 dentists (60 U.S-born), and 132 pharmacists (100 U.S.-born) served Nikkei community health needs on the West Coast.[29]

Four doctors and five nurses made up the Puyallup Assembly Center's primary medical staff with Dr. Kyo Koike, age sixty-four, in the role as senior physician. Born an only child into a family whose father and grandfather were *kanpo* doctors employing Chinese methods and herbs, Koike, like most medical students in Japan during the Meiji period (1868–1912), studied Western medicine in the German language. Graduating from Okayama Medical College in 1901, the young Koike practiced in Okayama city with an interest in surgery.

Koike left Japan for Seattle in 1917 at the invitation of a friend who agreed to sponsor him until he was settled. His push to leave the homeland may have been prompted by romantic feelings for a married woman, his friend's offer freeing him from an irreconcilable situation. Soon after arriving in Seattle, Koike set up a medical practice in the Empire Building on Main Street located in the center of *nihonmachi*, with treatment rooms adjoining his living quarters. A quiet man, he lived and practiced in Seattle until his departure for Camp Harmony with the advance group of essential volunteers on April 28, 1942.

A competent physician, Koike nevertheless felt drawn even more to the arts; his medical practice could financially support his pursuits of haiku poetry and pictorial photography. His study of haiku originated in Japan, while his interest in photography arose after his arrival in America, eventually earning him an international reputation.

Years after Koike's death, a contemporary recounted the dual focus of the doctor's life before the war: "A friend came to see Koike at his office and was told to come back after lunch. He came back—no Koike. He waited. 2 pm— no Koike. Much later—Koike never showed. The friend later suggested to Koike that he take his sign down because he was never around to practice medicine."[30]

The physicians serving under Koike at Camp Harmony were all younger. Nine years his junior, Seattle physician Dr. Shohei Sawamura, also an Issei, had graduated from the University of Oregon Medical School in 1924. Sawamura was licensed in 1925 and practiced at 613½ Jackson Street three blocks from Koike.

Dr. Paul Seikichi Shigaya graduated from the University of Oregon Medical School in 1927. Five years younger than Sawamura, he arrived in the United States in 1907. He was licensed in 1929 and practiced in Japantown on 6th Avenue South.

The youngest physician serving Camp Harmony inmates, thirty-eight-year-old Mitsuo Paul Suzuki emigrated from Japan at the age of thirteen and was raised in Tacoma by an aunt and uncle. After graduating from the University of Puget Sound, he received his medical training at Creighton University in Omaha. Graduating there in 1936, he returned to Seattle to complete an internship at Harborview Hospital. Two years later, Suzuki began slowly to build a practice on Jackson Street located within a block of Dr. Sawamura's.

For a month a fifth doctor shared duties at the Puyallup Assembly Center before reassignment to the Tule Lake Relocation Center in California. Dr.

George Taro Akamatsu, a Walnut Grove, California physician, graduated from Emory University School of Medicine in 1936. Shortly before the war's outbreak, he moved to Seattle to establish a practice in Japantown. However, on June 8, after receiving notice from the WCCA office in San Francisco, Akamatsu departed for Tule Lake, leaving the Puyallup Assembly Center with only four doctors to serve nearly 7,500 people.[31]

A month into his incarceration at Camp Harmony Dr. Koike wrote to a friend, "I am busy day and night." This statement spoke for all physicians from the moment they arrived at the center.[32] Their first priority was to set up aid stations to treat minor ailments and facilitate medical examinations and inoculations for new arrivals.

Despite optimism expressed by center manager Turner, who declared the hospital would be ready to receive patients the day the center opened, there was little progress in preparing it for patient admissions during the settling-in phase. The medical examinations mandated by USPHS for all new arrivals took up all their time, even with assistance from two USPHS physicians.[33]

Following completion of the intake examinations, doctors and nurses resumed the typhoid inoculation program.[34]

Food-borne maladies were the major problem medical personnel encountered. Minor epidemics of gastroenteritis, impossible to prevent, plagued most of the assembly centers. The outbreaks spread from numerous sources: improper food handling by inexperienced workers; inadequate dishwashing equipment; incomplete insect screening; insufficient numbers of poorly constructed and improperly placed latrines; inadequate refrigeration; and improper garbage storage. Most mess hall workers had never worked with food by trade. Joe Shiga, one of the few exceptions, had cooked at Seattle's Blanc's Cafe for twenty-three years. Few had any experience cooking for large numbers of people, so improper storage and food handling practices were common. The government's failure to have refrigeration and dishwashing equipment installed promptly was a significant cause of disease as was the failure to ensure adequate supplies of hot water.

In early May spoiled Vienna sausages caused a severe flare-up among inmates at Camp Harmony. Symptoms having emerged after the lights were out, the resulting commotion led to near panic on the part of sentries in the guard towers. Flashlights helped light the way to the latrines, a considerable walking distance from most barracks with outdoor lighting poor to nonexistent. All public stalls occupied meant pinpoints of light moved erratically in the darkness as victims hurried from one location to another. Fearing an insurrection, sentries manned the spotlights and called for reinforcements.

But with order quickly restored tragedy was averted, and the epidemic passed within twenty-four hours.[35]

Outbreaks of diarrhea were common in the assembly centers, particularly during the early days of occupancy. For instance, on the night of April 6 at Santa Anita improperly cooked and stored salmon loaf brought temporary misery to many inmates. The next day, at the Manzanar Reception Center nearly two hundred inmates fell victim to a week-long episode of food poisoning that occurred prior to the availability of hot water heaters and refrigeration.[36]

Given the crowded, unsanitary conditions of most assembly centers— including Puyallup—it is surprising more frequent, if not serious, outbreaks of gastroenteritis did not take place. According to Dr. W. T. Harrison, director of USPHS District No. 5, dishwashing with inadequate as well as unsanitary equipment and an insufficient hot water supply unable to meet peak loads resulted in the most serious health concern overall.[37] In time, vigilance by evacuee staff, eventual installation of adequately sized refrigeration units and hot water heaters, combined with detailed instructions on food handling safety to mess hall workers helped minimize camp-wide food poisoning outbreaks. Regardless, minor episodes persisted as a result of other unsanitary conditions.

Because the assembly centers were designed to function as way stations pending completion of the permanent relocation centers, their medical facilities were relegated to the status of infirmaries or emergency hospitals. Medical planners had equipped and stocked them to provide rudimentary care for minor emergencies and uncomplicated obstetrics cases. Nearby municipalities stood by to offer inmates comprehensive care at county hospitals located close to the assembly centers.[38]

With the majority of medical facilities located in typical theater of operation barracks, few built-in provisions existed to meet the special requirements required for a proper hospital setup. Camp Harmony's "E"-shaped hospital was sketched out on the back of a napkin by an engineer with little understanding of a medical care facility's construction requirements. Follow-up designs failed to provide for segregation of patients by age or gender, let alone by nature of physical illnesses. Shelving and cabinetry had been placed in inefficient locations, with sinks and drains installed only at the building's far ends. Despite repeated requests by inmate physicians and USPHS representatives, changes came slowly.

Supplies and essential equipment such as sterilizing units arrived incrementally. By May 18, as Camp Harmony's population neared its peak, the hospital remained unprepared to receive its first patient. This resulted in ongoing referral of patients to the Pierce County Hospital.[39] In the meantime, the Pierce County Board of Health, upon condemning the poor sanitary conditions at the center, demanded additional medical facilities be put into place.[40]

*   *   *

Life at Camp Harmony settled into a routine as its population inched toward its 7,390 apex, reached on May 25. Activities for diverting residents from the boredom of captivity included athletic programs with volleyball, softball, and other sports where area teams were pitted against each other. A library opened, its books donated by sympathetic organizations or on loan from the Seattle Public Library. Concerts employing phonograph records whose sounds amplified through speakers drew crowds to open areas, and movies were projected in community areas. A center store in Area D provided candies, soda pop, newspapers, and toiletry items, while kinks had been worked out making inter-area visits more manageable. Now people coming from the outside could enter a new visitors' house instead of lining up along the fence, and work opportunities had been created for those desiring to make constructive use of their time.

But most significantly, by now opportunities had begun to arise whereby individuals could make plans to leave the center.

7

Early Departures and a New Community

After May 26, the day Camp Harmony's population peaked at 7,390, the center's numbers slowly began to diminish as small groups of young adult Nisei began heading for agricultural work in the sugar beet fields in eastern Oregon and Montana and to college campuses outside Military Area No. 1. In addition, some Issei men and their families volunteered for repatriation to Japan. By the end of June, Camp Harmony's population had declined by 222.

As the 1942 growing season began in earnest, the nation's farm labor crisis deepened as many draft-age farm hands entered military service or took on higher-paying jobs in the expanding war economy. This development proved particularly troubling to the labor-intensive sugar beet industry in the high desert country of the Far West, for its money crop had to be blocked and thinned in the spring, hoed and irrigated in the summer, and harvested during October and November. The imminent exile of young adult Japanese Americans to the assembly centers caused sugar processors to turn to the centers as an untapped labor source.[1]

As the farm labor pool continued to shrink and imported sugar stocks dwindled, demand for the commodity rose. With memories of similar shortages during World War I still fresh, Americans rushed to stockpile sugar after the bombing of Pearl Harbor. Sugar, needed by U.S. troops and as a source of ethanol for fuel, imposed additional strains on existing supplies as imports from Latin America and the Philippines declined or dried up altogether. In May 1942, the government, attempting to dampen domestic consumption, issued coupon ration books initially limiting purchases to eight ounces per week.

Given wartime's intensifying demand for sugar and an inadequate farm labor force available to produce it, the Wartime Civil Control Administration (WCCA) became receptive to urgent requests by Amalgamated Sugar, Utah & Idaho (U&I) Sugar, and other processors to access inmates in the assembly centers even though they were scheduled to close before the end of harvest season. Although many residents of Idaho and Montana disliked having Japanese Americans in their midst, desperate farmers reconciled themselves to employing Nisei labor and provided written guarantees of fair treatment. The alternative of hiring Mexican labor would cause direct competition with California and the Southwest for available workers.

With the exile of Nikkei from the West Coast, a certainty as early as March 12, 1942, officials from the Federal Security Agency began formulating employment possibilities for them.[2] One month later, General DeWitt agreed to conditions set by the Agriculture Department that would enable growers to employ Japanese Americans under his jurisdiction:

1 That recruitment be on a voluntary basis, with placement to be made through the U.S. Employment Service;

2 That workers be paid wages prevailing for the type of work performed and not to displace other labor;

3 That employers provide, without cost to the government or the evacuees, transportation from assembly centers to the work-location and return;

4 That the State provide adequate protection and guarantee the safety of the evacuees and the communities in which they work; and

5 That employers provide suitable housing for evacuees at the work location.[3]

By this time significant opposition had arisen from state officials toward Japanese Americans coming to work in inland western states. A naïve War Relocation Authority (WRA) director, Milton Eisenhower, kept uninformed by WCCA officials, including Colonel Bendetsen, learned of this swelling antipathy at a conference of state officials in Salt Lake City on April 7. They came to the meeting to express unwillingness or inability to meet DeWitt's five conditions, in particular the provision requiring temporary laborers receive adequate protection and safety guarantees. Resentment toward Japanese Americans had magnified in the wake of Pearl Harbor as losses mounted in the Pacific and Australia came under threat of invasion. Those in attendance centered their concerns on several points: opposition to Japanese purchasing land in their states and, regardless of citizenship status, settling in their states during or after the war. The mood of the citizens could not be controlled, they warned, and most upheld the conviction that California used their interior states as dumping grounds for an old immigration problem.

While several officials advocated detention camps for all Japanese no matter where they resided, others expressed a more moderate view, proposing
Japanese workers be allowed entry only under federal guard and at the end
of the war be escorted out of the state.[4]

While such exclusionist views may have represented the electorate's sentiments, politicians remained out of touch with the needs of the region's farmers. Beet growers would not have to wait long for such attitudes to change.

The Amalgamated Sugar Company and Oregon public officials, including
Governor Sprague, signed the first private employment agreement on May
5, 1942. Processors sought four hundred workers for sugar beet thinning in
Malheur County lying east of the Cascades and outside Military Area No.
1. Amalgamated Sugar's refinery at Nyssa's company camp accommodated
ninety single workers and utilized an abandoned two hundred-man capacity Civilian Conservation Corps (CCC) camp situated nearby. Other CCC
and Farm Security Administration (FSA) camps available throughout areas
growing sugar beets also accommodated needed workers.

On May 20 recruitment started in the Portland Assembly Center. However,
the first contingent heading eastward consisted of only fourteen former Portland area high school students. Other volunteers, aware of public opposition
in nearby states and fearing for their safety, backed out at the last minute.

Even though seasonal agricultural work leave provided a sure way to get
out of the assembly centers, volunteers came forward slowly, with recruitment
lagging due to the uncertainty of Nikkeis' future status as farm workers. While
willing to work they wanted to know the nature of the reception they would
get in farming areas. Earlier, Idaho governor Chase Clark advocated for the
army to closely supervise the Nikkei already present in his state, having earlier described them in a public pronouncement as people "who act like rats"
and suggesting "[we] send them all back to Japan, then sink the island."[5]

Following publication of Clark's speech in local newspapers Puyallup Assembly Center recruitment efforts also suffered.[6] In fact, Idaho's sugar beet
company representatives encountered clippings of Clark's "rat" speech on
assembly center bulletin boards everywhere they went and little enthusiasm
from volunteers.[7]

That a vital source of badly needed labor might sit idle throughout the
war caused public hostility toward the Nikkei to abate in many farm regions
of the Far West. As incendiary attitudes quieted down, growers pressured
Idaho governor Chase Clark to change his stance in opposition of Japanese
coming into his state and "buying up land."

By mid-May, his demagogic utterances now clearly linked to the low volunteer rates, Clark revised his rhetoric and assured Nikkei they would receive

"the finest treatment" if they came to work on Idaho farms.[8] A Boise Idaho *Statesman* editorial noted: "Governor Clark tip-toed 'round to the back stoop Monday and gingerly sprinkled sand on his Jap-Issue incendiary, which, in our analysis, was mostly political smoke." Numerous editors of farm area newspapers had expressed similar sentiments by the end of May.

On May 22 six hundred potential recruits at Camp Harmony met representatives of the United States Employment Service and the "U & I" Sugar Company in Area A to hear promises of 45 cents per hour wages and a thirty-day trial period with transportation provided.[9]

As of June 1, seventy-four inmates left assembly centers to work on Malheur County farms in eastern Oregon with an equal number awaiting transportation into the area; the potential worker pool increased as the WCCA permitted recruitment at three additional assembly centers. Agreements with major sugar processors followed suit with the blessing of Idaho and Montana governors. By now formal requests for three thousand sugar beet hires had been recorded.[10]

On May 28 nine workers departed Camp Harmony for farm work in eastern Oregon's Nyssa area. Another twenty-five left for Montana on June 7, a total of seventy-two seasonal work leave volunteers reaching the beet fields by June 20.[11] The early workers from the centers were mostly Nisei, those from Puyallup averaging twenty-one years of age.[12]

Favorable worker conditions typified most reports sent back to the assembly centers. A scarcity of available jobs at the centers; financial inducement for outside work at prevailing wages exceeding the WCCA pay scale of $8 per month plus room and board and clothing allowance for unskilled labor; and Governor Clark's willingness to guarantee the safety of workers in his state combined to make recruitment of new workers proceed more smoothly.

By mid-June about 1,000 assembly center inmates were working the beet fields; by the end of the assembly center period 1,579 had moved onto farms in the high desert country of the American West on seasonal agricultural work leave.[13] The program proved a success at generating farm hands and provided a model for the much larger organized farm labor recruitment to occur later in the relocation centers.[14]

*   *   *

Nisei college students, their educations on West Coast campuses abruptly suspended, also encountered opportunities to leave their assembly centers. However, while over the next three years a student relocation program would enable more than four thousand Nisei to continue their educations at six hundred inland colleges and universities, the effort was slow to gain momentum with the number of transfers from the centers small.

At the start of 1941's fall session, 3,252 Japanese American students attended classes at West Coast colleges and universities. In Washington, 458 students were enrolled at the University of Washington, with 95 others attending colleges throughout the state.[15]

With the freezing of Issei assets in the wake of Pearl Harbor, many students had little hope of continuing in the winter term. A survey of 150 University of Washington Nisei students in April 1942 confirmed this when less than one-fourth of them reported possessing sufficient funds to enable them to continue their studies.[16] In the San Francisco Bay Area an earlier survey revealed over 80 percent of Nisei college students desired to continue their education, but the majority required financial assistance.[17]

Officials at the University of Washington and University of California, the two West Coast institutions with the largest Nisei enrollments, quickly grasped the developing problem. In Seattle Robert O'Brien, faculty advisor to the Japanese Student Club, brought students together to discuss the uncertain future of their educations. When students began to drop out, the university initiated a liberal leave of absence policy and refunded all prepaid fees. As the purge of Seattle's Nikkei community loomed, University of Washington President Lee Paul Sieg urged his counterparts throughout the country to accept his students as transferees. Soon the American Friends Service Committee (AFSC) became involved in the welfare of West Coast students, sending Tom Bodine to Seattle to assist in student resettlement work.

These largely uncoordinated efforts brought about resettlement of 216 Nikkei students from the West Coast prior to the March 29, 1942 deadline for voluntary migration out of Military Area No. 1. Anyone attempting to leave assembly centers after that time would face increased difficulty because the WCCA imposed heavy restrictions for granting travel permits. In fact, restrictions eased only after jurisdiction of students passed from the WCCA to the WRA.[18]

Before the March 29 voluntary migration deadline a modicum of Washington Nisei students succeeded in transferring to the Universities of Michigan, Minnesota, Idaho, and Chicago; transfers after that date continued on a case-by-case basis. By May 1, as Camp Harmony continued to take in inductees, fifty-eight University of Washington students had received placements in fifteen colleges and universities in eleven states.[19] Omitted from this list of states was Idaho, which earlier admitted six students to the University of Idaho in Moscow. Having just arrived in town, the new enrollees encountered Idaho governor Chase Clark's declaration insisting no out-of-state Nisei could enroll at any state-supported college or university. Two of these students spent the night in jail as protection from a Moscow mob. Soon after this incident the group enrolled at Washington State College located at Pullman, ten miles away.[20]

From the assembly center period's beginning in April until October and the start of fall term, overall only 360 students out of the eventual 4,000 applicants for release to attend school resettled to new campuses. This meant, at least temporarily, the majority of Nisei desiring to continue their college educations remained in the assembly centers.

On June 5, 1942, Marnie Schauffler of the AFSC, representing the newly formed National Japanese American Student Relocation Council (NJASRC), met with the first Seattle area students with acceptance letters in hand or pending applications to plan transfers in time for fall enrollments. The available data for forty-six of these students clarifies the inherent difficulties in achieving resettlement during the assembly center period.[21]

Ultimately, only three students departed the Puyallup Assembly Center. Eventually twenty-three transferees departed the Minidoka Relocation Center, but most not before 1943. Camp Harmony's mini exodus took place on August 22, 1942, when students boarded a train for the University of Colorado and Denver University just days before their scheduled move to Minidoka. Another three from Minidoka headed for the University of Utah in Salt Lake City on September 24. Before the end of 1942, only three more students left Minidoka, for a total of nine. From this 1942 group eight attended the institutions of their first choice. Among the later group, seventeen who left Minidoka in 1943 and 1944, only nine attended their preferred school as a result of delays in acquiring travel clearances.[22]

A small number of WCCA-approved institutions became available to students during the assembly center period. Choices by the Camp Harmony group included three in Ohio (Bowling Green, Oberlin, and Ohio State University), two in Colorado (University of Colorado and Denver University), University of Minnesota, Northwestern (Evanston, Illinois), University of Nebraska, University of North Carolina, Syracuse University (New York), University of Utah, and five colleges in Washington State east of Military Area No. 1 (Gonzaga, Spokane Junior College, Whitman College, Whitworth, and Washington State College.)[23]

Because he opposed student resettlement for national security reasons, Colonel Karl R. Bendetsen imposed layers of restrictions that allowed only a short list of approved colleges and universities. He forbade Nisei access to the NJASRC created to assist students with financial aid and their transfer to colleges willing to accept them. Bendetsen also imposed strict leave clearance regulations making it nearly impossible to meet enrollment deadlines. He required proof of financial resources to pay travel expenses, one year's tuition, and room and board. Further, students had to undergo FBI intelligence checks, while the colleges themselves had to be cleared.

Such obstacles caused many students to alter short-term plans; others abandoned their applications altogether. Family situations within the centers pressured some prospective college students to remain incarcerated. Most Nisei attempting to continue their college education during the war prepared their applications while residing in the relocation centers.

University of Washington freshman Kenji Okuda's experience illustrates the difficulties encountered by students seeking college placement during the assembly center period. In the spring of 1942, prior to evacuation to Camp Harmony, Okuda, an economics major, received his acceptance letter from Oberlin College in plenty of time to register for the fall term. But his father's detention at Fort Missoula elevated Kenji to the head of the household, resulting in his remaining in Seattle to see his mother and two sisters safely settled at the Puyallup Assembly Center.

Okuda himself planned to stay at the center for one month before leaving under the auspices of the NJASRC. Weeks passed, however, without word of his travel clearance from WCCA headquarters in San Francisco. On August 11, 1942, Okuda wrote "The War Department" regarding his status, stating he had filed the necessary paperwork with the WCCA, including his formal acceptance from Oberlin; a statement of his financial resources (a trust fund in his name exceeding $3,000); and multiple testimonies attesting to his loyalty from Caucasian friends. He asked if Oberlin appeared on the War Department's current approved list of colleges; if not, he would apply to "some other school which has secured your approval."

On August 12 shortly after Okuda mailed the letter, without warning, center manager J. J. McGovern, under instructions from the WCCA, ordered him and his family transferred to the Merced Assembly Center in central California. Branded a troublemaker because of his connection with the pacifist Fellowship of Reconciliation and its mimeograph publication, *Pacific Cable,* Kenji's associations unwittingly resulted in his family's banishment. In addition, Okuda's father remained under WCCA suspicion despite his recent parole from Fort Missoula. The army's failure to clear him resulted in loss of his 1942 fall term slot to another Oberlin student. This untoward experience delayed his education until the 1943 spring term.[24]

By August 1943, 169 former Puyallup and Portland Assembly Center in-mates had left Minidoka for inland colleges and universities, more transfers than from any other WRA center. However, by the end of 1942 fewer than half the students with college acceptance letters had actually enrolled and were attending classes.[25]

The fallout from Executive Order 9066 was not limited to University of Washington Nisei undergraduates. The civilian exclusion orders also im-pacted Nikkei teaching fellows and faculty. Assistant Professor Henry Tatsumi and Associate Professor John Maki of the Department of Oriental Studies, and Instructor Masako Takayoshi from the Department of Nursing Education, all left their positions before their eviction orders took effect. Ironically, Tatsumi headed to the University of Colorado to teach in the navy's Japanese Language Program. Takayoshi relocated as assistant head nurse in the women's surgi-cal ward at Colorado General Hospital, and sociology instructor S. Frank Miyamoto, a Nisei first incarcerated at the Puyallup Assembly Center and later at Tule Lake Relocation Center, found employment as a paid participant observer for the University of California–based Japanese Evacuation and Re-settlement Study . While incarcerated he utilized his sociological training to study life in a relocation center; his postwar doctoral dissertation written at the University of Chicago incorporated research conducted at Tule Lake.[26]

All five Nikkei teaching fellows had to leave their positions at the Univer-sity of Washington. Martha Okuda accepted a position at the University of Nebraska's School of Social Work. Nobutaka Ike, former student of Henry Tatsumi, left Camp Harmony on July 5 to join his mentor on the University of Colorado's Japanese Language School faculty, while Chihiro Kikuchi (Phys-ics) and Tashio Inatomi (Chemistry) moved to the University of Cincinnati. George Sawada, second-year fellow in the Anatomy Department, accompa-nied his family to Camp Harmony, never to resume academic life. Shortly after his transfer to Minidoka in August 1943, he volunteered for the all Nisei 442nd Regimental Combat Team. While serving as a medic in the 100th In-fantry Battalion, Sawada was killed by enemy fire in Italy on July 5, 1944.[27]

* * *

As Nisei students pursued avenues to continue their education and further invest in America, some Issei inmates chose to pursue repatriation. The State Department and Japan's Foreign Ministry negotiated two diplomatic ex-changes in which ships chartered by the two countries would carry the dip-lomatic corps of the two countries and other non-officials to neutral ports in Asia and Africa and be exchanged there.[28]

On June 6, 1942, twenty-seven-year-old Shizuye Iriye, Issei wife of detainee Tataki Iriye, who had been in Justice Department custody since December 7, their nine-month-old American-born son, Hidedi, and another Issei, twenty-seven-year-old Kiyoko Kanai, boarded an eastbound train at Puyallup station en route to New York under guard for a scheduled June 11 departure for Japan on the Swedish liner, MS *Gripsholm,* chartered earlier by the State Department. Traveling south to Portland, the train picked up five additional volunteer repatriates—three from the Portland Assembly Center and two from Pasco, Washington, outside Military Area No. 1.[29]

Winding southward through California then eastward picking up passengers along the way, the train had fifty-four repatriates aboard by the time it reached New York City's Pennsylvania Station early on the morning of June 10. State Department representatives and a military police guard met the group and escorted them to a nearby hotel to await the ship's sailing.[30]

At New York Harbor a thousand repatriates, including members of the Japanese diplomatic corps in the United States and Latin America just arriving from detention centers in the eastern United States and Texas, were joined by detainees and internees from Justice Department and army camps as well as voluntary repatriates from Hawaii. Family members born in the United States, including young Hidedi Iriye from the Puyallup Assembly Center, accompanied many Japanese nationals.[31] MS *Gripsholm* sailed from New York harbor on June 18, 1942.[32]

Over the next six months the State Department provided the WCCA additional lists of Japanese nationals to be considered for future repatriation.[33] One list included the names of 309 inmates from the Puyallup Assembly Center. The number of former Camp Harmony inmates actually repatriated remains unclear since the next sailing of the *Gripsholm* occurred September 3, 1943, nearly a year after the center closed.[34]

*   *   *

During May and June departures from Camp Harmony for seasonal work leave, student resettlement, and repatriation totaled fewer than a hundred persons, representing less than one percent of the center's peak population. Those remaining until the transfer to Minidoka in mid-August began to adjust to the dullness of incarceration's daily routine. Food improved; the hospital opened and took in obstetrics cases; inmate postal carriers delivered mail to the barracks; work and recreation opportunities opened up. And the weather began to improve.

Throughout the assembly center period WCCA administrators procured food supplies from the army quartermaster. During the settling-in phase most provisions consisted of army Field Ration "B" menus and accounted for the monotonous fare and dearth of fresh meats and produce many Camp Harmony survivors were to recall half a century later.

In 1939, the army classification system for feeding its troops categorized all rations as "Field Rations." Field Ration "A" consisted of fresh food products prepared for mess hall consumption at permanent military facilities; Field Ration "B" accommodated conditions lacking adequate refrigeration. This led to canned meats, vegetables, and dehydrated foods replacing the more palatable "A" ration meals.

Earlier incompetence by army planners resulted in hurried conceptualization, construction, and outfitting of the assembly centers and meant environments necessary for proper food preparation, including refrigeration, were either absent or inadequate to serve the needs of early arrivals. Until necessary equipment could be installed, the quartermaster shipped "B" rations in units of ten breakfasts and ten lunch/dinners, each unit designed to accommodate a hundred men.

Camp Harmony's food preparers served up "B" rations in the mess halls for approximately three weeks. Since a day's military ration consisted of two meals, until May 11, when "A" rations first appeared, extra rations for the supper meal had to be procured from these same lunch/dinner menus.

"B" rations, invented to supply the nutritional needs of troops in the field, proved inadequate for women and younger children, who made up more than half of Camp Harmony's population. Initially fresh milk, butter, and eggs remained scarce. Not part of the "B" ration diet, local producers of fresh dairy products had to be lined up quickly to create reliable supply lines for the inmates. The existing short-term supplies went primarily to children or to others with special dietary needs.

By mid-May, menus improved significantly in both quality and variety. In response to ongoing complaints about food in the assembly centers, center managers were directed to submit to San Francisco complete menus for a full month. Table 4 shows the Camp Harmony menu for the week of May 19–25: plentiful fresh fruit and vegetables with little evidence of main entrees from the can. The memo also reveals availability of both American- and Japanese-style dishes.[35]

Complaints about going hungry all but disappeared. However, chronic grumbling over being fed institutionalized food persisted at Camp Harmony and later at the Minidoka Relocation Center. As the transfer to Minidoka got under way journalist Bill Hosokawa, in the August 14, 1942 souvenir edition of the *Camp Harmony News-Letter*, put food-related issues into per-

Table 4. Menus for Puyallup Assembly Center Inmates for the Week of May 19–25, 1942

May 19, 1942

BREAKFAST	DINNER	SUPPER
Fresh apples	Beef stew/vegetables	Egg soup
Corn meal	Fresh tomatoes/lettuce salad	Rice
Pancakes/syrup/butter	Fruit cobbler	Boiled onion
Coffee/milk	Tea/milk/bread	Shoyu
		Dill pickles
		Canned peaches
		Tea

May 20, 1942

BREAKFAST	DINNER	SUPPER
Bananas	Hamburger	Sukiyaki
Corn meal	Rice	Japanese pickles
Toast/butter	Sliced onions	Vegetable soup
Coffee/sugar/milk	Shoyu	Boston cream pie
	Butterscotch pudding	Tea
	Bread/tea	

May 21, 1942

BREAKFAST	DINNER	SUPPER
Fresh apples	Meatballs	Soup
Cereal	Mashed potatoes	Tempura
Toast/jelly	Vegetable salad	Rutabagas
Coffee/sugar/milk	Pears	Dill pickles
	Bread/butter/tea	Bread/tea

May 22, 1942

BREAKFAST	DINNER	SUPPER
Nectarines	Cream of celery soup	Fresh fish
Oatmeal	American cheese	Rice
Pancakes/syrup/butter	Vegetable salad	Fresh spinach
Coffee/milk/sugar	Butterscotch pudding	Shoyu
	Bread/butter/tea/milk	Lettuce/tomato/radish
		Cake
		Tea/milk/bread

May 23, 1942

BREAKFAST	DINNER	SUPPER
Fresh apples	Baked Italian delight	Tempura
Rolled oats	Mashed potatoes	Shoyu
Hot cakes/syrup/butter	Rutabagas	Rice
	Canned pears	Apple/carrot/lettuce salad
	Bread/butter/tea/milk	Apricot cobbler
		Tea/milk/bread

May 24, 1942

BREAKFAST	DINNER	SUPPER
Bananas	Beef pot roast	Soup
Cereal	Rice	Spaghetti
Scrambled eggs	Peas	baked/tomato/cheese
Fried potatoes	Fruit salad	Bread/butter
Coffee cake/butter	Cookies	Tea/milk

May 25, 1942

BREAKFAST	DINNER	SUPPER
Applesauce	Cabbage roll/tomato sauce	Pork shoulder
Cereal	Carrots/raisin/lettuce salad	Rice
Pancakes/syrup/butter	Browned potatoes	String beans
Coffee/milk	Butterscotch pudding	Shoyu
	Tea/milk/bread	Green onions radishes
		Head lettuce
		Bread pudding
		Tea/milk/bread

Source: RG338, WDC & 4th Army WCCA + CAD, General Unclassified Correspondence, 1942–1946, file 323.3.

Young women smiling for the camera in a mess hall with fresh milk and "A" rations on the table. Sun glasses suggest the weather has improved. (National Archives)

spective. In a column entitled "Little Things," he looked back over three and a half months at the Puyallup Assembly Center: "At first the food was bad, then they got off the canned rations and the meals were better. Pretty soon we were getting cantaloupes once in awhile and raspberries three times a day while they were paying a dollar a crate for folks to pick them. Then one memorable day there was steak for lunch and three pork chops apiece for supper, and then they started to kick about too much meat on the menu."[36]

Although "B" rations disappeared after days, not months, their impression settled into the long-term memory of many former inmates. Incarceration's first weeks proved a shock as people moved from freedom into a prison environment while normal life beyond the barbed wire fences passed freely by. The attendant uncertainty compounded these early assaults to the senses.

Although food on mess hall tables soon became more palatable, a healthful physical environment for its preparation was slower to evolve and resulted in ongoing threats of gastrointestinal problems. Modifications to existing hot water systems in Areas A, B, and C on the former parking lot sites brought noticeably improved kitchen sanitation. Water boilers installed in Area D's kitchen on the main fairgrounds site, however, could never be augmented to adequately accommodate 2,800 people in a facility designed for 1,500: the supply of hot water only met about half the actual need.

Even when hot water sufficed, sanitation problems persisted because food workers could not or would not follow health department recommendations. Inexperience resulted in cooked foods being left on the floor uncovered, unrefrigerated, and vulnerable to contamination. In all four areas ongoing noncompliance with chlorine rinses during dish washing frustrated U.S. Public Health Service (USPHS) sanitation inspectors during periodic visits to the center. Standard practice required a two-minute bath in chlorine solution followed by air drying, a simple procedure widely available to control disease-producing bacteria. Sometimes workers employed the solution in soapy water, failed to immerse dishes in the chlorine rinse for the entire two minutes, towel dried the dishes, or bypassed the procedure altogether. Such noncompliance greatly reduced or destroyed the bactericidal effect of the chlorine.

Compliance increased slowly, and sanitation problems continued even after inspectors organized an education program for the workers in July. Until the center emptied in August and early September, workers everywhere ignored repeated suggestions to comply with established disease control practices.[37]

Camp Harmony's poor sanitary controls extended beyond unsafe food handling and dishwashing practices. Garbage handlers and workers assigned to clean showers and latrines were lax in controlling flies drawn to overfilled garbage cans. Propped-open screen doors in mess halls, meat cutting rooms, latrines, and shower areas defeated efforts to control pest-borne contamination, while drain holes and sumps for ground water lacked proper protection against fly breeding despite inspectors' recommendations.

The government, knowing the majority of workers had little or no prior work experience in institutional settings, failed to provide trained outside personnel to ensure inmates' good health. The desire to oppose their oppressors' authority may also have impacted a lack of compliance even as it worked against the inmates' own best interests.

In July McGovern learned of two sanitation problems involving the U.S. Army Corps of Engineers' master drainage system. Frequently backed up, the septic tanks had to be bucketed out manually; plans by center management to hire local professional septic tank cleaners had not materialized. The army never stepped in to alleviate the problem: ongoing hand bailing by inmates to fill garbage cans hauled to a dumpsite on the Puyallup River increased risk of disease and outbreaks to the center and surrounding community.[38] In an attempt to take control of the problem, McGovern's staff ordered weekly hosing and flushing out of septic tanks with the unfiltered effluent discharged into the communal sewer system. This practice defeated the septic tank system by allowing untreated sewage to pass through the lines. It compromised the entire sewer system consisting of an open drainage canal known as "Meeker Ditch"; two chlorinators feeding the ditch at the heads of the lines provided insufficient capacity for handling the increased load. During frequent breakdown periods no chlorine passed over liquid and solid wastes flowing through the system.

Meanwhile, even with danger signs (but no fences) properly posted, children from the surrounding Puyallup community played in the ditch, putting Camp Harmony inmates and Puyallup city residents at risk for disease and epidemic until the last inmate departed the center grounds.[39]

In their final report on August 12, 1942, USPHS sanitation inspectors expressed frustration over the program's shortcomings, knowing that little would be done to rectify the problem with the relocation to the Minidoka Relocation Center about to get under way:

> They still have the authority and the duty to the inhabitants to insist on such factors as proper chlorination of the dishes and utensils, sanitary methods of food handling and the preparation, and proper operation of the supply and disposal. Sanitation reports submitted by the health department since the inception of the program have continually stressed improvement of these various systems and some of the improvements suggested have been followed, but many have been ignored. The department will continue to stress these items until its services are rendered unnecessary due to completed evacuation.[40]

Sanitation woes constantly plagued visiting USPHS inspectors throughout the life of the assembly centers, later causing one senior public health official to write: "That there have been no more serious epidemics of gastro-intestinal disease is due to the constant vigilance and heroic efforts of the health departments and resident medical staffs and probably, considering the very inadequate sanitary facilities provided in the centers, to a great deal of good fortune."[41]

While sanitation problems remained ongoing at the Puyallup Assembly Center, public health care for individual inmates began to improve. As the medical staff brought closure to the examination and inoculation program its energies now turned toward providing routine health care for Camp Harmony's population. Essential hospital equipment and supplies began arriving and pharmaceuticals appeared on shelves, allowing the rudimentary hospital to accept its first admission, on May 31.

These advancements, like improvements in the sanitation situation, were slow in coming. On June 9, 1942, Dr. Kyo Koike wrote to a friend detained at Fort Missoula: "The medical services are not perfect yet, but we must try our best for the Japanese evacuees to keep them healthy and well. There are about eight thousand people in the four areas and we physicians are only five in number. Moreover, yesterday one of us, Dr. Akamatsu, was ordered to move to the Tule Lake Relocation Center with only one day notice. We are obliged to change our daily schedule very often. People are overanxious and we are called for nothing very often."[42]

By July 7, first aid stations operated in all areas with attendants on duty around the clock. But with sterilizing units not yet on hand, obstetrics cases continued to be outsourced to the Pierce County Hospital. The USPHS added a consultant physician for prenatal and obstetrics cases, and by the end of the following week the autoclaves finally were in place, permitting the hospital to operate at full capacity. With adequate supplies and equipment now a reality, all but the most difficult obstetrical cases could be treated in-house. On July 12 the hospital celebrated its first on-site birth. Five days later, Camp Harmony surgeons performed their first appendectomy, a second one following two weeks later. The number of minor surgical cases referred to outside hospitals decreased.[43]

Because of the center's peculiar physical layout doctors limited out-of-area visits to emergency cases only. Patients seeking treatment at the Area D hospital clinics therefore had to walk or be transported by an ambulance. Medical aides in Areas A, B, and C helped reduce some of the load by treating patients with minor maladies at the area first aid stations.

Ten dentists, each assigned to an aid station, assessed dental needs and provided minor care. USPHS regulations applying to all centers authorized only emergency dental care: tooth extractions, treatment of traumatic injuries and acute oral infection, placement of temporary fillings, and denture repairs. With most equipment and supplies lacking, dentists were challenged in efforts to provide even palliative care.

Dentists who thought ahead to continuing their professional lives while in captivity had brought hand instruments and supplies. Assisted by inmate

Nurses Natsuko Yamaguchi and Mayme Sembe going off shift from the hospital. Other hospital staff may be seen in the background. (National Archives)

carpenters, they constructed rudimentary dental chairs and improvised lighting. Government-provided essential dental equipment had not arrived by mid-July and may never have been ordered. This lack of planning created problems for all assembly centers. The Office for Emergency Management assessed the feasibility of leasing privately owned equipment from prewar practicing Nikkei dentists, eventually drawing up equipment leases with dentists at six assembly centers. Camp Harmony was excluded because of its scheduled closure in the near future. Possessing minimal instrumentation, no x-ray equipment, and no central facility in which to provide care, dentists often could do little more than relieve acute pain. This meant many Camp Harmony residents endured considerable discomfort from untreated dental disease, which in some cases affected their general health.

The center hospital gradually improved its ability to provide care as supplies trickled in and carpenters built cabinetry and erected wall barriers to segregate hospital populations. With the addition of a Caucasian hospital administrator in July, the efficiency of the Nikkei staff in the wards and communication between staff and central administration noticeably improved.

Although patients received universal access to medical and dental care and medical care was free, midwives played only a minor role. Because USPHS policy restricted delivery of babies to physicians midwives were limited to pre- and postpartum care for mothers and help and counseling with infant care.[44]

Camp Harmony mothers gave birth to thirty-seven babies at the Pierce County and center hospitals. The first was a baby girl born to John and Masue Hiyashi on July 12. In August, Camp Harmony's medical staff documented 2,260 outpatient treatments, most involving dental, surgical, and general medical treatments, including inoculations. During the same period the staff delivered five babies and recorded eleven deaths.[45]

* * *

Although physically isolated from their former communities throughout the Puget Sound region, English-speaking inmates had access to news and world events through AM band radio broadcasts and mail subscription newspapers and periodicals, including *Pacific Citizen,* the Japanese American Citizens League (JACL) weekly now published in Salt Lake City. Because Japanese-language print media was banned, such as *Utah Nippo,* also published in Salt Lake City, and similar periodicals published elsewhere, many Issei inmates received the news second hand.

To provide information on what was going on within the assembly centers, each center published and distributed free a newsletter produced by Nikkei editorial and production staffs. Some of them had evocative names: *Walerga Wasp*; *Turlock Fume*; *Santa Anita Pacemaker*; *Pinedale Logger*; *Tanforan Totalizer*; *Fresno Grapevine*. The two-sided paper editions were mimeographed, often on hand-stapled legal-sized paper.

The newsletters provided center managers with a means to communicate rules, regulations, and directives while editors reported center-wide happenings, such as social and sporting events, Sunday church schedules, and news from other centers. Vital statistics—marriages, births, and deaths—appeared regularly. These journalistic efforts served to improve morale and reduce feelings of isolation.

Officially sanctioned by the WCCA, center managers maintained ultimate control over policy and content and were heavy handed with censorship. Stories in the Japanese language were forbidden. In short, no story could be published without first being scrutinized by center management or its representatives. Some insisted on screening items announcing upcoming religious services.

J. J. McGovern and other center managers relied on press relations representatives assigned by the WCCA to each center to guide editors and see that news items were appropriate and fell within established censorship guidelines. Tom Montgomery, editor of the *Puyallup Valley Tribune* and local public relations representative of the T. W. Braun Company in Los Angeles, took charge of the *Camp Harmony News-Letter* following distribution of the sixth issue. He read the pre-published stories, reviewed the stencil after it had been cut, and finally checked the first copy off the mimeograph machine. Proximity to Camp Harmony enabled Montgomery to maintain daily contact with the administration and report his findings to Braun on a regular basis.[46]

Commenting on the centers' newsletters, the *Final Report* understated the public relations representatives' role: "The young editors had the assistance and guidance of the Public Relations Representative who confined news items to those of actual interest to the evacuees."[47]

The editors and staff took their work seriously. Prior to entering the Puyallup Assembly Center, Dick Takeuchi published the English section of the now defunct *Great Northern Daily News*, while several former writers helped make up his eighteen-member staff, including Bill Hosokawa, previously a journalist in Asia. He later became editor of the *Heart Mountain Sentinel* and after the war eventually launched a lifelong career with the *Denver Post*.[48] Takeuchi's staff, mostly young Nisei, also included area correspondent and photographer Kiyoshi Okawa, although prohibition of cameras in the center prevented him from utilizing his skills. Hisashi Hirai, a twenty-three-year-old commercial artist, and Eddie Sato, a high school student and winner of

· CAMP HARMONY · NEWS-LETTER

Vol. 1 No. 10   Puyallup, Wash.   July 18, 1942

PAY CHECKS MONDAY

M'GOVERN 1ST DONOR FOR PLASMA DRIVE

J. J. McGovern, center manager, became Camp Harmony's first "resident" to offer his blood in the current campaign for blood plasma as registration began this week to sign up voluntary donors for blood tests.

"This campaign is being carried on to supplement the reserve supply of the Red Cross blood bank which is being overtaxed by the great demand on overseas fighting fronts," Tom Kanno, headquarters campaign supervisor, declared.

The Red Cross blood bank is a reserve supply maintained principally for emergencies. Since the inception of war, however, it was the only organization with enough blood plasma qualified to meet the sudden requirement.

The drain on its reserve has necessitated a nation-wide campaign for blood donations.

Kanno revealed that the following persons were named to accept application. (Cont'd. on pg. 2)

$ 9,150 WILL GO TO 2,400.... 'D' WORKERS FIRST PAYEES

Area D workers will line up at the center's central cashier's office in their home area at 9 a.m. Monday, to receive 'initial paychecks covering the period extending from April 26 to May 27, WCCA Service Manager Kermit Livingston announced today.

Workers in other areas were assured that schedules are being arranged in an effort to guarantee distribution of the long-awaited checks to all eligible residents during the week following Monday.

Individuals applying for checks were requested to bring their work slips, or else be able to give their work numbers.

Finance Officer K. L. Harding declared the center's first checks total $9,150 in value and will go to 2,400 workers.

"Some of the checks," he explained, "are smaller than others, because they are for workers who were not on their jobs for a full month."

Harding added that additional checks for 2,458 persons and totalling $21,000 are expected to arrive from San Francisco "within ten days."

Pay checks may be cashed individually by mail through the holder's own bank, it was explained, or else be endorsed and turned over, together with a self-addressed envelope, to Center Cashier W. E. Hill who will arrange to have them cashed at the Puyallup Branch of the First National Bank. The latter procedure will entail a five-cent service charge for the local bank.

The paychecks may also be used for purchasing canteen coupon books from Cashier Hill, it was further explained.

JAPANESE PRINT BANNED IN CAMP; BIBLES EXEMPT..

Japanese books, newspapers and printed material of any kind still retained by residents within Camp Harmony must be turned ed 'into respective Area Head quarters immediately, J. J. McGovern center manager, announced today.

McGovern's order reiterated and emphasized the army order of a month ago which classified Japanese printed material as contraband and, as such, subject to seizure.

"Such material turned in will not be confiscated but will be stored in warehouses until circumstances permit their return to the owners," McGovern said.

The order excepted approved Japanese religious books such as Bibles and hymnals.

This Week's Angels

If there's anything purely and irrevocably American, it's that strident, gutty musical form we call Jazz.

Koichi Hayashi's crew may not yet be able to toot the "Jazz Me Blues" with the skillfully contrived abandon of Bob Crosby's Dixieland gang, but we like to think they're working toward it, and working in the tradition of Biederbecke, Armstrong, Goodman, Ellington, Spanier, Stacey and so on down the long line of immortal jazzmen.

In the meantime, the lads are keeping the center alive to one of the most pleasurable features of Americana. You can suck our lollipops in between licks, boys.

Front page of the July 18, 1942 edition of the *Camp Harmony News-Letter.*

a Seattle JACL-sponsored poster contest on national defense, contributed pen and ink drawings while moving through the center sketching vignettes of everyday life.[49]

Takeuchi and his staff produced twelve issues, the first on May 5; the last, a nine-page souvenir edition published on the center's imminent closure on August 14.[50] Regular newsletter editions from two to six pages in length were printed on 8½ x 14 inch mimeograph paper. Optimistic staff promised issues every Tuesday and Thursday, yet only met their goal once. On three occasions two weeks lapsed between issues, twice blamed on paper shortage.

Content originating with the staff centered on inter-area activities, the war bond effort, vital statistics, and work opportunities as reflected in the following headlines:

HDQTRS. MEET CLARIFIES SELF-GOVERNMENT SET-UP

200 VOLUNTEER FOR TULELAKE ADVANCE GROUP

BOY, GIRL ARE 1ST BIRTHS IN CAMP

WAITRESS'S SMILE STOPS D WORKERS' 'HABA-HABAS'

INTER-AREA SOFTBALL SLATED

'C' VOLLEYBALLERS BEATEN

Absence of editorial opinion revealed how little autonomy the staffers possessed. Montgomery excised the one attempt to convey serious comment. While inmate editors earlier had learned to restrain themselves with self-censorship, the August 1 *News-Letter* mockup made it to the stencil stage before Montgomery red-lined twenty column inches of text. Instead of re-cutting stencils, staff members mutilated the columns. When the paper reached the public, large blocks of empty space presented visible evidence of censorship, the white outs flanked by articles on free radio repair, two successful hospital surgeries, a plasma drive, and a wedding.

Takeuchi and editors everywhere were frustrated by their inability to publish freely. The editor of the *Manzanar Free Press* noted privately the only thing free about his newspaper was the subscription fee.[51]

Despite its irregular publication, the *Camp Harmony News-Letter* provided both useful information and momentary diversion from the inherent boredom of center life. Without access to earned income subscriptions, for most newspapers or national magazines became a luxury. And since few had brought their AM band radios because of rumors they, like shortwave radios, would be banned, the center newspaper may have alleviated some feelings of their intense isolation.

Because ordinary inmates had no access to telephones most communication with the outside world occurred via letter writing as expedited by the U.S. Post Office Department (USPOD), which set up classified stations and branches within the centers. These full-service facilities, staffed by civil service employees from nearby main post offices, sold postage stamps, postal money orders, U.S. Savings Bonds, and Defense Stamps, and handled registered, insured, and C.O.D. mail, as well as parcel post packages. City postmasters trained inmate orderlies to sort and deliver incoming mail while on the WCCA payroll at $8 per month.[52]

Mail to and from inmates in the centers circulated without restrictions, unlike in Justice Department and army-run internment camps, in which interned enemy aliens endured weekly quotas of outgoing mail and censorship of their correspondence. The army held no authority to limit the number of letters posted or to censor the incoming or outgoing mail. This left inmates free to communicate with whomever they pleased.[53]

The Puyallup Assembly Center's four-area layout complicated USPOD's efforts to provide postal service. The main post office was established in Area D with satellite facilities in the other three. Dispatched daily from the center to the Puyallup post office, a pickup truck driven by a Caucasian arrived at 8:00 a.m. to collect first-class and registered mail, packages, magazines, and newspapers. A bonded postal employee accompanied him back to the center with the incoming mail. All mail except registered letters was turned over to Mrs. Rubi Aoki, a Nisei serving as unofficial head postmistress. She and her staff of eighteen orderlies sorted the mail by area and dispatched it to the appropriate satellite stations. Inmate orderlies further sorted mail within each area before postal carriers made twice daily barrack deliveries. Because only bonded civil service employees could handle registered mail, volunteer foot messengers (runners) notified addressees to collect their letters by reporting immediately to the post office. In late afternoon the Caucasian driver and bonded postal employee retrieved outgoing mail accumulated during the day and returned to the Puyallup post office.[54]

The center's population more than doubled the volume of mail passing through the Puyallup city post office; each day nearly 1,000 letters and more than 270 parcels moved in and out of the Area D central post office. On July 6, 1942, after the Independence Day holiday, a record 2,000 first-class letters left the center. Residents purchased an average of 125 money orders per day, totaling $1,000, most of it in payment for mail order catalogue items.[55]

*　*　*

Because the WCCA insisted that Nikkei exiles bring into captivity only household items and personal effects they could carry, the settling-in phase proved harsh and austere. Inmates addressed their physical comforts by turning to mail order firms like Montgomery Ward and Sears Roebuck, which filled orders for clothing, dishware, lamps, pillows, small carpets, and small furniture items customers could not manufacture for themselves with lumber scraps, nails, and a cross-cut saw.

Because WCCA could not control transactions carried out through the mail the threat of contraband entering the gates was always present. Therefore, addressees were required to call for their parcels in person at the Area D post office, whereupon Internal Security Section employees opened them

Civil service employees from the Puyallup post office staffed a full-service classified station, located in Area D, with Nisei inmates hired as orderlies. (National Archives)

in their presence. Inmates were forbidden from importing firearms and other weapons, shortwave radios and radio transmitting sets, cameras, alcoholic beverages, any hypnotic or narcotic drugs, and, beginning in July, writing or phonograph records in Japanese. Contraband was seized on the spot.[56]

Although censorship of private correspondence was not authorized, Colonel Bendetsen and General DeWitt raised the question frequently during the early assembly center period. Both advocated martial law as a means to assure discipline and legitimize control of the mail, enabling them to monitor suspected subversive activity they were convinced was ongoing.

The precedent for wartime censorship had been established earlier. On December 19, 1941, President Franklin D. Roosevelt signed Executive Order 8985 establishing the Office of Censorship. Postal censorship of incoming and outgoing international mail became the office's largest administrative function, and averaged over one million letters per day through its fifteen field stations scattered throughout the nation.[57] Furthermore, censorship of Issei internee mail, permitted under the guidelines of the Geneva Convention of 1929, began right after Pearl Harbor.

But the army lacked authority to censor the personal mail of individuals impacted by Executive Order 9066. Gaining access to residents' mail by declaring martial law in the Western Defense Command (WDC) became a strategy conceived by Colonel Bendetsen, who sent a secret teletype over DeWitt's signature to the army chief of staff:

> Request authority to declare effective immediately martial law over all assembly centers within Western Defense Command now housing Japanese evacuees. Each area to include the center and a strip 100 yards wide around perimeter. Request based on military necessity of: (1) having exclusive military jurisdiction over administration of centers (2) having exclusive judicial jurisdiction vested in military commissions (3) having control of an censorship of mail and express (4) insulating evacuees from outside subversive contacts (5) having effective control over inside subversive groups (6) preventing, with present limited number of troops immediately available to centers, large scale escapes.[58]

In DeWitt's and Bendetsen's view, martial law in concert with effective censorship of the mail and other forms of communication isolated inmates from potential contact with enemy agents.[59] Such a mandate would further erode the civil rights of inmates without regard to citizenship status. But the recommendation failed to carry the day as War Department superiors squelched the plan. The mail passed freely.

Even so, isolated incidents of mail censorship occurred. On orders of the commanding officer of the military police stationed at the Tule Lake Relocation Center, mail originating from there was censored for two weeks in May 1942.[60] During this time, with the center occupied solely by advance work groups from the Puyallup and Portland assembly centers, outgoing mail was to be examined on the premise that subversive activity was taking place there. This resulted in vocal protests from evacuees, which reached WCCA headquarters. The provost marshal ordered the practice discontinued immediately. Further instances of unauthorized postal censorship at assembly centers were never reported.[61]

*   *   *

Camp Harmony life became routine in part because the Christian and Buddhist religious traditions observed prior to the war had been brought in and were allowed to continue. The Seattle Council of Churches, working through representatives Reverends E. W. Thompson and Emery Andrews, secured heavy army vehicles to transport pianos, pulpits, draperies, and communion sets for both Japanese- and English-language services. In addition to clergy, parishioners from churches in Puyallup, Sumner, and Fife with large contingents of prewar Japanese members also sent aid.

Each of Camp Harmony's four areas held church services and children's Sunday school. From the first to the last Sunday of occupancy Issei pastors from five Protestant churches offered services in Japanese for older inmates, assisted by Japanese-language Bibles and hymnbooks brought in from various Japanese churches. Caucasian pastors who spoke Japanese stood in the pulpit and participated in fellowship when needed.

However, Nisei eager to hear Caucasian preachers received the greatest focus. Assisting Reverend Tsutomu (Tom) Fukuyama, a recently ordained Seattle Nisei American Baptist minister, over fifty Seattle, Tacoma, Puyallup, and Sumner clergymen served without remuneration or reimbursement for expenses.[62]

At Camp Harmony and the other assembly centers the WCCA, viewing religious expression as a privilege not a right, permitted individual clergy from the outside to participate in services at the inmates' request and if they had established a preexisting constituency among the people.[63] Suspicious administrators feared religious services could serve to propagandize or incite inmates. This led to investigations of individuals before they could receive passes permitting entry into the center. Each had to sign a visitor's statement agreeing to abide by specific rules and regulations, and most passes were renewed weekly.[64]

Administrators nervous about use of Japanese that no one but the inmates could speak or read, banned it, Bibles and hymnals in Japanese being the only exceptions. In the event a congregation did not speak English, Japanese could be spoken during religious services or other activities, but only with the center manager's sanction, which it appears McGovern always provided.

Despite these petty regulations, religious events remained orderly with attendance at Camp Harmony's gatherings high. Separate Sunday services in Japanese and English, Sunday school, and prayer and Bible study meetings occurring midweek attracted over 2,500 people. Sunday services alone drew 1,500 Christian and Buddhist worshipers to the mess halls with their makeshift pews.[65]

It took many pastors to minister to Camp Harmony's sizable number of Christians. Clergy from Seattle as well as from the Puyallup city Methodist and Episcopal churches held entry privileges by mid-May.

Apparently, Robert Turner and his successor, J. J. McGovern, authorized entry for all clergy requesting it as no evidence has surfaced indicating any of them to have been untrustworthy. Only rarely was a clergyman's request to enter the center for a particular day refused. McGovern denied passes to evening speakers for Sunday, June 21, citing a seven o'clock visitors curfew and insufficient details provided in the application in regard to activities for the four speakers involved.

∗   ∗   ∗

While Camp Harmony was administered by former Works Progress Administration (WPA) administrators and a small staff of former WPA workers, inmates made up the bulk of the center's workforce necessary for it to function on a day-to-day basis. From occupational information gathered at civil control stations prior to evacuation, 3,641 individuals listed occupations, the majority laborers (1,641), sales clerks (225), watchmen (120), cooks (154), foremen (154), and office clerks (129). By June 6, 2,058 had been assigned to work, half of them in mess and lodging activities. Each employee was added to the WCCA payroll at the rate of $8 per month for unskilled labor, $12 for skilled, and $16 for professional workers, the latter including, for example, physicians and teachers.[66]

Putting food on the mess hall tables occupied the greater numbers, while other inmates with specialized skills worked independently. Barbers, an especially important group, provided haircuts to almost half the population. First mention of them came in the May 14 issue of the *News-Letter* with announcement of the "Second Avenue Barber Shop" opening in Area A. The operator, Mrs. S. Ishikawa, charged 25 cents for adult haircuts, 15 cents for youngsters.[67] By July 9, barbers settled on 15 cents per cut, with needy cases exempt from charge.

Barbers brought in their own equipment and supplies from their prewar businesses—clippers, shears, brushes, and combs. Sterilizers, however, were not available, and the barber chairs were improvised from found materials. Of the fifty hair cutters who had earlier identified themselves as barbers during the pre-evacuation registration period, thirty became employed. Each area offered five chairs per shop. Together the four shops averaged two hundred customers per day. Razor shaves, a popular service most prewar barbers had provided, could not exist at Camp Harmony in the absence of hot running water and sterilizing equipment in the shops.

With leisure time plentiful and many women tending to their own grooming needs in order to preserve scarce money, beauty shops never materialized at Camp Harmony. This left idle fifteen skilled beauty operators even though some had brought their professional equipment with them.

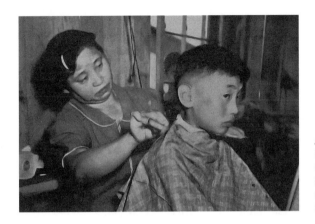

A Nikkei barber practicing her trade in a multi-chair barber shop set up in a barracks unit. Barbers charged 15 cents per cut. (National Archives)

Shoe repair became essential; four cobblers set up operations at one centrally located shop. They also provided their own equipment and tools, including sewing machines, cutters, knives, and hammers. The center provided supplies, mostly leather and cement, and inmates received basic shoe repair services without charge. Beginning July 1, repairmen offered new half soles, heels, and patches, performing all of their work by hand. But without benefit of a finishing machine some work, especially women's shoes, had to be sent to shops in Puyallup with inmates bearing the expense.

One individual handy with small tools began producing *geta*. These wooden clogs soon became popular during the wet spring as people passed back and forth to the showers. Toyonosuke Fujikado converted a corner of his room in Area A into a workshop where he fashioned more than seven hundred pairs of the wooden shoes in all sizes, shapes, and heights, refusing to charge anyone for his work.[68]

Camp Harmony stores opened the first week of June. Managed by McGovern's administration, they provided employment for twenty-nine inmates. Here center residents purchased daily "essentials" not provided by the WCCA: cigarettes and lighter fluid, handkerchiefs, ink, nail polish, hair oil, pencils, playing cards, powder puffs, razor blades, shoelaces, toothbrushes, canvas gloves, and talcum powder. Available luxuries were candy bars, soda pop, ice cream bars, popsicles, and chewing gum—in all, over 130 items for sale.[69]

Each of the four areas had access to a store located near a center of activity and staffed by inmate clerks. Open seven days a week, from eight to eleven in the morning, one to four in the afternoon, and six to eight in the evening, sales were brisk, averaging $500 per day from an inventory valued at $18,000.

Transactions utilized WCCA-issued cash coupons, with no cash exchange permitted. For the month of June inmates purchased coupons with their own funds. Beginning July 1, free coupon books became available in denominations of $1, $2.50, and $4, with a maximum monthly allowance of $2.50 per individual, $4 per couple, and $1 for each individual under 16 years of age. Depending on size, families could receive up to $21 in coupon books per month. For July's allotment the administration distributed scrip worth more than $14,000.[70]

Essential services not available in the center were outsourced to businesses in Puyallup or other nearby communities. Without laundry facilities, inmates brought dirty clothes to an inmate clerk in charge of collecting and delivering bundles on Mondays and Thursdays. Twice-weekly deliveries averaged $50 in transactions.

Optometry and dental laboratory services did not exist at the center. Without available examination equipment optometrist Duncan Tsuneishi could do little more than repair eyeglasses frames. More sophisticated repairs had to go to laboratories in Seattle or Tacoma. Denture repairs and other minor dental laboratory procedures were outsourced as well.

With an abundance of typewriters, paper, carbon paper, and file cabinets, evacuee clerical staff helped produce memos, accountings, orders, lists, letters, instructions, and countless other documents driving Camp Harmony's bureaucracy. Among 231 available clerks, secretaries, stenographers, and typists, 125 individuals found employment in the administration office, warehouses, hospital, and other sectors at Camp Harmony.[71]

Some workers organized recreational activities to help stave off boredom and restlessness and to boost morale. Recreation director "Chick" Uno, a former college athlete and prewar friend of Jimmie Sakamoto, set up boxing, kendo, sumo, softball, volleyball, tennis, basketball, ping pong, and horseshoe pitching programs, as well as other games for young people. With separate softball leagues set up in each area for boys and girls, inter-area rivalries soon blossomed. Ball scores and league standings as well as marble, ping pong, and golf tournament outcomes made their way to the News-Letter's expanding sports section, echoing the Courier Leagues Sakamoto's prewar Seattle newspaper had reported on weekly. The "Haba-Haba Country Golf Club," a par 27 nine-hole golf course in Area A, became popular immediately.

Sports leagues thrived as spectator sports. In late July, an inter-area boxing tournament hosted in Area D brought 1,500 spectators to the ring.[72]

Organized non-athletic activities sprouted up whenever a small group of people discovered shared interests. Women formed knitting, sewing, and crochet groups, while older men organized *go* and *shogi* tournaments and card games to wile away long hours. Intra- and inter-area swing dances became common occurrences after organization of *The Harmonaires*, a twelve-piece dance band complete with vocals. The band, in demand by dance-crazy young people in attendance, circulated throughout the four areas every week with up to nine hundred dancers jamming the dance floor of Area D's mess hall. Outside, as the weather improved loudspeakers broadcast concerts of popular and classical recorded music to audiences sitting in grassy outdoor areas.[73]

In Area D a central lending library supervised by Bill Makino with volunteers Yoshi Hosokawa and Toshiko Baba opened in mid-June. Initially only five hundred books existed for all four areas, many of them donated by evacuees who had brought them from home. During the first week of June the Seattle Public Library loaned the center another 1,500 titles. Added to the inventory were women's and children's books donated by the Seattle Civilian War Defense Commission, provider of books and magazines to soldiers and sailors. The Seattle Public Library came forth with another two hundred volumes in July. Makino designed the lending program to give each area access to the complete inventory. Divided into four groups, the entire collection rotated through the areas once every three weeks. However, because Japanese-language books had been banned from the collection many first-generation Japanese had little access to reading materials.[74]

In June, as public school summer vacation began in the Pacific Northwest, vacation school came to Camp Harmony. After a month of inactivity, three hundred grammar school children returned to classes under the tutelage of sixteen inmate teachers and volunteers.

Camp Harmony inmates smoking and playing rummy. (National Archives)

Because the forced evacuation had occurred a month before the end of the school year students attending both Seattle public schools and the University of Washington could not complete their coursework. Nevertheless, school and university officials agreed to assign full credit for the term to students who did passing work at the time of their evacuation. Four hundred and twelve high school seniors received diplomas at ceremonies held in the grandstand with their families and friends in attendance. On June 6, the principal of Seattle's Garfield high school presented diplomas to forty seniors in a formal ceremony followed by a short dance and social hour for graduates and families and friends. At another gathering nine seniors from the University of Washington's Class of 1942 participated in graduation services attended by President Lee Paul Sieg, an event not duplicated elsewhere.[75]

The education department also offered adult evening education classes: creative writing, public speaking, journalism, parliamentary law, and German. Other offerings emphasized etiquette, first aid, knitting, pattern drafting, costume designing, shorthand, sketching, and Americanization classes.[76]

Without a primary focus, such as employment or volunteerism, time passed slowly for most people. With the mud of the springtime giving way to the baking summer sun, Tamako Inouye remembered the summer boredom she and friends experienced: "There was this space between the barracks. When it was really hot everybody would go to one side of this lane and lean against the building and just sit there. And later on in the day when the sun changed its course we'd go to the other side."[77]

Nevertheless, while a community formed and a semblance of normal life emerged, individuals lived under constant stress. Rising tensions existed not only between inmates and their captors, but also between inmates and their own leaders. In August, shortly before the move to the Minidoka Relocation Center began, discord came to a head.

8

Dissension

Feelings of Japanese Americans crowded inside the assembly centers ranged from numbness to rage. And with Nisei leaders now in control, the Issei elders' world turned upside down. For many the anger, confusion, fear, and anxiety that had rippled through West Coast Nikkei communities during the weeks between Pearl Harbor and their expulsion the following spring had evolved to rejection, hopelessness, helplessness, betrayal, and in many cases loss of self-esteem.

Restrictions imposed on the new inmates resulted in a new community norm of hoarding and stealing from the government scarce lumber scraps and nails necessary for building furniture. Rebellious acts manifested in breaking administrative rules, such as gambling, flaunting curfew hours, and otherwise opposing control of community leaders, parents, or oppressors. As parental authority disintegrated peer groups competed with nuclear family units. Boredom, frustration, and aggression erupted into fights. A light on after curfew, snoring, or an unruly child increased tensions that magnified under the lens of confinement.

Their new positions of authority led some Nisei leaders to exercise old or discover new ways to intimidate others, show favoritism, and curry favor with center administrators. Social and political hierarchies developed that ran the spectrum from aggression to obedience and submission.

These extremes in behavior slowly moderated when resources at relocation centers became more plentiful, as school systems came into existence, and as meaningful work opportunities increased. A more liberal leave clearance policy served to instill hope for the future. Even so, being uprooted from their homes to incarceration in crowded assembly centers created shock waves few of the exiles anticipated. Moreover, as Japanese forces continued tightening their hold in Asia and moved into French Indo-China and the Dutch East Indies, hopes for a quick end to either the conflict or incarceration faded or extinguished altogether. In the spring of 1942, assembly center inmates looked to a dubious future.

As truth and logic waned scapegoating began to surface; people sought out individuals or organizations on whom to project their feelings. Fingers pointed at the Japanese American Citizens League (JACL) for advocating compliance with government orders it hoped would be perceived as patriotic. Opponents urged resistance toward the JACL for selling out the people. And Wartime Civil Control Administration (WCCA) and center management personnel became targeted for blame as well.

Inmates at the Puyallup Assembly Center shared in this oppressed group psychology. Unrest centered on Jimmie Sakamoto and his council, as both were unpopular and perceived as unrepresentative. Dissension grew quickly against existing conditions with details soon reaching the national media.[1]

Appearance of Ted Nakashima's article "Concentration Camp: U.S. Style" in the June 15, 1942 edition of *The New Republic* turned national attention toward WCCA's assembly center policies. Nakashima, a young architectural draftsman who had worked in Seattle before the war, wrote an impassioned and angry essay bringing multiple grievances against the government for penitentiary-like living conditions, poor food and sanitation, restrictive curfews, and inadequate housing construction. Citing shiplap floors on two-by-fours laid directly on the mud, "which is everywhere," Nakashima, frustrated at his inability to contribute to the war effort, exclaimed, "I can't take it! I have 391 defense houses to be drawn . . . We're on this side and we want to help. Why won't America let us?"[2]

Colonel Bendetsen quickly responded to *The New Republic* article, acknowledging problems at Camp Harmony to editor Bill Blivens. But he minimized Nakashima's claims and altogether ignored the young Nisei's frustration and heartfelt question. Bendetsen asserted Nakashima's complaints described conditions that existed only during the first two weeks of operation. Because assembly centers sat within in a war zone, he wrote, separation of the loyal from the disloyal presented an unsolvable dilemma. Bendetsen justified the guard towers and barbed wire fences, assuring Blivens that extraordinary measures had been taken to guarantee the well-being and comfort of inmates under his jurisdiction, and he defended using theater-of-operation troop barracks adapted for civilian use.

Neither lies or exaggeration, Nakashima's article accurately described conditions existing during the first several weeks of his confinement that started May 1.[3] By June 15, when *The New Republic* article appeared, conditions had improved; Bendetsen's letter to Blivens reflected this time lag.

Bendetsen turned down the editor's offer to publish his response. However, at his urging Blivens sent a *Seattle Post-Intelligencer* reporter to Camp Harmony in early August to assess local conditions in preparation for a follow-up piece to appear the following January.[4]

Although Bendetsen accurately portrayed improved conditions at Camp Harmony existing in the latter part of May, this episode put the army on the defensive; Nakashima's testimonial revealed a brewing unrest within the center's population.

Bendetsen was already aware of rising tensions between the center's Caucasian administration and the Nisei-led group headed by Jimmie Sakamoto. Camp Harmony's first center manager, Robert Turner, left Puyallup on May 23, 1942, on reassignment to WCCA headquarters in San Francisco and was replaced by another former Works Progress Administration (WPA) administrator, J. J. McGovern. Soon McGovern initiated a series of weekly narrative reports on evolving conditions at his center, which he submitted to superiors in San Francisco. On May 26 he addressed a growing problem pertaining to an arrogation of power by Sakamoto's group: "I am going to have some trouble with the Japanese administration within the center. If I allow them to continue the way they are headed, they will soon take over the center. In order to head that off, I am having a meeting with their headquarters group tomorrow, and, no doubt, there will be some fireworks there."[5]

McGovern's report coincided with a concurrent visit by a team of army officials headed by Lieutenant Colonel William Boekel, sent to inspect the center's interior security section. This inquiry stemmed from earlier reports citing incompetence on the part of Caucasian personnel that centered on the dominant role of Nisei staff in internal police positions. Advised by McGovern on the broader power currently being wielded by the Japanese administration at the expense of WCCA's authority and effectiveness, Boekel sought and received authority from superiors to expand the investigation.

Boekel concluded that Sakamoto's staff was involved in an efficient top-down operation filled with enthusiasm, energy, resourcefulness, and effectiveness in its dealings with the community. In defense of his group's actions Sakamoto stated that prior to evacuation the army devised a plan to run the center, then dumped it in their laps. This interpretation contradicted Lieutenant Colonel Paul Malone's recollection in which the JACL group requested that the army furnish a skeletal organization framework for self-government, one he subsequently provided as a matter of accommodation. Permission of Sakamoto to implement hinged upon approval by the center director and WCCA headquarters.

The inspectors also reported this well-organized, ingrained local government to be fostering discontent within the general inmate population as well as among workers and professional staff. Citing supportive evidence, the report included a May 17, 1942 memo from Chief Supervisor Sakamoto to Nisei administration personnel imparting an impression the WCCA, charged with responsibility to oversee the affairs of Camp Harmony, had left actual administration of the center to the Nisei headquarters staff, which was also to serve as intermediary between the residents and the WCCA. Sakamoto informed head physician Dr. Kyo Koike that "since the WCCA is administering the camp through the Evacuation Administration Headquarters staff, made up of Japanese personnel, the hospital staff will function through this office." The Nisei leader, placing his position as administrator beyond the cultural norm that would call for deference to his elders, the Nisei leader demanded doctors and nurses, Issei and Nisei alike, display the standard of courtesy and efficiency expected of all center personnel.[6]

Boekel concluded that the JACL group had usurped power at the expense of the WCCA administration. His investigation suggested a similar infiltration of power to exist within the interior security section. He reported that Sakamoto had installed an interior police system of 148 inmates, one apparently accommodated by Turner that, in Boekel's view, ultimately compromised the manager's own administrative control. McGovern, Boekel, and Boekel's superiors agreed that self-government within the center had gone too far.[7]

Action ensued prior to Boekel's telegraphic report and departure from the center at the end of the day on May 26. McGovern received orders from San Francisco to take back the center's administration and reconstitute the Nisei headquarters staff as solely an advisory body. In his June 2 weekly narrative report to San Francisco, the center director reported on his subsequent May 27 meeting with the Nisei headquarters staff, stating "a definite understanding in line with the administration's policy has been reached with the prefabricated Japanese center organization."[8]

A week later, on June 9, McGovern provided additional details: "The situation in regard to self-government by the evacuees has been straightened out, and there will be no more misunderstanding on their part in this center. I am pleased that some of the so-called Headquarters group was removed from here, as Colonel Boekel suggested, until these matters had been ironed out."[9]

In response Sakamoto submitted a letter of resignation, expressing regret that his responsibilities as chief Japanese supervisor and of his headquarters staff had come to an end: "I feel that you W.C.C.A. officials can go directly to our area directors and their staffs or have the latter come directly to your office to expedite the schedules of work."[10] He concluded the letter with a question on how he might be of further use to the center director. Having accepted Sakamoto's resignation, McGovern turned to forming a new purely advisory group, one he expected to be more representative of the center population.[11]

Perceived excesses by Sakamoto's forces at Camp Harmony may have helped bring about elimination of self-government in all assembly centers, to which the WCCA had either paid lip service or never planned for. On May 31, 1942, following Boekel's report on conditions at Camp Harmony, R. L. Nicholson, chief of the Reception Center Division, ordered all center managers to permit elected councils to serve only in advisory roles.[12]

Created by fiat prior to the Seattle community's expulsion, Camp Harmony's Nisei administration was not representative. In other assembly centers inmates elected their all-male spokesmen by secret ballot. In that era, of course, no one thought of women as community leaders, although certain auxiliary roles were deemed appropriate. About a month later the WCCA further limited the options of inmates by banning Issei from elective office, from voting for elective members of advisory committees, and from serving on committees. Recent elections at Tanforan, Merced, and elsewhere were nullified and self-government, such as it was, became solely a Nisei activity.[13]

One month later, the WCCA dissolved all semblance of self-government. Henceforth center managers would select advisory committees from panels made up of three times the number of members authorized for each center based on its population size. Following background investigations, English-speaking Issei and Nisei over sixteen years of age would be eligible to vote and to serve on impotent committees, with each representative holding office at the manager's pleasure and subject to dismissal at any time.[14]

By the first week of August, six centers had been emptied and the Pomona Assembly Center was slated to close within a week. Eight centers remained open to hold all but meaningless elections. In a matter of weeks all assembly centers would be emptied, leaving little incentive for going through the motions of balloting. Tanforan's community council members declined to pursue what they saw as useless advisory council positions. With nine available positions the top twenty-seven candidates would appear on a panel roster from which the center manager would select nine candidates to eventually serve. The election failed to materialize when the election committee could not attract enough candidates. The manager eventually appointed a nine-man council from his own "panel" of volunteers.[15]

The new WCCA policy had little direct impact on Camp Harmony inmates having a representative voice because of the non-representative nature of the Sakamoto administration. Many there may have gloated over the group finally being cut down to size. McGovern, however, following his June 9 report to San Francisco must have had second thoughts about his decision to replace Sakamoto and his well-organized, entrenched staff. With Camp Harmony scheduled to close within two months, the manager's available timeline to assemble, train, and establish an efficient operation was too short, making organization of a new advisory council impossible. The problem, he ultimately realized, lay not with the organization, but with the manner in which the group had conducted business. With Sakamoto neutralized, why not utilize these hardworking, if overzealous Nisei and avoid inevitable uncertainties inherent with a new administration?

Sakamoto's ongoing unpopularity among some center residents stemming from his heavy-handed practices and the headquarters group's apparent hyper-cooperation with WCCA policies left McGovern conflicted. The extent of Sakamoto's unpopularity unknown, McGovern therefore decided to test residents' attitudes prior to recommitting to the former chief supervisor.

On June 14, five days after the center manager had dissolved the headquarters group, McGovern met with Sakamoto and his former staff to discuss their future as a newly constituted advisory council. The group agreed to a confidence vote by the residents; a plebiscite would test the validity of criticism directed against the former headquarters staff. McGovern promised Sakamoto that a positive outcome would breathe new life into the group.

Leaving the Nisei staff to decide how and when the voting process should occur, Sakamoto and the four area directors charged with carrying out balloting within their respective jurisdictions met to discuss logistics. Early action essential in light of Camp Harmony's scheduled closure in early September, they briefly considered and rejected public meetings prior to voting. Instead, at curfew when checkers normally moved through the center counting heads they planned to conduct secret balloting by residents sixteen years of age and older. Incorporating voting into an established routine assured eligible voters access to the ballot box, but by precluding an organized debate of the issue Sakamoto denied any opposition a forum.

The group produced ballot forms approved by McGovern with the following Yes/No question written both in English and Japanese: "Please signify whether or not you have confidence in the Japanese administration of the Camp."[16]

Voting took place at twilight on June 16. An appointed Issei oversaw the process in each area as curfew checkers carried slotted boxes to hold ballots. Allowed no organized discussion of the issue, abstainers were instructed to place their unmarked ballot in the box. Ballots were then submitted to the area directors who met the next morning with the former headquarters group to tally votes and determine the outcome.[17]

Plebiscite results headlined the June 17 issue of the *Camp Harmony News-Letter*: LANDSLIDE MAJORITY VOTES TO RETAIN JAPANESE STAFF. Of 5,545 votes counted, 4,064 (73.3 percent) checked "Yes," interpreted as overwhelming confidence in the headquarters administration.

An elated Sakamoto looked to the future: "The vote of confidence given us by residents of Camp Harmony will pave the way toward a smoother functioning at our relocation centers. Camp Harmony is merely a stop at a wayside but the experience we gain here will go a long way toward unity, mutual cooperation and harmony at our future community."[18]

Satisfied with the balloting outcome, on June 20 McGovern summarized in writing for the reconstituted council how it should function in the future. With a name change from "Evacuee Administration Headquarters" to "Japanese Advisory Council" it became the only group authorized to interact with the WCCA center administration in all matters pertaining to policy and procedure. Center administrators were to disseminate information to the inmate community through the Japanese Advisory Council and area councils. Suggestions, complaints, and requests originating in each of the four areas ascended from the area councils to the WCCA center administration via the Advisory Council.[19]

With this new arrangement in place autonomy for the new Japanese Advisory Council and its area councils all but disappeared. Moreover, McGovern became personally involved in supervising hospital activities and its staff. Any instructions and suggestions related to the hospital would now go out over McGovern's signature to Dr. Koike, physician-in-charge. McGovern specifically excluded Area D director Hiroyuki Ichihara from hospital policy matters, thus assuring Koike's independence from advisory council meddling.[20]

Some center residents, upset by how the confidence vote had been carried out, sought clarification. A week after the election petitioners from Area A demanded a review of the vote by insisting the balloting protocol had left a poor impression with the people. Already rankled by the prior installation of an unrepresentative administration, protesters cited the undemocratic process that denied debate prior to voting. Further, according to petitioners no one clarified for voters the significance of a "no" choice. Some curfew checkers allegedly warned if the "no" vote prevailed the army would step in, a vague threat leaving selecting "yes" the only alternative. Petitioners demanded an official response from Japanese headquarters and insisted on another election whereby voters could debate the issue beforehand.[21]

On July 2 a seventy-three-word response by Sakamoto stated the confidence vote took place by order of the center manager. "The instruction was to have no open discussion on the subject in order that persons casting ballots shall do so in accordance with their judgment without the pressure of any outside influence."[22]

It appears the protest died at that point, leaving unrevealed if the ballot issue was orchestrated by the former headquarters staff. Regardless, the incident deepened suspicions in regard to Sakamoto's complicity with the center's Caucasian administration. A small group of Issei noted the former chief supervisor's vision for himself and would soon initiate plans to prevent it from happening.

Demotion of the former chief Japanese supervisor failed to dampen the friction between many inmates and Sakamoto. Two days later, attitudes worsened when the advisory council distributed a six-page "Kibei Survey" soliciting personal information from this Nisei subgroup who had received some formal education in Japan. This caused rumors to circulate that Sakamoto had colluded with the JACL to produce the survey, further angering the Kibei and many of their supporters.

On June 25 intelligence officers in civilian clothes, one from the Office of Naval Intelligence (ONI), the other from Army G-2, brought 1,500 copies of the Kibei Survey to McGovern's office for distribution to relevant inmates. The questionnaire, a preliminary step in compiling information about every Kibei in the assembly centers, originated three weeks earlier not with the JACL but with representatives from ONI and the Seattle FBI office.[23]

The questionnaire solicited information on education and military service in Japan; membership in organizations, associations, unions, and clubs; records of departures and re-entries into the United States; relatives in Japan; and religious affiliation, including the nationalist Shinto sect. The Kibei viewed such information in the government's hands to be harmful given ongoing suspicions over their cultural and political ties to Japan.

Intelligence officers from the ONI and FBI arranged for Sakamoto's advisory council to distribute the questionnaires under the auspices of the JACL, thereby leaving an impression the national organization had initiated the survey. The plan backfired when center residents questioned Sakamoto's authority to collect such sensitive information in the first place. The JACL's attempt to acquire similar information on the Kibei group prior to evacuation also failed when the Kibei refused to cooperate even under pressure from national JACL staff.[24] With Sakamoto having come under increasing fire for issuing unpopular edicts such as strict curfew hours, a unilateral ban on Japanese-language books, magazines, and phonograph records, plus additional restrictions viewed as kowtowing to the center management, and now the vote of confidence controversy, few Kibei chose to cooperate. The forms remained blank, and damage to Sakamoto's reputation, in this case undeserved, broadened.[25]

The negative view of Sakamoto and the advisory council intensified in mid-August with the sudden banishment to other centers of several popular residents and their families. On August 12, 1942, McGovern summoned Bill Hosokawa to his center office and announced he should be ready to leave the center with his wife and infant son within four hours. He had orders to send the family to the Heart Mountain Relocation Center, which opened the same day. Denying knowledge of the decision and claiming compliance with an order issued from San Francisco, McGovern promised to put in a good word for Hosokawa should future employment opportunities arise.[26]

The same day Nisei attorneys Thomas Masuda and Kenji Ito, gambler Kiyoshi Roy Suyetani, and their families received transfer orders with only four hours' advance notice. And five days later, student leader Kenji Okuda and attorney William Mimbu were given orders to depart Camp Harmony on short notice. These transfers occurred as fellow inmates were preparing for the move to the Minidoka Relocation Center.[27]

After the first group's departure word spread quickly; soon a conspiracy theory began to circulate accusing Sakamoto of engineering the whole affair. Many residents believed he stood to gain from his rivals' exile. Attorneys Ito and Masuda, fluent in Japanese, had held sway with Isseis and Niseis and vocalized opposition to the JACL's earlier power grab. Prior to the war these charismatic individuals had competed for Issei clients with Clarence Arai, Sakamoto's close ally. Rumor held that Hosokawa, who also had minor differences with Sakamoto concerning acquiescence to army control over policy issues, became another of his enemies.[28] Only social outlier Suyetani, a non-participant in the political scene at Camp Harmony, seemed not to conform to the conspiracy theory incubating in the center.

The impossibility of Sakamoto influencing events appeared to matter little to many inmates, and the banishments may have alienated him from the center population once and for all. This stigma followed him into the Minidoka Relocation Center. There, center director Harry L. Stafford would receive advice from Issei spokesmen that elevating Sakamoto to a leadership position would create significant internal problems.[29]

Whatever Sakamoto's political and human failings, on this occasion opponents judged him unfairly. Any influence the controversial leader previously enjoyed with center administrators ended with Colonel Boekel's visit in late May. The respective backgrounds of the exiles from Camp Harmony themselves may hold clues to understanding the true reasons for banishment of these six inmates and their families.

With plans to transfer inmates into relocation centers and close the assembly centers in the weeks and months ahead, army planners in San Francisco viewed this transitional phase as an opportunity to isolate individuals who center managers believed exhibited disruptive behaviors within the inmate communities. The imminent transfer of Puyallup Assembly Center residents to Minidoka brought a WCCA recommendation to separate political antagonists Masuda, Ito, and Hosokawa to minimize future agitation at the relocation center.[30] Western Defense Command (WDC) G-2 described these individuals as "disturbing factors" and their prewar activities "unsatisfactory from a counter-intelligence standpoint."[31]

In 1941, Thomas Shinao Masuda had served as an officer of the North American Japanese Association/Japanese Chamber of Commerce, a dual organization engaged in charitable activities in the United States and Japan and dominated by Issei. According to army intelligence gathering, it sponsored Japanese-language schools and fencing clubs whose activities served to hold in check Americanization of the Nisei. A practicing attorney since 1930, Masuda had a list of clientele that included many Issei, as well as Seattle-based Japanese business concerns, clubs, and associations, some of them suspected of engaging in espionage activities. Masuda also served as counsel to Seattle's Japanese Association and the Japanese Consul. Never having traveled to Japan, he spoke but did not write Japanese.[32]

Despite war hysteria and prevailing fears on the West Coast, a federal jury acquitted Masuda of the charges he had served as a Japanese government agent. Sent directly to the Puyallup Assembly Center following release from jail, he spoke out publicly against Sakamoto and his group. While this drew significant support from center residents it also attracted the attention of his captors.[33]

The WCCA marked Kenji Ito as a troublemaker in part because he accused Sakamoto's administration of being unrepresentative and demonstrating favoritism to a privileged few. Ito, professionally four years Masuda's junior, had been vice president of the Seattle JACL prior to evacuation, but in the center argued against the organization's practices. He too was acquitted of all federal charges related to being an unregistered agent of a foreign government. However, the WCCA, apparently convinced the verdict reflected

having "7 women on the jury and because of the oratory of [Ito] and his attorney," continued to insist on Ito's guilt and recommended he be separated
from the main body of inmates.[34]

According to the ONI, calm prevailed at the Puyallup Assembly Center
until Ito's and Masuda's arrival; once there the attorneys challenged the validity of Sakamoto's authority on two counts. First, because the group's members
appointed themselves to positions of power, thereby making it undemocratic
and un-American. And second, the JACL, to whom the vast majority of the
group's officers belonged, had become closely aligned with government intelligence gathering agencies and failed to fight civilian evacuation orders
directly targeting Nisei, the organization's primary constituency. Adding
fuel to the pair's claims, Issei parolees trickling in from Justice Department
camps informed Masuda and Ito that detainees there enjoyed far better living conditions.[35]

For these reasons the ONI marked "the Masuda faction" as troublemakers
and agitators. An Area C informant, advising McGovern's office of support
among Issei for future leadership positions at the Idaho center for Masuda
or Ito, compounded this belief.[36]

On the surface, Bill Hosokawa's removal seems puzzling, since his prewar
liaison work between the WCCA and the Nikkei community, his testimony
as a government witness in the Masuda and Ito trials, and his role as chief
adjutant to Sakamoto served both the government's and Sakamoto's needs.
Although Hosokawa's differing views over the conduct of operations by the
Nisei administration may have antagonized him, Sakamoto, because of his
blindness, nevertheless depended upon Hosokawa to communicate with
people outside his office.[37]

Ironically, this close association may itself have led directly to Hosokawa's
ouster. Sakamoto's unpopularity among residents on the rise, center management, with their sights now on the transfer to Minidoka, perceived him
as a growing liability. Sakamoto's dependency on Hosokawa to carry out his
orders provided a means to neutralize the leader. Hosokawa had to go.

Besides, Hosokawa's prewar work for the Japanese consulate and as journalist for a Japanese owned newspaper in Singapore had brought government suspicions against him that dogged him throughout his incarceration.
His high visibility and intelligence agents' distrust of him arising from his
prewar activities singled him out for special treatment.[38]

Intelligence reports associated Kiyoshi Roy Suyetani with espionage. FBI
agents arrested him the day after Pearl Harbor. Operating as a professional
gambler, Suyetani had allegedly served as bodyguard and gunman for Kane-

kichi Yamamoto, former head of Seattle's Toyo Club. Yamamoto reportedly held close ties with Japanese naval officer Lieutenant Commander Shigeru Fujii, who had arrived in Seattle on an espionage mission. After admitting he also knew Fujii personally, the FBI attempted to intern Suyetani as an enemy alien but was forced to release him when the Hawaiian-born Nisei satisfactorily established his U.S. citizenship.[39]

Camp Harmony administrators became aware of Suyetani's prewar Japantown activities. In July, the Interior Security Section discovered a book in his possession published by a blacklisted pro-Japanese organization, the Black Dragon Society. Thereupon section chief Charles E. Johnston asked FBI informant Clarence Arai to help uncover incriminating details of Suyetani's past activities and associations. Having utilized Arai as an informant in previous investigations, Johnston knew him to be reliable. Earlier Arai had provided reliable information on several ongoing cases under investigation by the Interior Security Section.[40]

Arai provided intelligence on Suyatani's prewar Seattle activities, including his role as head of the Toyo Club, an operation linked to a flourishing gambling chain up and down the West Coast in the late 1920s and early 1930s. Suyetani became its leader following Kanekichi Yamamoto's deportation for income tax evasion and the re-migration to Japan before the outbreak of the war of Yamamoto's successor, a Mr. Ichikawa.

The WCCA, in possession of the FBI's prewar dossier on Suyetani and additional intelligence provided by Arai, ordered Suyetani's removal to the Gila River Relocation Center in Arizona. This transfer succeeded in ending his professional gambling associations at Camp Harmony along with the accompanying social disruption.[41]

With Hosokawa, Ito, Masuda, and Suyetani relocated, army intelligence soon noted an improvement in order at Camp Harmony: "Not only has it removed these four subversive characters to separate locations, but it has indicated to the persons remaining at the Camp that disciplinary action may be the result of un-American agitation."[42]

After this transfer of "undesirable elements" and their families, three days later McGovern received instructions from San Francisco to expel Kenji Okuda, Bill Mimbu, Setsugo Hosokawa, and Frank Kinomoto. The WCCA advised they be sent to separate relocation centers for an added "salutary effect on all concerned." To "throw them off balance for a few days" they should be transferred to centers other than Minidoka.

McGovern held the orders for Mimbu and Okuda until August 17. On that day these men and their families departed on the same train from Puyallup station; Mimbu with his wife and two children went to the Stockton Assembly Center, while Okuda and his family journeyed on to the Merced Assembly Center.

William Yoshiya Mimbu served as past president of the Seattle Junior Japanese Association, an alleged subsidiary of the Japanese Association of North America/Japanese Chamber of Commerce. Both organizations reportedly solicited contributions for the Japanese government, conducted a census for the Japanese Consul, and published and distributed propaganda. However, intelligence reports failed to directly implicate Mimbu in any of these activities. His wife, Merry, had helped publish the pacifist newsletter, *Pacific Cable*, and formerly served as executive secretary of the Japan Society. She was attorney Thomas Masuda's sister. Mimbu, leader of Area A in mid-May, allegedly became upset when Sakamoto usurped power upon arriving at Camp Harmony. A retrospective 1943 WDC report branded him an "agitator, troublemaker, and because of activities within the assembly center and relocation project classified as dangerous."[43]

Awaiting release from the Puyallup Assembly Center so he could attend Oberlin College in the fall, Kenji Okuda, a bright, articulate, charismatic student leader little more than half Masuda's and Ito's age, appeared to pose minimal danger to the government. Still, the WCCA viewed him as a threat in part because of his father, Henry, an influential Issei in the Nikkei community. In their view, the elder Okuda should have been interned by the Justice Department and not paroled. Kenji personally drew the WCCA's attention because of his pacifist leanings, strong support for Gordon Hirabayashi's refusal to accept incarceration, and helping publish and distribute *Pacific Cable*. He was also a member of the pacifist organization Seattle Youth Fellowship of Reconciliation.[44]

Frank Kinomoto had three marks against him—he was a Kibei, enjoyed a close association with Thomas Masuda, and was actively involved with the Junior Japanese Association.[45] A general auditor with the Washington State Tax Commission, he was one of forty-one state employees to lose their positions in the wake of Executive Order 9066.[46]

Finally, army intelligence gatherers viewed Bill Hosokawa's father, Setsugo Hosokawa, former head of Togo Realty Company and influential community leader, as instrumental in encouraging Thomas Masuda to assume an active role in the Japanese Association. It further associated him with the Hiroshima Prefectural Club.

Transfer orders for Kinomoto and the elder Hosokawa arrived too late, the two families having relocated to Minidoka earlier in the month as part of a routine transfer. The WCCA deferred from moving the Kinomotos out of Minidoka or recommending Hosokawa be interned once again although G-2 held the option open to advise WCCA regarding these individuals "at a later date." In fact, the army had no authority over persons in War Relocation Authority (WRA) custody and could never have exercised the option.[47]

Only five days passed between Hosokawa's summons to McGovern's office and the Mimbu and Okuda families' southbound departure from the Puyallup station. Virtually every adult resident learned of the transfers during this interval, and many grew enraged over the events and their own situation. A small group of Issei men who had earlier noted with alarm Sakamoto's vision for himself at Minidoka, according to statements made decades later by a person associated with them, now banded together to plan Sakamoto's assassination.

According to Shosuke Sasaki, then a thirty-year-old prewar Seattle apartment building manager and one of the youngest Issei in Seattle, plot organizers asked him to serve as their spokesman after the execution had been carried out. They instructed him to explain to authorities their actions had been motivated by revenge. Intending to withhold details of the crime until after it had taken place, conspirators selected Sasaki for his fluency in Japanese and English and impeccable reputation in the Japanese community.[48]

Revealing this episode half a century later, Sasaki said he balked at the plan and instead offered a compromise. Since Camp Harmony would soon close with everyone moving to a new location, he advised postponing the action until the new center administration could be approached. If Sakamoto subsequently acquired a position of authority, he would carry out the assassins' wishes.

Subsequently, Sasaki and other Issei met with Minidoka center manager Harry L. Stafford in an effort to convince him Sakamoto should not be permitted to assume any position of authority. Likely Stafford had been forewarned by the army and was unlikely to give Sakamoto any position of authority. Nevertheless, feeling they had succeeded with their mission, Sasaki said the plotters then abandoned their plan, thereby averting a possible tragedy.[49] Although the story remains unverified to the present day, Sasaki's vivid recollection illustrates how the eviction of popular leaders from Camp Harmony contributed to the extremes of anger toward Sakamoto.

In all, Sakamoto appears innocent of participating in any conspiracy to banish these people. Driven by military intelligence, the decisions came from WCCA personnel in San Francisco, who likely generated similar transfer orders for "troublemakers" in other assembly centers. Table 57 from the *Fi-*

nal Report, for example, documents 779 individuals as "Other Transfers" to relocation centers in contrast to the 90,477 moved by "Transfer Order." The origin of some of these "other transfers" may have arisen from attitudes existing in the San Francisco headquarters toward certain inmates.[50]

For most inmates anger toward Sakamoto and the Japanese Advisory Council moved into the background as preparations for relocation to Minidoka got under way. On August 9 an advance detachment of 213 volunteers left the Puyallup train station to prepare the relocation center for the mass movement scheduled to begin six days later from Camp Harmony.

9

Leaving Camp Harmony

The moon in the water;
Broken and broken again,
Still it is there.
—Chosu

During the first week of June 1942 U.S. and Japanese naval forces clashed in the Battle of Midway, an engagement fought almost entirely from the air. U.S. forces inflicted a staggering loss on the Imperial Japanese Navy by sinking four aircraft carriers. It marked the Pacific War's turning point and, in retrospect, eliminated the possibility of invasion of the West Coast. In the midst of this, without orders from superiors in the War Department to curtail operations, determined Wartime Civil Control Administration (WCCA) officials continued efforts to move the West Coast's Nikkei into relocation centers.

At the end of May word spread throughout Camp Harmony of the impending mass transfer to California's Tule Lake Relocation Center. The earlier departure of the voluntary crew to help prepare the new center for the first transferees from several assembly centers and the June 12, 1942 issue of the *News-Letter* fueled this speculation. An article citing Colonel Bendetsen, with an accompanying map detail of the center, informed Camp Harmony residents they would soon move to the northern California project to join transferees from four other assembly centers.

Throughout June as transferees from California began filling Tule Lake the army remained silent regarding plans for Pacific Northwest inmates to join them.[1] Developing events spoke for themselves. After weeks of continued speculation at Camp Harmony, on July 18, 1942, the *News-Letter* reported the population's transfer to California unlikely. The Pinedale Assembly Center's four thousand inmates, recently inducted into Tule Lake, filled the center to near capacity, leaving no available room for Camp Harmony's seven thousand residents.

Now speculation turned to Idaho as an ultimate destination for the center's residents. Hearsay soon gave way to reality on August 5, when a representative from WCCA's Operations Division arrived from San Francisco. Assisting center manager McGovern and his staff, they prepared for the en masse transfer to a relocation center currently under construction in Idaho's Jerome County near Twin Falls.[2]

As early as August 2, McGovern learned unofficially that Minidoka would become the permanent location. This early notification allowed him sufficient time to organize an advance crew through the help of the Japanese Advisory Council.[3] McGovern hand picked 213 volunteers who left for Minidoka on August 9 to prepare for receiving, feeding, housing, and readying medical services for new arrivals who would begin to appear in units of five hundred six days later. The families of the volunteers would be included in the first large group of transferees.[4]

The final issue of the *News-Letter*, a souvenir edition published on August 14, included details from a War Relocation Authority (WRA) information bulletin that had arrived the day before. They promised a regular school system, improved water and sanitation, and a local governing body with hints at free elections. The information bulletin, however, also warned that construction was not yet complete and temporary housing was in place for the advance crew. The well water supply was not yet in place or the plumbing to supply hot water. Implied was that the new arrivals would have to make do in the early days of the new relocation center. This news put aside many weeks of speculation on the inmates' final destination, allowing the center's residents to now focus on the realities of their impending move.[5]

Supplies and moveable equipment from Camp Harmony followed to Idaho incrementally, thereby avoiding the need to re-purchase beds, mattresses, and utensils for cooking and eating. Such quartermaster properties accompanied each train movement.[6]

Upon receiving official orders from San Francisco, McGovern's office first halted residents' ongoing practice of switching barracks to be closer to friends or families or to find improved quarters. With inmates frozen in place, roll call boards could prepare comprehensive family rosters and expedite upcoming train movements. Throughout the next week McGovern's staff counted out blocks in units of five hundred persons, collected their personal and medical records, and prepared the alphabetized train lists from apartment manifests. Two days prior to their transfer individuals in affected areas received notice of their hour of departure, allowing adequate time to pack personal belongings.

On the day prior to each movement army officials selected Nisei train monitors, one for every fifty passengers, to personally check family units and match them with the original roster. On the appointed moving day monitors checked each family into their bus for transport to the Puyallup train station to reduce the likelihood of anyone wandering off. McGovern was able to process five hundred transferees in a single hour by borrowing from similar procedures previously put into practice at Sacramento, Marysville, Salinas, Pinedale, and Turlock assembly centers.[7]

A typical train unit for the journey to Idaho consisted of eleven passenger cars for five hundred people, two diners, two baggage cars, and two Pullmans with sleepers reserved for children under age four, expectant mothers, physically compromised adults, and the infirm. Each passenger car in the chain was identified with an affixed distinct block letter. Families boarding buses at the center received tags marked with corresponding letters assigning each to a particular car. This practice served to eliminate confusion when passengers disembarked from the bus. Rousing send-offs from other residents who would soon be leaving launched the short bus ride to the Puyallup train station.[8]

On August 18, 1942, the Baba family from Area D boarded the Minidoka-bound train; Toshiko, then a twenty-one-year-old, succinctly recalls this event: "There were MPs [military police] all over, the train was filthy, and all the window shades were drawn."[9]

Wartime demands to move troops on the nation's rail lines forced the WCCA to employ re-commissioned passenger cars, hulks that generated universal complaints from both passengers and officials. One woman described "an old relic of a train adorned with gas lights, rococo wall paneling, and stiff mohair seats."[10] These inferior accommodations for transferees of all assembly centers produced headaches for WCCA schedulers who, between May 26 and October 26, assembled travel manifests for a total of 171 special trains consisting of more than 1,700 passenger cars that moved more than 90,000 people from assembly to relocation centers.[11]

Table 5 shows the dates when the 16 trains departed from Puyallup station for Minidoka and the numbers of people moved at one time. The first movement consisting of the advance crew of 213, departed from Puyallup station on August 9. The last movement, on September 12, included all remaining inpatients at the center hospital and the remainder of the hospital staff. The other 14 movements averaged 500 evacuees per train.

The thirty-hour ordeal in the decrepit coaches sitting upright on stiff seats burdened many of Camp Harmony's seven thousand residents. Nikkei physicians accompanying trains leaving Puyallup on August 15 and 16 complained to Dr. McGowan of the U.S. Public Health Service (USPHS) about sanitation

Boarding a train at the Puyallup train station headed for the Minidoka Relocation Center. (History of Museum and Industry, Seattle P-I Collection, 28081)

Table 5. Transfers from Assembly to Relocation Centers

Transfer Order No.	Assembly Center	Relocation Center	Date of Departure	Date of Arrival	Number of Persons Moved
—	Puyallup	Tule Lake	May 26	May 26	196
10	Puyallup	Minidoka	August 9	August 10	213
10	Puyallup	Minidoka	August 15	August 16	493
10	Puyallup	Minidoka	August 16	August 17	516
10	Puyallup	Minidoka	August 17	August 18	508
10	Puyallup	Minidoka	August 18	August 19	524
10	Puyallup	Minidoka	August 19	August 20	511
10	Puyallup	Minidoka	August 20	August 21	525
10	Puyallup	Minidoka	August 21	August 22	516
15	Puyallup	Tule Lake	August 25	August 26	53
10	Puyallup	Minidoka	August 29	August 30	517
10	Puyallup	Minidoka	August 30	August 31	512
10	Puyallup	Minidoka	August 31	September 1	503
10	Puyallup	Minidoka	September 1	September 2	505
10	Puyallup	Minidoka	September 2	September 3	505
10	Puyallup	Minidoka	September 3	September 4	412
10	Puyallup	Minidoka	September 4	September 5	297
13	Portland	Minidoka	September 6	September 7	500
13	Portland	Minidoka	September 7	September 8	494
13	Portland	Minidoka	September 8	September 9	501
13	Portland	Minidoka	September 9	September 10	506
13	Portland	Minidoka	September 10	September 11	317
10	Puyallup	Minidoka	September 12	September 13	92

Source: *Final Report*, Table 33, 282.

and other potential health concerns. Toilet closets lacked lighting; several toilets failed to flush or leaked into corridors. Plumbing problems in one Union Pacific car that was subsequently condemned compounded the misery throughout the journey. While gas lanterns helped restore lighting, their generated heat in combination with the outside atmosphere baking down on the carriage roofs endangered passengers' health. Dirty prior to occupancy, some coaches also had inadequate water pressure and faltering air conditioning, and their sealed windows prevented air circulation. In other cars air conditioning in the diners failed altogether.[12]

Dr. McGowan forwarded his list of deficiencies with an accompanying directive to WCCA planners in San Francisco: "Take the necessary steps to force the Railroad Company to provide cars in good working order and to insist that when defects in the cars appear en route that they be promptly and satisfactorily corrected."[13]

Despite myriad mechanical problems in the obsolete coaches, many childless passengers unaffected by the malfunctions found the experience a novelty. For some transferees train travel was a first-time experience; eating in a dining car with linens and silverware and being served by stewards brought a semblance of pleasure. Although Margaret Baba found the train to be dirty, hot, and stuffy, her diary recorded the dining car as cool and the food good.[14] And word circulated: if they were going to eat in the dining car, everyone should have change to leave for tips.[15]

Children didn't always grasp the reality of their situation, many believing they were headed to summer camp: "I remember being excited, I got to be on a train. And we were riding along and one of the things that I remember is hearing the older kids singing 'Don't Fence Me In,' a song popular at the time. I didn't realize how prophetic that would be."[16]

For a large number of Nikkei the train ride to Minidoka meant their first journey east of the Cascade range; few remained indifferent to the changing geography. First they headed south from Puyallup, passing through Centralia and Vancouver and across the Columbia River into Oregon. Turning eastward, they paralleled the Columbia before moving southeastward toward Idaho. The last leg of the journey took them through Twin Falls and finally to Eden, the train's final stop located six miles south of the Minidoka Relocation Center.

As verdant western Washington and Oregon landscapes transitioned to the desert country's treeless aridity, where "wisps of moldy-looking, gray-green sagebrush" dotted the land, passengers became engrossed in the unfamiliar scenery despite their physical and emotional discomforts.[17] Tamako Inouye, who participated in the August 21 trip, wrote in her diary: "In the evening, passing the Columbia River, the hills became bald one after another, like quiet moles crouched one after another with their brown suede backs. At sunset the hills looked like purple dust and the rivers were lighted with orange and gold. I saw a heron standing among the rocks in the river. Also I saw jackrabbits scampering among the sagebrush."[18]

A number of former Camp Harmony passengers recalled traveling with their window shades drawn for the duration of the trip. Passing through congested areas or at depot rest stops faces of Japanese peering through train windows, officials believed, might alarm the local populace. Therefore, accompanying MP guards ordered the shades be drawn to minimize visual contact.

Orders to keep shades drawn for the entire trip, however, would certainly have complicated the guards' task of maintaining calm and discipline and made little sense. The landscape passing outside the windows helped shorten long stretches sitting upright in uncomfortable coaches even as the open shades permitted access to latches on still functional windows that when opened might circulate the stifling air. Nevertheless, for some the humiliation of shades ordered drawn at rest stops carried over to the entire, seemingly endless, journey to Minidoka.

They migrated eastward at a crawl, shunted to sidings to allow oncoming trains to pass, almost all of which had a higher priority. After a night of minimal sleep and a morning with stiffened joints and sweat-soaked clothing, the train came to a final stop at Eden, where a fleet of buses waited to transport the weary passengers the last few miles. An early editorial in the center's newspaper, the *Minidoka Irrigator*, describes what they saw: "Minidoka . . . is a vast stretch of sagebrush, stubble, and shifting, swirling sand—a dreary and forbidding, flat expanse of arid wilderness. Minidoka in September 1942 is the sort of place people would normally traverse only to get through to another destination."[19]

Margaret Baba's diary corroborates this observation succinctly: "Disgusting. Dusty. Mosquitoes, sagebrush, no mountains, no grass."[20]

When the last train bringing 317 transferees from the Portland Assembly Center on September 11, 1942, put the center's population at 9,467, construction of the facility's basic infrastructure was not yet complete.[21] The day before, project director Harry L. Stafford relayed his initial message in the first issue of the *Minidoka Irrigator*: "I deeply appreciate the cooperation of the colonists of this center in meeting the chaotic conditions which presently exist. It is only a matter of a few weeks when the basic construction work will be completed and we can begin planning improvements to our community."[22]

The basic construction reference reflected the War Department's obligation to provide the minimum essentials of living. However, the blueprints failed to include buildings needed to house schools, churches, and other community services. Such additions and an irrigation ditch to provide water for crops would have to be built later utilizing labor provided by the new "colonists."[23]

Although initial conditions at the new center provided marginal improvement over the assembly centers Pacific Northwest Nikkei had left behind, the moving-in period would again repeat the trying experience of Type "B" rations, pit latrines, compromised medical services without adequate equipment, and long lines in the mess halls. In addition the new arrivals suffered from ever-present wind and swirling dust and an unappeasable sun.

Without running water in the apartments, care for infants and the elderly immediately turned problematic. Residents partitioned open rooms to gain privacy; shelves, tables, and chairs were constructed by hammer and nail or they arrived by parcel post. In preparation for the region's hard winters carpenters installed wallboard covering exposed 2 x 4 studs that comprised the inner walls. Additional electrical circuits would appear later.[24]

The site's atypical sloping topography required layout of blocks to differ substantially from the rectangular configuration in relocation centers sited on flat, unobstructed landscapes. Here the blocks angled downward and formed a crescent, conforming to the arc of the Twin Falls–North Side Canal running along the project's south boundary. This spread-out configuration posed problems for inmates. As observed by James M. Sakoda, hired by the Japanese Evacuation and Resettlement Study to observe daily life in the relocation centers: "It was one block following another block strung along a long string in a semi-circle, so that allowed for less concentration of the people, less interaction. In other words, if you lived in Block 1 and you had to go over to the last block, it would be a long walk. It might take about half an hour. The administration was way off, too, well to the center upon the hill, so that kept everybody more or less separated."[25]

Green lumber used in construction soon warped, producing the same cracks in barracks walls and floors that inmates had endured at Camp Harmony. Howling wind and fine dust penetrated family living areas. As inmates confronted extreme temperatures, ranging from below-zero teens in the winter to 110 degrees Fahrenheit in the summer, raging dust storms appeared suddenly and persisted with ferocity. A visitor to the center wrote: "The earth is a fine dust that blows all over when dry and turns to slidey gooey grease when wet."[26]

In doing battle with the elements one survivor of the incarceration experience recalled how her mother took matters into her own hands: "Mom used to come home from the bathroom with toilet paper . . . I'd see her making little wads and plugging up the holes so she wouldn't have to clean all the time . . .

There were no inside walls . . . just outside walls. So, like around the windows there would be little holes, and the dirt would just kind of pile up."[27] In her postwar memoir Monica Sone described a fellow resident caught in a windstorm: "A miniature tornado enveloped her and she disappeared from sight. A few seconds later when it cleared, I saw that she had been pulling a child behind her, shielding it with her skirt. The little girl suddenly sat down on the ground and hid her face in her lap. The mother ripped off her jacket, threw it over her daughter's head and flung herself against the wind, carrying the child. Someone pulled the two inside the mess hall."[28] Many refused to venture outdoors without heavy scarves to protect against the choking sand.

* * *

On November 1, 1942, six days after the last transfer from the Santa Anita Assembly Center to the Manzanar War Relocation Center, the WCCA, under prior agreement with the WRA, turned over jurisdiction of 111,155 Nikkei in its custody to the civilian agency.[29] The assembly center period finally came to a close. But not all had made the journey into captivity.

In the evacuated areas more than 1,200 Nikkei remained behind in public institutions, the vast majority individuals whose illnesses made travel impossible. Most of the infirm, because of insufficient resources or medical staff at the assembly center infirmaries and hospitals, occupied beds at tuberculosis sanitaria.[30]

In preparation for transfer to the relocation centers, USPHS personnel examined each patient; inmates too ill to be moved remained in or were moved to public institutions to be maintained at federal government expense.[31] Of those still institutionalized on November 1, 1942, 753 never entered a relocation center.[32]

Puget Sound area residents assigned to Camp Harmony contributed to these numbers. Accompanied by their caregivers, on September 12, 1942, the last ninety-two inpatients from the center hospital departed the Puyallup train station en route to Minidoka. Ten former Camp Harmony residents remained behind as patients in area hospitals—one at Mountain View Sanitarium in Pierce County established to care for tubercular patients; three at the Tacoma White Shield Home for unwed mothers; one at Western State Hospital for psychiatric patients; and five at Tacoma's Pierce County Hospital.[33]

The transfer of their families to Minidoka meant isolation for these patients for the foreseeable future. On the eve of their departures family members were permitted under escort to visit loved ones still institutionalized.[34]

In addition to the ten inpatients with medical conditions who remained in hospitals in Washington state, twenty-nine other Nikkei from the Pacific

Northwest were relegated to long-term care in mental hospitals; prior to February 19, 1942, sixteen Pierce County patients had been committed to Western State Hospital at Steilacoom. Because they resided within the boundaries of Military Area No. 1 the WCCA held jurisdiction over them until November 1. The army's method of handling individuals exempted from evacuation is illustrated by the Western State Hospital experience.[35]

Experimental treatments like lobotomy, insulin shock, and electric shock began in the 1940s and soon became the standard of care. Use of such "cures" may seem extreme, but psychodynamic treatment had yet to take hold and at the time remained underutilized. Whether Nikkei patients at Western State Hospital experienced such clinical interventions or the hospital served only as caretaker for the government remains unclear.

On March 25, 1942, one month prior to the exile of Seattle's Nikkei, the Washington State Department of Social Security, acting on behalf of the WCCA, requested data on every Japanese American patient who resided in an institution west of the Cascades. The next day Western State Hospital forwarded data on its nineteen Nikkei patients, the majority with chronic mental conditions and poor prognoses for recovery. Transfer to an assembly center would require long-term care in a hospital setting that no assembly center hospital, including Puyallup's, could provide. Therefore, Japanese American inpatients at Steilacoom, all admitted prior to evacuation, would remain for the duration of the war. Only two patients, both institutionalized after first entering the Puyallup Assembly Center, would ever undergo the experience of a relocation center.[36]

New WCCA orders issued on May 25, 1942, stipulated ten days' advance notification of the release or parole of any institutionalized Nikkei patient, an interval necessary for army officials to assign an assembly or relocation center and alert project managers. Periodic updates of the number of Nikkei under institutionalized care were to be provided by hospital officials.[37]

The WCCA reimbursed Western State Hospital a portion of the per diem for Nikkei patients under its jurisdiction, which by mid-May had increased to twenty-one. It also agreed to provide transportation and medical attendants in the course of transfer to the centers for those who might eventually be released.[38]

On August 1 WCCA closed its Seattle office that had provided services to the small number of individuals granted deferments from evacuation, including the twenty-one psychiatric cases. Its responsibilities temporarily passed to the State Department of Social Security, which followed the directive to provide ten days' advance notice per release. At this point 109 Japanese Americans resided in state-funded institutions—hospitals, jails, and custodial homes.[39] On September 1, 1942, the USPHS assumed full responsibility for assistance to all deferred evacuees, relieving Washington State from all obligation to Nikkei who fell under federal jurisdiction.[40] Eight days later, the Western State Hospital admitted a fourteen-year-old girl from the Puyallup Assembly Center.

Following WCCA's transfer of jurisdiction to the WRA, state institutions received federal funds earmarked for those institutionalized Japanese Americans admitted after evacuation orders had been handed down. Just three Western State patients fell into that category.[41]

As the last train departed Puyallup station on September 12, the Puyallup Assembly Center became a ghost town; McGovern retained a skeleton crew in the administrative area to sign off transfer of all leased buildings and permanent infrastructure and turn over keys to Fort Lewis army personnel. A similar exercise was repeated as each assembly center, with the exception of Manzanar, shut down operations.

All but two of the assembly centers remained under army control, providing facilities and open spaces for ordnance, signal, quartermaster, and transportation corps service schools. Tiny Mayer Assembly Center, a former Civilian Conservation Corps (CCC) site in Arizona, returned to the Forest Service on June 27, 1942, while the Manzanar center had long since been turned over to the WRA and remained in use for the duration of the war. Army Ordnance took control of Santa Anita, the largest assembly center and the last to close, on November 30, 1942.[42]

The Puyallup Assembly Center site officially became attached to the Fort Lewis Ninth Service Command on September 30, 1942, which used it as a training facility. Since the number of servicemen passing through on temporary duty never approached the numbers of Nikkei once confined there, the city of Puyallup returned to its slow-paced existence. Its seven thousand permanent residents began to look forward to return of the annual Western Washington Fair, a four-year wait ending in 1946, a year after the conclusion of the war.

* * *

In mid-September 1942, Minidoka Relocation Center's new arrivals wondered about a future that remained uncertain. Inmates speculated as to when they would leave this inhospitable terrain where nothing green reminded them of home. Faintly visible mountains on the distant western horizon became a hopeful reminder of the place where one day they might return. Defying the elements, they planted trees and flowers; rock gardens and *koi* ponds adorned their living quarters.[43]

Glimpses of eventual freedom soon became evident, for in the first month of their Idaho captivity Nisei farm workers steadily left for the state's sugar beet fields. By the end of the 1942 growing season, 1,850 workers from Minidoka harvested nearly one-quarter of the state's crop, receiving the gratitude of the region's growers. Many farm hands never returned to the center. At about the same time the trickle of students leaving for inland colleges and universities became a stream.[44]

Permanent "leave clearance" for families seeking to live on the outside began in earnest before the end of 1942. Shortly after the beginning of 1943, the War Department, in a change of policy, allowed Nisei to volunteer for military service. In the ensuing months more volunteer recruits departed Minidoka for military service than from any other relocation center. Some would eventually pay the ultimate price for their freedom.

As jurisdiction shifted from the military to the civilian-run WRA, restrictions loosened on daily life in the center. As the ban on possession of Japanese-language materials eased, the *Minidoka Irrigator* published a Japanese-language section, while a form of limited self-government slowly evolved with Issei eligible to participate. A combined effort involving Issei leaders and members of the administration helped thwart initial moves of Japanese American Citizens League (JACL) leaders to dominate key positions on the WRA payroll. The ever controversial Jimmie Sakamoto never rose above a position of block delegate, while FBI informant Clarence Arai remained an obscure figure in the Legal Aid Department. As Nisei continued engaging in center politics Issei assumed a role in the process. The JACL's hold over the people began to loosen as an attempt to set up a JACL chapter within the center failed.[45]

Nevertheless, changes came slowly. Three years after the Minidoka Relocation Center opened, with major portions of Hiroshima and Nagasaki reduced to rubble by nuclear blasts, almost half the residents still remained in their tarpaper barracks. From the onset of their Idaho interlude inmates from the Pacific Northwest remained dependent on their captors for food, housing, clothing, education, health, and law enforcement, as well as for other forms of sustenance. Government administrators, more focused on the overriding objectives of the incarceration than individual needs of its residents, continued to hand down policy decisions.

In a postwar reflection on the activities of the WRA, unnamed authors wrote: "Although many decisions were related to perceived needs, no provision was made on the level of policy determination for the participation and advice of the evacuees in formulating decisions . . . The result, of course, was a rather thorough and efficient institutionalization of the population."[46]

Epilogue

Even though life in the Minidoka Relocation Center was physically difficult and emotionally trying for the inmates from the Puget Sound region, the earlier four-month transition to captivity at the Puyallup Assembly Center may have helped the Nikkei prepare for their several years of subsequent confinement in Idaho. Although her response was likely atypical, Sharon (Tanagi) Aburano provided insight from her own experience: "I think that was the best adjustment really the army could give us, to herd us all together to get us used to queuing up in lines and being a bit more patient and learning to get along because we were in such tight quarters. I think without them knowing, it was the greatest thing to do."[1]

In 1978, thirty-six years after the Camp Harmony experience, an organized return to the former assembly center for a day of remembrance helped galvanize a Nikkei community poised to seek government redress for those who had endured and survived the incarceration experience.

At its annual convention in July 1978, a new generation of Japanese American Citizens League (JACL) national council members unanimously passed a resolution proposing legislation for a $25,000 individual payment and community trust fund, and writer Frank Chin conceived of the Day of Remembrance to draw national attention to this action.[2] While researching a story about redress in Seattle for the *Seattle Weekly,* Chin and members of the Seattle Evacuation Redress Committee (SERC), a local group formed to consider redress, helped organize the event. Included among them was Shosuke Sasaki, the young Issei conspirator from the alleged plot to assassinate Jimmie Sakamoto. A written invitation disseminated throughout the community encouraged participants to join a car caravan from Seattle's Rainier Valley to the Western Washington Fairgrounds in Puyallup on November 25, 1978, to "Raise the flag over Camp Harmony to remember the years of hardship Japanese America endured to make the United States home for their parents, themselves, their children, and all the Nikkei generations to come."[3]

More than two thousand people attended these festivities accompanied by a potluck, talent shows, dance performances, and a Japanese American play. Politicians and former inmates made speeches, and for the first time since the end of World War II survivors shared with each other and their children memories of Puyallup and Minidoka kept locked in their minds for a generation.

For Sasaki and fellow SERC organizer Henry Miyatake, the Day of Remembrance would be a freeing experience. Hours after the event Chin unexpectedly encountered them in Seattle's International District, and later related this meeting in print:

> "You know," Shosuke said, in a mood to speak in whole sentences, "I was a little leery of going out there. I haven't set foot on those premises since the days it was Camp Harmony. And, much to my surprise, all the horrible feelings and memories I expected to assail me there were of no matter. Standing there by that grandstand, alone with Henry there tonight, I found to be the strangest elation."
>
> "I'm free! I'm free!" Henry Miyatake yelled, not too loud, and jumped up and down, and nodded at Shosuke.
>
> "Shosuke, you didn't!" I said, and realized we looked dumb chatting and jumping in the middle of a Chinatown street.
>
> "It wasn't until I was standing there tonight that I really felt released from camp. I think it was because I went there of my own free will."[4]

This sense of free will may have been felt by others attending the first Day of Remembrance, a gathering that is held annually in the Pacific Northwest and other cities throughout the country. Four years after this first Day of Remembrance, on August 21, 1983, Governor John Spellman and other state representatives active in their support of the redress movement helped dedicate a ten-foot cylindrical silicon-bronze sculpture at Puyallup's Western Washington Fairgrounds, formerly Area D, a memorial to those incarcerated forty years earlier. This geometric sculpture's ascending abstract figures depict, in the words of its creator, George Tsutakawa: "Human people—old people, young people, men, women, children, even babies. They are gathered around in a circle holding each other in a happy relationship."[5]

The sculpture seems to convey that, despite the wartime travails of most persons of Japanese ancestry, family ties, cultural values, and group cohesion enabled the Nikkei community to survive, to grow, and finally, to prosper.

Notes

Introduction

1. *Seattle Times*, August 31, 1896.

2. Malone, *James J. Hill*, 167–68.

3. Ichioka, "Japanese Immigrant Labor Contractors."

4. Ichioka, *The Issei*, 63; Ichioka, "Japanese Immigrant Labor Contractors," 332.

5. For a compelling story of Nikkei life in a rural setting in western Washington, see Flewelling, *Shirakawa*; Ito provides a broad spectrum of immigrant life in the Pacific Northwest in *Issei*.

6. Ichioka, "Japanese Immigrant Labor Contractors," 334.

7. For a narrative on Japanese immigration and the anti-Japanese movement, see Daniels, *Asian America*, 100–155.

8. Ichioka, *The Issei*, 72.

9. Miyamoto, *Social Solidarity*, 9–11.

10. Ito, *Issei*, 904–16.

11. Ichioka, *The Issei*, 164.

12. For a description of the picture bride process, see Ichioka, *The Issei*, 164–75.

13. Miyamoto, *Social Solidarity*, 14. The term *Nikkei* is commonly used by Japanese Americans to indicate all members of the Japanese community, both immigrant (Issei) and U.S.-born.

14. Ichioka, *The Issei*, 173–75.

15. For several discussions of the Tanforan Assembly Center, see Sandra C. Taylor, *Jewel of the Desert*; Modell (ed.), *The Kikuchi Diary*; and Linke's unpublished master's thesis, "Tanforan." For discussions of other assembly centers, see, for example, Feeley, *A Strategy of Dominance*; Gorfinkel (ed.), *The Evacuation Diary of Hatsuye Egami*; Bailey, *City in the Sun*; Lehman, *Birthright of Barbed Wire*.

Chapter 1. Prewar Japantown

1. For a general history of Seattle during World War II, including the expulsion of the Japanese community and the return after the war, see Berner, *Seattle Transformed*.

2. Sale, *Seattle, Past to Present*, 4–5.

3. Fujita-Rony, *American Workers, Colonial Power*, 108–38.

4. For a history of the Chinese in the canning industry, see Friday, *Organizing Asian American Labor*.

5. Schmid, *Social Trends in Seattle*, 131–50.

6. In 1940, King County's Japanese population was 9,863; in the state, 14,565.

7. Demographers of the day employed street names to define boundaries of the geographic areas home to most of Seattle's minority population. They avoided popular, ethnocentric terms like Japantown, Chinatown, Little Manila, or Cross-Town.

8. Dubrow with Graves, *Sento at Sixth and Main*, 62–79; Tsutakawa and Lau (eds.), *Turning Shadows Into Light*, 47–53; *Polks Seattle City Directory*, 1930–42.

9. "Statement by Emergency Defense Council, Seattle Chapter, Japanese-American Citizens League, Seattle Wash.," in U.S. Congress, House, *Hearings before the Select Committee Investigating National Defense Migration, Part 30 Portland and Seattle Hearings*, 11450–70 (hereafter Tolan Hearings followed by page numbers).

10. Sone, *Nisei Daughter*, 8–10.

11. Tolan Hearings, 11459.

12. Cited in Fujita-Rony, *American Workers, Colonial Power*, 126.

13. Miyamoto, *Social Solidarity*, 16.

14. Takami, *Divided Destiny*, 28.

15. Shigeko (Sese) Uno interview.

16. Tamako (Inouye) Tokuda interview.

17. Emery E. Andrews Papers, 1925–1969, University of Washington Libraries, Special Collections, Accession No. 1908.

18. Ochsner (ed.), *Shaping Seattle Architecture*, 38–39, 240–45. For a discussion of Christian and Buddhist institutions in Seattle's Nikkei community in the decade leading up to World War II, see Miyamoto, *Social Solidarity*, 45–50.

19. U.S. War Department, *Final Report*, 333–36.

20. Jim Akutsu interview.

21. U.S. Bureau of the Census, *Sixteenth Census of the U.S., 1940, Population*, vol. 2, 401.

22. Cited in Fujita-Rony, *American Workers, Colonial Power*, 123.

23. Schmid, *Social Trends in Seattle*, 149.

24. *Polks Seattle City Directory*, 1941, 1942; Fujita-Rony, *American Workers, Colonial Power*, 122–28.

25. Fujita-Rony, *American Workers, Colonial Power*, 129.

26. Schmid, Nobbe, and Mitchell, *Nonwhite Races, State of Washington*, 61.

27. A good historical account of African Americans in Seattle may be found in Taylor, *The Forging of a Black Community.*

28. de Barros, *Jackson Street After Hours,* 36–38.

29. Ibid., 37; *Polks Seattle City Directory,* 1940.

30. *Polks Seattle City Directory,* 1940; Tolan Hearings, 11455.

31. Tolan Hearings, 11454–55.

32. Ibid., 11457.

33. Miyamoto, *Social Solidarity,* xx.

34. *Final Report,* 403.

35. *The Pacific Citizen,* May 19, 1941.

36. *Polks Seattle City Directory,* 1940–42; War Relocation Authority, "Final Accountability Roster of the Minidoka Relocation Center, October 1945," Records of the War Relocation Authority (RG210).

37. *Seattle Times,* May 14, 1942.

38. Bill Hosokawa interview. See also Hosokawa, *Out of the Frying Pan,* 12–14.

39. The biographical information in this section derives from Tsutakawa's unpublished master's thesis, "The Political Conservatism of James Sakamoto's Japanese American Courier"; and Ichioka, "A Study in Dualism," 49–81.

40. *Japanese American Courier,* January 1, 1928.

41. Hosokawa, *JACL,* 29; Niiya (ed.), *Encyclopedia of Japanese American History,* 219–20.

42. Hosokawa, *JACL,* 33–47; Niiya (ed.), *Encyclopedia of Japanese American History,* 219–20.

Chapter 2. War Comes to Japantown

1. Kimmett and Regis, *The Attack on Pearl Harbor.* For a fuller historical account of the attack, see Prange, *At Dawn We Slept.*

2. *Seattle Times,* December 7, 1941.

3. Shosuke Sasaki interview.

4. Sharon (Tanagi) Aburano interview.

5. Jim Akutsu interview.

6. Sharon (Tanagi) Aburano interview.

7. Hosokawa, *Out of the Frying Pan,* 25–26.

8. Jim Akutsu interview.

9. Shigeto Ishikawa interview.

10. Whitehead, *The FB_ _* see "Instructions for the _ Attorney General," CWRI_

11. Biddle, *In Brief Author_ Americans,* 61–64.

12. Kashima, *Judgment Witho_*

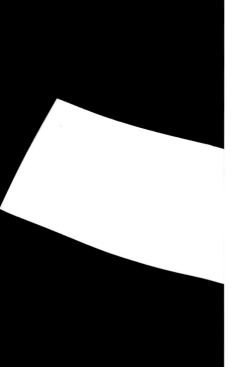

13. Robinson, *By Order of the President,* 64–65; Commission on Wartime Relocation and Internment of Civilians, *Personal Justice Denied,* 54.

14. *Seattle Times,* December 9, 1941.

15. Kenji Okuda interview.

16. Fiset, *Imprisoned Apart,* 11–26.

17. Tamako (Inouye) Tokuda interview.

18. Sharon (Tanagi) Aburano interview.

19. Sone, *Nisei Daughter,* 156.

20. Together they would soon be heading for the INS detention station at Fort Missoula, Montana.

21. Kashima, *Judgment Without Trial,* 234n27.

22. Shigeko (Sese) Uno interview.

23. On January 28, 1942, Takahashi and Ozawa were arraigned by a federal grand jury on charges of conspiring to export war materiels to Japan. The Takahashi trial began May 12 and resulted in a deadlocked jury, as did the second trial. The jury from a third trial convicted him, but the case was overturned by the U.S. Court of Appeals on grounds of illegal search and seizure. Following the successful appeal, Takahashi was escorted to the Minidoka Relocation Center.

24. "Leave Clearance Hearing for Kenji Ito," April 12, 1944, in Kenji Ito File, Records of the War Relocation Authority (RG210), National Archives, Washington, D.C.

25. *Seattle Post-Intelligencer,* February 1, 1942.

26. Nobuko (Yanagimachi) Suzuki interview.

27. *Seattle Times,* December 12, 1941.

28. Ibid., December 15, 1941.

29. *Japanese American Courier,* December 19, 1941.

30. Shigeko (Sese) Uno interview.

31. *Seattle Times,* December 9, 1941.

32. Shorett, "A history of the Pike Place marketing district," unpublished manuscript, 1972, 95.

33. *Seattle Star,* May 6, 1942.

34. Shorett and Morgan, *The Pike Place Market,* 111.

35. *Seattle Post-Intelligencer,* December 11, 1941.

36. Ibid., December 8, 1941.

37. Congressional Record, 77th Congress, Appendix, December 8, 1941, A5551–4.

38. *Japanese American Courier,* January 1, 1942.

39. Bill Hosokawa interview.

40. For a brief discussion of the anti-axis committee of Los Angeles, see Deborah K. Lim, "Research Report Prepared for the Presidential Select Committee On JACL Resolution #7," 11–21.

41. *Great Northern Daily, December 15, 1941;* War Relocation Authority, "Final Accountability Roster of the Minidoka Relocation Center, October 1945."

42. Bill Hosokawa interview.

43. *Great Northern Daily,* December 16, 1941.

44. *Japanese American Courier,* December 19, 1941.

45. *Seattle Post-Intelligencer,* December 24, 1941.

46. Ibid.

47. Ibid.; *Great Northern Daily,* December 26, 1941.

48. *Seattle Times,* December 23, 1941.

49. Ibid.

50. Daniels, *Asian America,* 209.

51. Fiset, "In the Matter of Iwao Matsushita," 215–35; Kumamoto, "The Search for Spies," 57.

52. Fiset, "In the Matter of Iwao Matsushita," 215–35.

53. *Seattle Times,* January 21, 1942.

54. Ibid., January 31, 1942.

55. *Seattle Post-Intelligencer,* January 24, 1942.

56. *Japanese-American Courier,* January 23, 1942. Repeated in *Seattle Times,* January 31, 1942.

57. *Pearl Harbor Attack: Hearings Before the Joint Committee on the Investigation of the Pearl Harbor Attack,* Part 39, 1–21.

58. Daniels, *Prisoners Without Trial,* 37–38.

59. Grodzins, *Americans Betrayed,* 72–80.

60. *Seattle Post-Intelligencer,* January 26, 30, February 5, 13, 18, 1942.

61. Ibid., February 7, 1942.

62. Lippmann's syndicated column appeared in newspapers throughout the nation on February 12, 1942.

63. *Seattle Post-Intelligencer,* February 21, 1942.

64. Daniels, *Prisoners Without Trial,* 46. For a discussion of politics leading up to Executive Order 9066, see Daniels, *The Decision to Relocate the Japanese Americans.*

65. *Final Report,* Table 47, 363–66.

Chapter 3. Preparing for Exile

1. Daniels, *Concentration Camps USA,* 74–81.

2. Tolan Hearings, Arthur B. Langlie testimony, 11397–404.

3. Ibid., Earl Milliken testimony, 11409.

4. Ibid., Smith Troy testimony, 11503.

5. Ibid., Harry P. Cain testimony, 11415.

6. Ibid., Floyd Schmoe testimony, 11526–35.

7. Ibid., Jessie F. Steiner testimony, 11557–64.

8. Ibid., Hildur Coon testimony, 11590–91.

9. Ibid., Miller Freeman testimony, 11536–38.

10. Ibid., 11433.

11. For a fuller discussion of the dismissal of the school clerks and other Nisei public employees, see Fiset, "Redress for Nisei Public Employees."

12. *North American Times,* February 23, 1942.

13. *Great Northern Daily News,* February 23, 1942.

14. Ibid., February 25, 1942.

15. *North American Times,* February 26, 1942.

16. Sally (Shimanaka) Kazama interview. On April 2, 1986, Washington Governor Booth Gardner signed a redress bill authorizing local governments in the state to pay monetary compensation to former Japanese American employees dismissed from their employment in 1942. Each of the school clerks, then living, received $5,000 from the Seattle School District. See *Pacific Citizen,* April 11, 1986; *Seattle Times,* April 3, 1986. See Fiset, "Redress for Nisei Public Employees."

17. *Seattle Times,* February 28, 1942.

18. Interestingly, Sakamoto devoted little attention to the incident in the *Japanese American Courier.*

19. Fiset, "Redress for Nisei Public Employees," 27.

20. Kumamoto, "The Search for Spies," 71.

21. I am indebted to Yukiko (Kawakami) Sato for providing details of her family's World War II experience and a copy of her father's FBI record obtained through the Freedom of Information Act. Documents are in the author's possession.

22. Social Security Administration, after July 16, 1946.

23. Yukiko (Kawakami) Sato documents.

24. Ito, *Issei,* 868; Sharon (Tanagi) Aburano interview.

25. *Seattle Times,* March 19, 1942.

26. Biweekly INS compilations of detainees held at the Seattle immigration station, beginning February 15, 1942, are instructive. On that day seventeen Japanese detainees occupied its jail, presumably from December's initial arrests. Two weeks later, on February 27, their numbers jumped to 108; two weeks after that to 150. "Alien Enemies in Temporary Detention," Records of the Immigration and Naturalization Service (RG85)—Records Related to the Detention and Internment of Enemy Aliens during World War II, Box 2410, file 56125/35 (hereafter RG85).

27. "Alien Enemies in Temporary Detention," RG85, Box 2410, file 56125/35.

28. Daniels, *The Decision to Relocate the Japanese Americans,* 115.

29. Ibid., 53.

30. *Final Report,* Table 1, 79. 84.6 percent of the Japanese population in the United States resided in the four-state region defined by Military Area No. 1.

31. Ibid., 101–13.

32. Ibid., Figure 8, 87.

33. Ibid., 65–67.

34. Niiya (ed.), *Encyclopedia of Japanese American History,* 129. For a fascinating view of Bendetsen, see deNevers, *The Colonel and the Pacifist.*

35. U.S. Department of the Interior, *WRA: A Story of Human Conservation,* 26.

36. *Final Report,* Table 6, 110.

37. Takahashi, "Japanese Americans in the Pacific Northwest."

38. *Final Report,* 412.

39. Takahashi, "Japanese Americans in the Pacific Northwest."

40. Sims, "The 'Free Zone' Nikkei," 243.

41. Fiset, "Thinning, Topping and Loading."

42. Tolan Hearings, James Y. Sakamoto testimony, 11449–81.

43. James Y. Sakamoto to General DeWitt, March 23, 1942, James Y. Sakamoto papers, Box 15, Folder 9, University of Washington Libraries (hereafter Sakamoto papers).

44. Sakamoto to Milton Eisenhauer [*sic*], April 2, 1942, Sakamoto papers, Box 15, Folder 9. See Tolan Hearings, 11602–3, for a statement submitted by the president of the Seattle Glove Company.

45. Frank Y. Toribara to James Y. Sakamoto, March 27, 1942, Sakamoto papers, Box 15, Folder 2.

46. Eric Peterson to M. S. Eisenhower, April 9, 1942, Sakamoto papers, Box 15, Folder 4.

47. Fiset, "Thinning, Topping and Loading."

48. *Seattle Times,* March 12, 1942.

49. Sakamoto to Saburo Kido, March 5, 1942, Sakamoto papers, Box 4, Folder 45.

50. I am indebted to William Seltzer and Margo Anderson for much of the information contained in this section. See "The Dark Side of Numbers" and "After Pearl Harbor." See also Daniels, "The Bureau of the Census."

51. Seltzer, personal communication with the author, March 29, 2005. Schmid appears to have been opposed to the incarceration even though he agreed to work for the WCCA during the spring of 1942. In his subsequent study, *Social Trends in Seattle,* he presented a positive picture of the excluded population even as he demonstrated the same graphic and cartographic skills in data presentation that can also be found in many of the reports of the WCCA and the Western Defense Command's *Final Report.* Schmid, a teenager during World War I, may have recalled his own German American roots when the government interned more than two thousand resident German nationals living in the United States. In a 1975 interview, Robert O'Brien provides an erroneous impression that Schmid helped set the boundary between Military Areas No. 1 and No. 2, thereby saving Japanese Americans in eastern Washington and Oregon from incarceration and allowing his own group to place college students at Washington State College, Whitman College, and other eastern Washington institutions. See Robert W. O'Brien interview.

52. Additional preliminary reports were issued on December 19 and February 2. On December 12, 1941, the Bureau disseminated a report on foreign-born Germans and Italians in selected cities.

53. 46 Stat 21, at 25,26, 18 June 1929, as cited in Okamura, "The Myth of Census Confidentiality."

54. U.S. Code Congressional Service, 1943, P.L. 507, 77th Congress, 2nd Session (S2208); Seltzer and Anderson, "After Pearl Harbor," 15.

55. Figure 6 of the *Final Report* at page 83 reveals the level of resolution of population in its population density maps. Although others wrote most of the text for the *Final Report*, Dedrick edited the statistical tabulations in the chapter titled "Statistical Summary" (Chapter XXVIII), 352–427. See Daniels, "The Bureau of the Census."

56. Seltzer and Anderson, "After Pearl Harbor," 28–30.

57. *Final Report*, 77.

58. Tule Lake, Colorado River (Poston), and Gila River (Rivers) Relocation Centers.

59. *Final Report*, Table 47, 363–66.

60. The 3,497 Washington Nikkei sent to the Pinedale Assembly Center fell under CEOs No. 39 (989 persons), No. 67 (868), No. 68 (166), No. 79 (1,016), No. 80 (458). The remainder went directly to the Tule Lake Relocation Center under CEOs No. 88 (339), No. 89 (151), and No. 90 (157). These numbers do not include parolees or detainees under Justice Department jurisdiction. 12,892 were actually removed by the army. See *Final Report*, Tables 47 and 48, 363–68.

Chapter 4. Puyallup Assembly Center

1. Dumond, *Doin' the Puyallup*.

2. Telegraph, Jay L. Benedict to Arthur B. Langlie, February 5, 1942, Arthur B. Langlie papers, folder Japanese Internment, Box 2M-1-13, Washington State Archives, Olympia, Washington.

3. *Final Report*, 151.

4. The Mayer Arizona Assembly Center, with only 250 inmates, eventually occupied one such abandoned CCC camp. The center remained open for six weeks.

5. For a history of the 360,000 German and Italian POWs held in the United States during World War II, see Krammer, *Nazi Prisoners of War in America*, and Keefer, *Italian Prisoners of War in America, 1942–1946*.

6. *Seattle Star*, April 2, 1942.

7. *Great Northern Daily*, April 2, 1942. The owner, Joe Gottstein, claimed he never knew the site was being considered.

8. *Seattle Star*, April 4, 1942.

9. Lease between Western Washington Fair Association and The United States of America, July 1, 1942, lease between John and Josephine Svoboda and The United States of America, June 4, 1942, and lease between Frank S. and Lettie N. Martin and The United States of America, March 28, 1942, RG338 WDC & 4th Army, WCCA and CAD Central Correspondence, 1942–46, Box 92, file 601.53II.

10. *Tacoma News Tribune*, March 29, 1942.

11. RG338 WDC & 4th Army WCCA & CAD, microfilm copy of Records of Assembly Centers 1942–45, Box 3, Roll 36—Toppenish.

12. *Engineering News-Record* 128, no. 24 (June 11, 1942): 952–53.

13. *Tacoma News Tribune*, March 29, 30, 1942.

14. *Engineering News-Record* 128, no. 24 (June 11, 1942): 952–53.

15. *Tacoma News Tribune*, March 30, 1942.

16. Roy Wingate, "Housing Survey of Evacuation Centers."

17. Hosokawa, *Out of the Frying Pan*, 35.

18. See, for example, Sharon Aburano interview.

19. *Tacoma News Tribune*, April 19, 1942.

20. *Seattle Post-Intelligencer*, April 23, 1942.

21. Japanese Evacuation Report #9, April 9, 1942, Joseph Conard Collection, box 3, folder Notebook, April 1942, Hoover Institution Archives (hereafter Joseph Conard Collection).

22. Japanese Evacuation Report #12, May 20, 1942, box 4, Joseph Conard Collection.

23. Inspection Report on Assembly Center at Toppenish, April 18, 1942, RG338, WDC-4 WCCA General Correspondence 1942–1946, box 90, file 600.4, National Archives, Washington, D.C.

24. Ibid.

25. Bill Hosokawa interview.

26. Emergency National Council Meeting at JACL Headquarters in San Francisco, March 8, 1942, minutes, Sakamoto papers.

27. Bill Hosokawa to Office of the National Secretary, May 7, 1942, Sakamoto papers, box 11.

28. *Japanese American Courier*, January 1, 1941; *Pacific Citizen*, December 23, 1955, A-11.

29. Miyamoto, "The Seattle JACL and Its Role in Evacuation," 32–34, Japanese American Evacuation and Resettlement Records (BANC MSS 67/14 c), folder T6.24, Bancroft Library, University of California Berkeley.

30. Bill Hosokawa to Office of the National Secretary, May 7, 1942, Sakamoto papers, box 11.

31. DeWitt to Senior Surgeon W. T. Harrison, March 28, 1942, in Daniels (ed.), *American Concentration Camps*, vol. 6.

32. Nobuko (Yanigamachi) Suzuki testimony before the Commission on Wartime Relocation and Internment of Civilians, Seattle, Washington, September 9–10, 1981, manuscript copy in the possession of the author; telephone interview with the author, December 18, 1995.

33. *Great Northern Daily News*, April 4, 8, 11, 13, 1942.

34. Ibid., April 17, 1945; *Final Report*, 193.

35. *Fellowship*, July 3, 1995.

36. For a biography of Abraham John Muste, see Hentoff, *Peace Agitator*.

37. Teletype message from Braun to Bendetsen, April 28, 1942, RG338, WDC & 4th Army, WCCA-CAD, General Correspondence, 1942–46, Box 22, file T. W. Braun.

38. *Seattle Times,* April 28, 1942.

39. Correspondence regarding FOR in RG338 WDC-4 WCCA CAD General Correspondence, 1942–46, box 15, file 080/Fellowship of Reconciliation. FOR helped care for the property of those incarcerated, and provided employment, sponsorship, and travel loans for those able to leave camp and settle in the East. In the United States FOR took action when the U.S. government ordered Japanese Americans into the assembly centers in 1942. FOR held public protests of the action and extended concrete help to the victims (such as caring for the property of those forcibly evacuated). A FOR member, Gordon Hirabayashi, refused to register for evacuation; his case went to the Supreme Court. FOR provided for visits to the camps and set up a travel loan fund to help resettle people after they were released from the relocation centers. The national office added a young Japanese American to its staff to inform school, church, and FOR groups what was happening to people of Japanese ancestry.

40. The family returned to Seattle from the Minidoka Relocation Center on January 22, 1945. Eight days later Sanzo died, leaving Matsuyo and the adult children to carry on the business. When the store was remodeled in 1957 while under the management of the two sisters, the name was changed to Higo Variety Store. Takami, *Divided Destiny,* 28, 48.

41. Sone, *Nisei Daughter,* 165–66.

42. Shigeko (Sese) Uno interview; *Japanese American Courier,* October 3, 1941.

43. Tamako (Inouye) Tokuda interview.

44. Jim Akutsu interview.

45. Sharon Aburano interview.

46. *Seattle Post-Intelligencer,* April 12, 1942.

47. Ads appearing in the classified advertising sections of the *Seattle Post-Intelligencer* and *Seattle Times,* from March 1 through April 30, 1942.

48. Houston and Houston, *Farewell to Manzanar,* 12–13.

49. John H. Tolan to Secretary of War Henry L. Stimson, February 23, 28, 1942, in Daniels (ed.), *American Concentration Camps,* vol. 3.

50. Taylor, "The Federal Reserve Bank and the Relocation of the Japanese in 1942"; Taylor, "Evacuation and Economic Loss," in Daniels, Taylor, and Kitano (eds.), *Japanese Americans,* 163–67.

51. Report of the Select Committee Investigating National Defense Migrations, HR Report No. 1911, 77th Congress, 2nd Session (March 19, 1942), 19–20, in Daniels (ed.), *American Concentration Camps,* vol. 6.

52. *Seattle Post-Intelligencer,* March 12, 1942.

53. *Personal Justice Denied,* 129–30.

54. For an account of a bureaucrat's mission to ensure that agricultural products were fully maintained and Japanese farms were transferred to "safe hands," see Hewes, *Boxcar In the Sand,* 159–75.

55. Tolan Hearings, Floyd Oles testimony, 11423.

56. *Seattle Post-Intelligencer,* March 5, 1942.

57. Quote cited in *Personal Justice Denied,* 126.
58. *Personal Justice Denied,* 126.
59. Tolan Hearings, Floyd Oles testimony, 11423.
60. *Seattle Times,* April 2, 1942.
61. *Great Northern Daily News,* April 2, 1942.
62. Tolan Hearings, Floyd Oles testimony, 11428. Tacoma Mayor Harry P. Cain made similar suggestions.
63. *Seattle Times,* April 15, 1942; *Great Northern Daily News,* April 16. 1942.
64. *Japanese American Courier,* April 17, 1942.
65. Farm Security Administration press release, April 17, 1942.
66. *Seattle Post-Intelligencer,* April 24, 1942.
67. *Seattle Times,* May 5, 6, 1942.
68. Shigeo Wakamatsu testimony, cited in *Personal Justice Denied,* 127.
69. Dick Nishi testimony, cited in *Personal Justice Denied,* 126.

Chapter 5. Exile

1. *Final Report,* 297–98; *Seattle Times,* March 24, 1942.
2. Daniels, *The Decision to Relocate the Japanese Americans,* 124–26.
3. Kenji Okuda to Norio Higano, May 12, 1942, Norio Higano Papers, box 1, file Kenji Okuda, Special Collections, University of Washington Libraries, Accession #2870.
4. James A. Hirabayashi, "Four Hirabayashi Cousins," in Fiset and Nomura (eds.), *Nikkei in the Pacific Northwest,* 155–58. See also Gordon Hirabayashi interview with Roger Daniels, February 3, 9, 1981, transcript of Tapes 536b/c, Special Collections, University of Washington Libraries.
5. Gordon Hirabayashi interview with Roger Daniels, February 3, 9, 1981; Irons, *Justice At War,* 84–93.
6. Gordon K. Hirabayashi, "Why I refused to register for evacuation," Ring Family Papers, box 1, file 17, Special Collections, University of Washington Libraries, Accession #4241-1.
7. Hirabayashi's case reached the Supreme Court in 1943. For details, see Irons, *Justice At War,* 219ff.
8. *Final Report,* 100.
9. For biographical details of Dr. Kyo Koike, including his life as an artist, see Zabilski, "Dr. Kyo Koike, 1878–1947."
10. *Japanese American Courier,* April 24, 1942.
11. *Seattle Post-Intelligencer,* April 23, 1942.
12. Naske, "The Relocation of Alaska's Japanese Residents."
13. An additional nine male German nationals and one Italian were included in the transfer. See "Alien enemies and Japanese evacuees," May 27, 1942, Office of Provost Marshal, Fort Richardson, Alaska, Headquarters, Alaska Defense Command, CWRIC 35:0426–0429.

14. The expulsion of Alaska's Nikkei population should not be confused with the evacuation of Aleuts from the Aleutian Islands, which began after the occupation of Attu and Kiska by Japanese Imperial forces in early June 1942. For details of this unrelated event, see Kohlhoff, *When the Wind Was a River.*

15. Buckner served as commander of the Alaska Defense Command and its successor the Alaskan Department until 1944, long after the threat of a Japanese invasion had passed. In 1944, he was given command of the newly formed Tenth U.S. Army and with it the task of taking Okinawa. The battle for Okinawa won on June 18, 1945, four days earlier Lieutenant General Buckner was killed by a shell fragment to the chest while directing his forces from an advanced observation post, the highest-ranking officer to die on the battlefield in the Pacific Theater.

16. Telegram, S. B. Buckner to Bartlett (acting governor), April 2, 1942, in Ronald K. Inouye, "The World War II Evacuation of Japanese-Americans from the Territory of Alaska," 75, unpublished 1973 compilation of archival documents, in CWRIC 35:435–644 (hereafter "The World War II Evacuation of Japanese-Americans from the Territory of Alaska," followed by document page numbers).

17. *Fairbanks Daily News Miner,* April 2, 1942, in "The World War II Evacuation of Japanese-Americans from the Territory of Alaska," 73. The proclamation reads as follows:

"By authority of Executive Order 9066 of the President of the U.S., dated February 20, 1942, and as an Army Commander designated thereunder by the Secretary of War, I, Simon B. Buckner, Jr., Commanding General of the Alaska Defense Command, do hereby declare the Territory of Alaska to be a military area which requires every possible protection against espionage and against sabotage to national defense material, national defense premises and national defense utilities as defined in Section 4, Act of April 20, 1918, as amended by the Act of November 30, 1940, and the Act of August 21, 1941, from which all persons being of Japanese race 16 years of age of half blood shall be excluded.

"Now, therefore, it is ordered and directed that all persons of Japanese blood as aforesaid whether American citizens or otherwise, to on April 20, 1942, report to the commanding officer of the army post most convenient to them in order that they may be transported to the continental limits of the U.S.

"In accordance with the above Executive order of the President of the U.S., it is required that all Executive departments, independent establishments and other federal agencies and other civil authorities give aid and assistance to said persons and the military authorities designated to the end that these orders may be carried out effectively and with a minimum of hardship to persons effected hereby."

18. Conn, Engleman, and Fairchild, *The Western Hemisphere,* 231.

19. *Fairbanks Daily News Miner,* April 18, 1942.

20. *Anchorage Daily Times,* April 18, 1942, in "The World War II Evacuation of Japanese-Americans from the Territory of Alaska," 91–92.

21. In a letter to acting Governor Bartlett Russell Maynard, director of the Department of Public Welfare, pleaded his case that the majority of the sixteen families eligible for relief concerned "native people living in the native manner," and should fall within the jurisdiction of the Office of Indian Affairs. In any event, the relief funds at his disposal would run out by the end of June 1942.

22. Russell G. Maynard to E. L. Barnett, April 22, 1942, in "The World War II Evacuation of Japanese-Americans from the Territory of Alaska," 98–101; Naske, "The Relocation of Alaska's Japanese Residents," 129, 132.

23. E. L. Bartlett to Alice Stuart, April 29, 1942, in "The World War II Evacuation of Japanese-Americans from the Territory of Alaska."

24. For additional details on the removal of Alaska's Japanese community in World War II, see Naske, "The Relocation of Alaska's Japanese Residents," 124–32.

25. "Japanese Evacuation Report #11," May 12, 1942, box 4, Joseph Conard Collection.

26. *Final Report,* 186; a collection of original CEO posters and pamphlets may be found in the Calvin F. Schmid papers, box 3, Special Collections, University of Washington Libraries, Accession #2591-76-26.

27. Chin, (ed.), *Born in the USA,* 288–89.

28. Tamako (Inouye) Tokuda interview.

29. For example, on May 8 nine private automobiles with a total of ten occupants drove in a convoy to Camp Harmony, escorted by army military police.

30. "Japanese Evacuation Report #10," April 30, 1942, box 3, folder Notebook, April 1942, Joseph Conard Collection.

31. "Japanese Evacuation Report #11," May 12, 1942, box 4, Joseph Conard Collection.

32. U.S. Department of Commerce, Weather Bureau, "Climatological Data Washington Sector," vol. 46 (Nos. 4–9), 1942.

33. Sone, *Nisei Daughter,* 171.

34. "Japanese Evacuation Report #11," May 12, 1942, box 4, Joseph Conard Collection.

35. U.S. Department of the Interior, *The Evacuated People,* 8.

36. Shigeko Uno interview.

37. Ibid.

38. "Civilian Exclusion Order No. 40" (CEO No. 40), Calvin F. Schmid papers.

39. For a discussion of mixed marriages in the Japanese community through the World War II period, see Spickard, *Mixed Blood,* and Spickard, "Injustice Compounded," 5–22.

40. *Final Report,* 145–47.

41. Memorandum from Major Herman P. Goebel, Jr., July 12, 1942, RG338, Records

182 · NOTES TO PAGES 93–100

of U.S. Army Commands Western Defense Command & 4th Army, WCCA-CAD Microfilm copy of the records of the Assembly Centers, 1942–1945, Box 9, Reel 108.

42. E. Sandquist to All Assembly Center Managers, July 17, 1942, RG338, Records of U.S. Army Commands Western Defense Command & 4th Army, WCCA-CAD Microfilm copy of the records of the Assembly Centers, 1942–1945, Box 9, Reel 108.

43. *Final Report*, 145–47.

44. *Seattle Star*, April 24, 1942.

45. "Evacuation Population Changes of Puyallup Assembly Center by Days: April 28, 1942–September 12, 1942," RG338, WDC & 4th Army, WCCA-CAD, General Correspondence, 1942–46, box 15.

46. *Final Report*, Table 52, 374.

47. The policy extended into the early relocation center period. A total of 465 individuals of Japanese ancestry were released for residence in the evacuated area. *Final Report*, 146.

48. *Northwest Enterprise*, May 15, 1942.

49. Ibid., May 23, 1942.

50. Ibid., February 27, May 15, 1942.

51. For details of employment of African Americans in Seattle during World War II, see Berner, *Seattle Transformed*, 50–55, and Taylor, *The Forging of a Black Community*, 160–66.

52. Miyamoto, "Reminiscences of JERS," 144.

53. Former evacuees revealed their feelings publicly during testimony before the Commission on Wartime Relocation and Internment of Citizens in 1981. For excerpts from this testimony, see *Personal Justice Denied*.

54. Sone, *Nisei Daughter*, 177–78.

Chapter 6. Settling In

1. Tamako (Inouye) Tokuda interview.

2. Sharon (Tanagi) Aburano interview.

3. "Narrative Report—Puyallup Assembly Center," May 2, 1942, RG 338, Records of U.S. Army Commands WDC & 4th Army, WCCA & CAD Microfilm copy of the records of the Assembly centers, 1942–1945, Box 9, Reel 108.

4. "Narrative Report—Puyallup Assembly Center," May 6, 1942.

5. Hosokawa, *Out of the Frying Pan*, 35.

6. Tamako (Inouye) Tokuda interview; Sharon (Tanagi) Aburano interview.

7. Paul S. Shigaya, M.D. prescription, July 13, 1942, RG 338, Records of U.S. Army Commands WDC & 4th Army, WCCA & CAD Microfilm copy of the records of the Assembly centers, 1942–1945 (General Correspondence), Box 1, ACB Roll #7.

8. Shosuke Sasaki diary entry, in Chin, *Born in the USA*, 290.

9. Sone, *Nisei Daughter*, 175.

10. "Japanese Evacuation Report #11," May 12, 1942, box 4, Joseph Conard Collection.

11. Jim Akutsu interview; "Narrative Report—Puyallup Assembly Center," June 1, 1942.

12. "Narrative Report—Puyallup Assembly Center," May 18, 1942.

13. Tolan Hearings, Rev. Harold V. Jensen testimony, 11568.

14. Dye, "For the Sake of Seattle's Soul," 127–36.

15. Duntley, "Japanese and Filipino Together"; "Maryknoll Pupils Say 'Goodbye' to their School Here," *Catholic Northwest Progress*, April 20, 1942.

16. Duntley, "Japanese and Filipino Together"; *Pacific Citizen*, August 6, 1942.

17. "Consolation of Faith Cheers Japanese Catholics under Evacuation Ordeal," *Catholic Northwest Progress*, May 1, 1942.

18. DeBiase, "Neither Harmony nor Eden."

19. Sone, *Nisei Daughter*, 185–86.

20. Emery E. Andrews papers, boxes 1–3, Accession #1908-001/003, Special Collections, University of Washington Libraries (hereafter Emery Andrews papers).

21. American Friends Service Committee Bulletin No. 2, February 25, 1942, box 2, folder 9, Emery Andrews papers.

22. For an account of Buddhists and their general incarceration experience, see Williams, "Camp Dharma."

23. *Camp Harmony-Newsletter*, July 18, 1942; Magden, *Furusato*, 139. Reverend Pratt spent the next forty-five years teaching Nisei and Caucasian study groups in Seattle, White River, and Tacoma. See Tacoma Buddhist Church History at www.tacomabt .org/history.htm; Williams, "From Pearl Harbor to 9/11," 67.

24. Smith, "New Deal Public Works at War," 63–92.

25. *Final Report*, 46–47. *Camp Harmony News-Letter*, August 14, 1942.

26. "Assigned Personnel as of May 6, 1942: Puyallup Assembly Center," RG 338 WDC & 4th Army WCCA & CAD General Correspondence, 1942–1946, box 58, folder Puyallup AC.

27. R. L. Nicholson to Robert F. Turner, April 28, 1942, RG 338, Records of U.S. Army Commands WDC & 4th Army, WCCA & CAD Microfilm copy of the records of the Assembly centers, 1942–1945, Box 9, Reel 108.

28. *Camp Harmony News-Letter*, May 7, 1942.

29. U.S. Department of the Interior, *The Evacuated People*, Table 22, 70.

30. Interviews with Iwao Matsushita, December 15, 1975–April 12, 1976, by Carol Zabilski, transcripts in author's possession; Zabilski, "Dr. Kyo Koike, 1878–1947"; Lee, "'Good American Subjects Done through Japanese Eyes.'"

31. Fiset, "Public Health in World War II Assembly Centers for Japanese Americans."

32. Dr. Kyo Koike to Iwao Matsushita, June 9, 1942, Iwao Matsushita Papers, Box 9, Special Collections, University of Washington Libraries.

33. "Narrative Report—Puyallup Assembly Center," April 25, 1942; *Camp Harmony News-Letter*, May 5, 1942.

34. "Service Division Report," RG 338, Records of U.S. Army Commands WDC &

4th Army, WCCA & CAD Microfilm copy of the records of the Assembly centers, 1942–1945, Box 9, Reel 108.

35. Takezawa, *Breaking the Silence*, 88.

36. "Report of Activities in the Japanese evacuation from the West Coast, June 2, 1942," 9, in Daniels (ed.), *American Concentration Camps*, vol. 6.

37. "Report of Activities in the Japanese Evacuation from the West Coast, June 2, 1942," 8–9.

38. Three exceptions to this rule were Manzanar, Santa Anita, and Pomona, where, combined, more than thirty thousand residents were housed. Here hospitals were established to handle all medical, surgical, and obstetrical cases except those requiring specialized treatments and sophisticated equipment.

39. "Narrative Report—Puyallup Assembly Center," May 18, 1942.

40. Ibid., May 26, 1942.

Chapter 7. Early Departures and a New Community

1. Between 1939 and 1945, nearly 1.5 million farm workers left for military service or for defense industry jobs, representing 30 percent of the farm labor force. See Wilcox, *The Farmer in the Second World War,* 54–56. For a history of the participation of Japanese Americans from assembly centers and relocation centers as agricultural workers, see Fiset, "Thinning, Topping and Loading."

2. "Tolan Report 2124," 197–98, in Daniels (ed.), *American Concentration Camps,* vol. 5.

3. M. S. Eisenhower to Claude R. Wickard, April 10, 1942, in Daniels (ed.), *American Concentration Camps,* vol. 4.

4. "Report on meeting, April 7, at Salt Lake City, with governors, attorneys general, and other state and federal officials of ten western states," in Daniels (ed.), *American Concentration Camps,* vol. 4.

5. Caldwell, *Idaho News-Tribune,* May 26, 1942.

6. *Idaho Free Press,* May 22, 1942.

7. Sims, "Japanese Americans in Idaho," 106.

8. *Boise Capital News,* May 23, 1942.

9. *Camp Harmony News-Letter,* May 23, 1942.

10. Milton Eisenhower to John J. McCloy, assistant secretary of war, June 8, 1942, in Daniels (ed.), *American Concentration Camps,* vol. 4.

11. "Evacuee Population Changes of Puyallup Assembly Center by Days: April 28, 1942–September 12, 1942," RG338, Box 15 (hereafter Puyallup Census).

12. Puyallup Census; *Final Report,* Table 52, 374.

13. Milton Eisenhower to the president, June 18, 1942, in Daniels (ed.), *American Concentration Camps,* vol. 4.

14. For more details on the seasonal work leave program, see Fiset, " Thinning, Topping and Loading;" see *Final Report,* 245, and 373–75 for an alternate handling of data.

15. O'Brien, *The College Nisei*, 135–37; Okihiro, *Storied Lives.*

16. *University of Washington Daily*, April 2, 1942.

17. Austin, *From Concentration Camp to Campus*, 7.

18. Ibid., 14, 23.

19. Colorado, Illinois, Iowa, Massachusetts, Missouri, Minnesota, New York, North Carolina, Ohio, South Dakota, and Washington. Austin, *From Concentration Camp to Campus*, 23.

20. *University of Washington Daily*, May 12, 1942.

21. Thomas R. Bodine to J. J. McGovern, June 4, 1942, RG338, Reel 108; "Final Accountability Roster of the Minidoka Relocation Center October 1945," RG210, Records of the War Relocation Authority. This database lists the first address for each person leaving Minidoka and the type of leave clearance granted.

22. "Final Accountability Roster of the Minidoka Relocation Center October 1945."

23. For a list of most approved colleges and universities from this time period, see O'Brien, *The College Nisei*, 135–48.

24. Kenji Okuda interview; RG210, entry 22, file: Kenji Okuda; Oberlin, however, anxious to have this promising student, reserved a place for him for the second term, to begin in February 1943. After a visit to Oberlin College the previous June, Robert O'Brien reported "Kenji was the first student that they were most anxious to receive." Leave clearance would come on January 1, 1943, via a terse teletype message to the Granada (Amache) Relocation Center Project director from John H. Provines: "Kenji Okuda may be granted indefinite leave for student relocation."

25. Austin, *From Concentration Camp to Campus*, 96.

26. For greater detail of the dismissal of Nisei public employees in Washington State, including the University of Washington, see Fiset, "Redress for Nisei Public Employees in Washington State after World War II."

27. Ibid.; Nisei Veterans Committee, *Uncommon American Patriots*, 50.

28. For a diplomatic history of these two voyages, see Corbett, *Quiet Passages.*

29. "Narrative Report—Puyallup Assembly Center," June 9, 1942. Actual sailing of the exchange ship, destined for Lourenço Marques, Mozambique, via Rio de Janeiro, was June 18, at 11:22 p.m. U.S. Department of State, *Papers Relating to the Foreign Relations of the United States, 1939–1945*, vol. I, 434–35. All Japanese officials in the United States at the outbreak of war and all Japanese officials brought to the United States from Latin American countries at war with Japan repatriated on this voyage. Also on board were Japanese newspapermen and nonofficial Japanese nationals, including repatriates from the assembly centers and Justice Department camps and from Canada. The ship rendezvoused with the Japanese exchange vessels *Conte Verde* and *Asama Maru* July 22–26, 1942. On the return trip the *Gripsholm* sailed from Lourenço Marques on July 28 with 1,510 repatriating Westerners, matching the number of Japanese repatriates.

30. Memorandum of Captain Albert H. Moffitt Jr. to Colonel Karl R. Bendetsen,

June 15, 1942, Albert H. Moffitt papers, Box 4, File "Japanese Repatriation Trip to N.Y. 6/6/42," Hoover Institution archives; "List of Japanese Searched for Repatriation Purposes," Karl R. Bendetsen papers, Box 315, File Assistant Secretary of War—Mr. McCloy, Hoover Institution archives.

31. Moffitt memorandum.

32. An additional 417 Japanese repatriates boarded at Rio de Janeiro, bringing the total to 1,500.

33. The MS *Gripsholm* made eleven diplomatic voyages during World War II to repatriate civilians and wounded POWs on both sides of the conflict. See Fiset, "MS *Gripsholm* & the 1942–1943 Diplomatic Exchange Voyages with Japan."

34. *Final Report*, Table 42, 323.

35. RG338, WDC & 4th Army WCCA + CAD, General Unclassified Correspondence, 1942–1946, file 323.3 (hereafter RG338 Unclassified Correspondence, followed by box number and file).

36. *Camp Harmony News-Letter*, August 14, 1942.

37. "Report on Sanitation Facility—Japanese Assembly Center, Puyallup," May 28–29, June 26, July 16, July 31, August 12, 1942, RG338, Reel 108 (hereafter "A Report on Sanitation Facilities," followed by date).

38. N. E. Magnussen to J. J. McGovern, July 16, 1942, RG338, Reel 108.

39. "A Report on Sanitation Facilities," July 16, 1942.

40. "A Report on Sanitation Facilities," August 12, 1942.

41. U.S. Public Health Service District #5, "Report of activities in the Japanese evacuation from the West Coast, June 2, 1942," 9, in Daniels (ed.), *American Concentration Camps*, vol. 6.

42. Dr. Kyo Koike to Iwao Matsushita, June 9, 1942, Iwao Matsushita papers, box 9, file 4, Special Collections, University of Washington Libraries.

43. *Puyallup News-Letter*, August 1, 1942.

44. Smith, *Japanese American Midwives*, 170–72.

45. *Final Report*, Tables 19, 20, and 24, 199–200, 202.

46. Tom Montgomery to B. D. Box, June 13, 1942, RG338, Unclassified Correspondence, box 58, file Puyallup Assembly Center.

47. *Final Report*, 213.

48. For an autobiographical account of Hosokawa's life as a journalist, see Hosokawa, *Out of the Frying Pan*.

49. Eddie Sato Camp Harmony Sketchbook and Drawings (art original) 1942, Special Collections, University of Washington Libraries, Photograph Collection 664.

50. The text of all *News-Letter* issues may be found at www.lib.washington.edu/exhibits/harmony/Newsletter/; for a microfilm version of the originals, see *Japanese Relocation Camp Papers World War II*, Microform and Newspaper Collections, University of Washington Libraries, uncatalogued No. 316.

51. Girdner and Loftis, *The Great Betrayal*, 184.

52. The one exception was the Mayer Assembly Center, in Arizona, which held

245 inmates. The center manager arranged for twice daily trips to the post office in the nearby town.

53. Lester S. Diehl to All Assembly Center Managers, May 25, 1942, RG338, Reel 108.

54. E. V. Livingston to J. J. McGovern, May 22, 1942, RG338, Reel 108.

55. *Camp Harmony News-Letter,* July 18, 1942.

56. "WCCA Operations Manual," paragraphs XVII, XXV, RG 210, Entry 7, Box 5, file WCCA, National Archives, Washington, D.C.

57. Broderick and Mayo, *Civil Censorship.*

58. DeWitt to Army Chief of Staff, May 26, 1942, RG338, Unclassified Correspondence, box 15.

59. Colonel Karl R. Bendetsen to Commanding General, WDC & 4th Army, May 27, 1942, RG338, Unclassified Correspondence, box 15.

60. For an example of censored mail from Tule Lake, see letter to Kiyoka Kumagai, June 30, 1942, James Y. Sakamoto Papers, box 10, File 15, Special Collections, University of Washington Libraries. Girdner and Loftus, *The Great Betrayal,* 185, discuss censorship of incoming mail to Tanforan Assembly Center.

61. Memorandum from Colonel Karl R. Bendetsen to chief of staff, WDC & 4th Army, July 13, 1942, Karl R. Bendetsen Papers, Box 312, Folder Confidential Staybacks, C.A.D. Hoover Institution on War, Revolution and Peace, Stanford University. For a discussion of censored mail in the Justice Department camps, see Fiset, *Imprisoned Apart,* chap. 6.

62. "Japanese Assembly Center at Puyallup," September 8, 1942, Church Council of Greater Seattle Records, box 15, folder 17, Accession 1358-7, Special Collections, University of Washington Libraries.

63. Perceived by the army to be a form of state religion, Shinto services were forbidden in all assembly centers.

64. "Council of Churches Visitors' Agreement," May 20, 1942, Church Council of Greater Seattle Records, box 15, folder 21.

65. Everett Thompson to Frank Herron Smith, June 24, 1942, Church Council of Greater Seattle Records, box 15, folder 1.

66. Unsigned report to Lowell White, June 6, 1942, RG338, Reel 108.

67. *Camp Harmony News-Letter,* May 14, 1942.

68. Ibid., June 17, 1942.

69. Until June 1, Camp Harmony inmates had access to the post exchange store (canteen) for the army's military police contingent assigned to guard them. Ibid., July 18, 1942; "WCCA Operations Manual," Paragraph XV.

70. Camp Harmony News-Letter, June 25, July 18, 1942.

71. Unsigned report to Lowell White, June 6, 1942, RG338, Reel 108.

72. *Camp Harmony News-Letter,* August 1, 1942.

73. Ibid., June 2, 1942.

74. Ibid., June 12, 1942.

75. Richard Weir to J. J. McGovern, June 8, 1942, RG338, Reel 108. On May 18, 2008, during a ceremony at the University of Washington honoring Japanese Americans whose educations there were interrupted by the war, 200 in attendance, of the 450 former students, received honorary degrees. *Seattle Times*, May 19, 2008.

76. *Camp Harmony News-Letter*, various issues.

77. Tamako (Inouye) Tokuda interview.

Chapter 8. Dissension

1. Kitano, "The Effects of Evacuation on the Japanese Americans"; "Concentration Camp: U.S. Style," *The New Republic*, June 15, 1942.

2. "Concentration Camp: U.S. Style," *The New Republic*, June 15, 1942.

3. Nakashima's reference to "scant portions of canned wieners and boiled potatoes" puts the period he writes about at early to mid-May. Nakashima and his wife, Masako, were evacuated from Seattle on May 1 under Civilian Exclusion Order No. 18.

4. "Conditions at Camp Harmony," *The New Republic*, January 18, 1943.

5. "Narrative Report—Puyallup Assembly Center," May 26, 1942, RG338, Records of U.S. Army Commands, Western Defense Command and Fourth Army, WCCA and Civil Affairs Division, Microfilm Copy of the Records of the Assembly Centers, 1942–1945, Box 9, Roll 108, National Archives, College Park, Md. hereafter RG338, WCCA Puyallup Assembly Center Microfilm Records, followed by roll number).

6. Sakamoto to Dr. Kyo Koike, May 25, 1942, cited in "Report of Inspection Puyallup Assembly Center," May 29, 1942, RG338 WDC-4th Army, WCCA and Civilian Affairs Division, General Correspondence 1942–1946, box 58, file—Puyallup Assembly Center.

7. "Report of Inspection Puyallup Assembly Center," May 29, 1942, RG338 WDC-4th Army, WCCA and Civilian Affairs Division, General Correspondence 1942–1946, box 58, file—Puyallup Assembly Center.

8. J. J. McGovern to R. L. Nicholson, June 1, 1942, RG338, WCCA Puyallup Assembly Center Microfilm Records, Roll 108.

9. J. J. McGovern to R. L. Nicholson, June 9, 1942, RG338, WCCA Puyallup Assembly Center Microfilm Records, Roll 108.

10. Sakamoto to J. J. McGovern, June 9, 1942, James Y. Sakamoto papers, Box 10, Folder 19, Special Collections, University of Washington libraries, Accession #1609-001.

11. J. J. McGovern to R. L. Nicholson, June 16, 1942, RG338, WCCA Puyallup Assembly Center Microfilm Records, Roll 108.

12. Nicholson to assembly center directors, May 31, 1942, cited in Taylor, *Jewel of the Desert*, 79.

13. Girdner and Loftis, *The Great Betrayal*, 185–89.

14. "W.C.C.A. Operation Manual," Chapter XXVIII (revised August 1, 1942), Headquarters Records, RG 210, Entry 7, Box 5, File—WCCA, National Archives, Washington, D.C.

15. Modell (ed.), *The Kikuchi Diary,* 216, 230–31.

16. Sakamoto to J. J. McGovern, June 15, 1942, Sakamoto papers, Box 10, Folder 19, Accession #1609-001.

17. Sakamoto to All Area Directors, June 15, 1952 (*sic*), Hiroyuki Ichihara papers, Special Collections, University of Washington Libraries, Accession 4761-001, Reel 1.

18. *Camp Harmony News-Letter,* June 17, 1942.

19. McGovern to Japanese Advisory Council, June 20, 1942, Hiroyuki Ichihara papers, Special Collections, University of Washington Libraries, Accession 4761-001, Reel 1.

20. McGovern to Dr. Koike, June 16, 1942, Hiroyuki Ichihara papers, Special Collections, University of Washington Libraries, Accession 4761-001, Reel 1.

21. Area "A" residents to James Sakamoto, June 23, 1942, Sakamoto papers, Box 10, Folder 14, Accession #1609-001.

22. Sakamoto to The Area A Petitioners, July 2, 1942, Sakamoto papers, Box 10, Folder 19, Accession #1609-001.

23. "Japanese (Nisei-Kibei) Questionnaire," July 9, 1942, CWRIC 23:193–200.

24. Lim, "Research Report prepared for Presidential Select Committee on JACL Resolution #7."

25. Major W. B. Parsons to Assistant Chief of Staff G-2, (CIB), July 9, 1942, CWRIC 23:193–200.

26. Perhaps McGovern made good on his promise since Hosokawa later became editor of *The Heart Mountain Sentinel.*

27. Masuda and family were sent to the Colorado River (Poston) Relocation Center; Ito to the Tule Lake Relocation Center; Hosokawa to the Heart Mountain Relocation Center; Mimbu to the Stockton Assembly Center and subsequently to the Rohwer (McGehee) Relocation Center; Okuda to the Merced Assembly Center and relocated to the Amache (Granada) Relocation Center; and Suyetani to the Gila River Relocation Center.

28. Bill Hosokawa interview.

29. Chin, *Born in the USA,* 292–93.

30. Lieutenant Colonel A. K. Stebbins Jr. to assistant chief of staff, WDC-4th Army, August 3, 1942, RG338, WDC & 4th Army WCCA + CAD, General Unclassified Correspondence, 1942–1946, file—000.51.

31. Major W. F. Durbin to Mr. Fryer, WRA, August 7, 1942, RG338, WDC & 4th Army WCCA + CAD, General Unclassified Correspondence, 1942–1946, file—000.51.

32. Masuda later attempted to enlist in the army to serve as a linguist with the Military Intelligence Service. He was turned down because of his poor mastery of Japanese. Robert P. Patterson to Honorable Warren Magnuson, July 12, 1943, Thomas Masuda personal file.

33. RG210, Entry 22, file—Thomas Masuda.

34. Kenji Ito leave clearance hearing, RG210, Entry 22, file—Kenji Ito.

35. "Japanese Evacuation and Relocation in the Thirteenth Naval District to March 10, 1943," CWRIC 2:1534–73.

36. Internal Security Section internal memo, August 8, 1942, RG338, WCCA Puyallup Assembly Center Microfilm Records, Roll 108.

37. Hosokawa writes about his banishment in *Out of the Frying Pan* (40–45), citing archival documents he "pried from federal archives through the Freedom of Information Act [FOIA]." Earlier, in preparation for a 1995 interview, the author provided Hosokawa copies of these same documents to assist him with recall of events occurring half a century earlier. The National Archives in Washington, D.C., currently provides open access to the personal files of incarcerated Japanese Americans, thereby making use of FOIA unnecessary.

38. Bill Hosokawa to Dillon S. Myer, March 9, 1943, RG210, Entry 22, file—William K. Hosokawa.

39. Suyetani's detention ended on April 20, one week prior to the first mass movement of evacuees from Seattle, RG210, Entry 22, file—Roy K. Suyetani; Ito (ed.), *Issei*, 749–54.

40. Charles E. Johnston to J. J. McGovern, July 18, 1942, RG338, WCCA Puyallup Assembly Center Microfilm Records, Roll 108.

41. Ibid. Later Suyetani's wife and children sought and received a transfer to Minidoka, leaving Suyetani behind at Gila River. While in Idaho she filed divorce proceedings. Suyetani ran a large gambling operation out of his apartment at Gila River, was caught, and was subsequently denied leave clearance. RG 210, Entry #22, file—Kiyoshi Roy Suyetani.

42. "Conditions Existing at Japanese Evacuation Center, Puyallup, Washington," August 14, 1942, RG338, WDC & 4th Army WCCA + CAD, General Unclassified Correspondence, 1942–1946, file—Thirteenth Naval District.

43. Ibid.; Philip Glick to War Relocation Authority director, November 26, 1943, RG210, Entry 22, file—William Mimbu.

44. Internal Security Section internal memo, August 8, 1942.

45. "Conditions Existing at Japanese Evacuation Center, Puyallup, Washington," August 14, 1942.

46. Fiset, "Redress for Nisei Public Employees," 27.

47. "Conditions Existing at Japanese Evacuation Center, Puyallup, Washington," August 14, 1942.

48. In the 1970s, Sasaki helped form a Seattle group dedicated to seeking redress from the U.S. government for the incarceration.

49. Chin (ed.), *Born in the USA*, 292–93; Shosuke Sasaki interview. Sasaki's assassination plot narrative has never been corroborated, and by now all of the participants are dead.

50. *Final Report*, Table 57, 381–82.

Chapter 9. Leaving Camp Harmony

1. *Camp Harmony News-Letter*, May 13, June 12, 25, 1942.

2. *Final Report*, Table 33, 282; *Camp Harmony News-Letter*, July 18, 1942.

3. *Camp Harmony News-Letter,* August 14, 1942.

4. *Final Report,* 287–88.

5. *Camp Harmony News-Letter,* August 14, 1942.

6. *Final Report,* 275–76.

7. "Report of the Evacuation of Puyallup Assembly Center," no date, RG338, WCCA Puyallup Assembly Center Microfilm Records, Roll 108.

8. "Report of the Evacuation of Puyallup Assembly Center," no date, RG338, WCCA Puyallup Assembly Center Microfilm Records, Roll 108. For a complete list of transfer dates and the number of transferees in each movement, see *Final Report,* Table 33, 282–84.

9. Tsuchida (ed.), *Reflections,* 237–62.

10. Sone, *Nisei Daughter,* 190.

11. *Final Report,* 282–84, 288.

12. T. S. McGowan, MD, to Sector Transportation Office, 44th Infantry, Fort Lewis, August 19, 1942, RG338, WCCA Puyallup Assembly Center Microfilm Records, Roll 108.

13. Ibid.

14. Margaret (Baba) Yasuda diary entry for August 18, 1942, copy in the author's possession.

15. Tamako (Inouye) Tokuda interview.

16. May K. Sasaki, transcript of videotaped interview, October 28, 1997, *Densho: The Japanese American Legacy Project,* www.densho.org/.

17. Sone, *Nisei Daughter,* 191.

18. Tamako (Inouye) Tokuda interview.

19. *Minidoka Irrigator,* September 10, 1942, 4.

20. Margaret (Baba) Yasuda diary entry, August 19, 1942.

21. The regular movement by transfer orders to Minidoka included 7,149 from the Puyallup Assembly Center and 2,318 from the Portland Assembly Center. See *Final Report,* Table 33, 282–83.

22. *Minidoka Irrigator,* September 10, 1942.

23. *Final Report,* 248.

24. Burton, Farrell, Lord, and Lord, *Confinement and Ethnicity,* 203–14.

25. Sakoda was employed by the University of California–sponsored Japanese Evacuation and Resettlement Study (JERS). He was at Minidoka Relocation Center from 1944 to 1945. Hansen (ed.), *Japanese American World War II Evacuation Oral History Project,* 401.

26. Chase, "'My Dear Bishop.'"

27. Mary Hirata, transcript of videotaped interview, March 22, 1998, *Densho: The Japanese American Legacy Project,* www.densho.org/.

28. Sone, *Nisei Daughter,* 193.

29. By transfer order—89,698; by direct evacuation—18,249; and by other movement—2,414. See *Final Report,* Table 32, 279.

30. Forty-six others were confined in penal institutions completing sentences for petty crimes.

31. Victor Nielsen, "Supplemental Report," unpublished manuscript, 470–72, Edward N. Barnhart Papers, Box 1, Hoover Institution, Stanford University.

32. U.S. Department of the Interior, *The Evacuated People*, Table 1, 9. Tables 86 and 87 also provide data on institutionalized persons.

33. "Evacuee Population Changes of Puyallup Assembly Center by Days: April 28, 1942–September 12, 1942," RG338, Box 15.

34. Teletype message from R. F. Turner to J. J. McGovern, August 8, 1942, RG338, WCCA Puyallup Assembly Center Microfilm Records, Roll 108. Camp Harmony inmates serving sentences in the King County jail were returned to the center prior to September 12 in time to participate in one of the scheduled transfers to Minidoka. Thus, no one remained behind in penal institutions.

35. U.S. Department of the Interior, *The Evacuated People*, Table 87, 189; Western State Hospital Records 1871–1979, General Subject Files, Box 29, Folder—Japanese Patients 1942–1945, Accession #95–A-213, Washington State Archives, Olympia (hereafter Western State Hospital records).

36. Western State Hospital Records 1871–1979, General Subject Files, Box 29, Folder—Japanese Patients 1942–1945, Western State Hospital records. As of February 28, 1942, the total patient population at Western State Hospital was 2,809, of which 1,149 (41 percent) were from King County. Thus, Japanese Americans represented less than one percent of the total patient population there.

37. Supervisor of State Institutions R. A. McGee to All Superintendents, May 28, 1942, Western State Hospital records.

38. Hospital census dated July 17, 1942; W. T. Harrison to Superintendent Western State Hospital, August 18, 1942, Western State Hospital records.

39. Memorandum #628 from State Department of Social Security to State Staff, July 29, 1942, Western State Hospital records.

40. Memorandum #651 from State Department of Social Security to State Staff, September 1, 1942, Western State Hospital records.

41. Elizabeth Ahrens to R. A. McGee, September 17, 1942, Western State Hospital records.

42. *Final Report*, 183–84.

43. Helphand, *Defiant Gardens*, 155–200.

44. Fiset, "Thinning, Topping and Loading," 134.

45. Sakoda, "Minidoka," 121–22; *Minidoka Irrigator*, April 24, May 15, 19, 1943.

46. U.S. Department of the Interior, *Community Government in War Relocation Centers*, 5.

Epilogue

1. Sharon Aburano interview.

2. For a history of the redress movement in the United States, see Maki, Kitano,

and Berthold, *Achieving the Impossible Dream*. For details focusing on the redress efforts in Seattle, see Shimabukuro, *Born in Seattle*.

3. Shimabukuro, *Born in Seattle*, 44.

4. Frank Chin, "Days of Remembrance," unpublished manuscript, 1978–79, cited in Shimabukuro, *Born in Seattle*, 43.

5. *Pacific Citizen*, September 9, 1983. Tsutakawa served with the Military Intelligence Service in World War II teaching Japanese to linguists at Fort Snelling, Minnesota. Some forty of his relatives were in assembly centers and relocation centers during the war, and several repatriated during the war. For details of Tsutakawa's life as an artist, see Kingsbury, *George Tsutakawa*.

Bibliography

Secondary Sources

Austin, Allan W. *From Concentration Camp to Campus: Japanese American Students and World War II.* Urbana: University of Illinois Press, 2004.

Bailey, Paul. *City in the Sun: The Japanese Concentration Camp at Poston, Arizona.* Los Angeles: Westernlore Press, 1971.

Berner, Richard C. *Seattle Transformed: World War II to Cold War.* Seattle: Charles Press, 1999.

Biddle, Francis. *In Brief Authority.* Garden City, N.Y.: Doubleday & Co., 1962.

Broderick, Wilfrid N., and Dann Mayo. *Civil Censorship in the United States during World War II.* Kansas City, Mo.: Civil Censorship Study Group, 1980.

Burton, Jeffery F., Eleanor Roosevelt, and Irene J. Cohen. *Confinement and Ethnicity: An Overview of World War II Japanese American Relocation Sites.* Seattle: University of Washington Press, 2002.

Chase, Jane. "'My Dear Bishop': A Report from Minidoka." *Idaho Yesterdays* 44, no. 2 (2000): 3–6.

Chin, Frank (ed.). *Born in the USA: A Story of Japanese America, 1889–1947.* New York: Rowan & Littlefield Publishers, Inc., 2002.

Conn, Stetson, Rose C. Engleman, and Byron Fairchild. *The Western Hemisphere: Guarding the United States and Its Outposts.* Washington, D.C.: Department of the Army, 1964.

Corbett, P. Scott. *Quiet Passages: The Exchange of Civilians between the United States and Japan during the Second World War.* Kent, Ohio: The Kent State University Press, 1987.

Daniels, Roger. *Asian America: Chinese and Japanese in the United States Since 1850.* Seattle: University of Washington Press, 1988.

———. "The Bureau of the Census and the Relocation of the Japanese Americans: A Note and A Document." *Amerasia Journal* 9, no. 1(1982): 101–5.

———. *Concentration Camps USA: Japanese Americans and World War II.* New York: Holt, Rinehart and Winston, Inc., 1971.

———. *The Decision to Relocate the Japanese Americans.* New York: J. P. Lippincott Company, 1975.

———. *Prisoners Without Trial: Japanese Americans in World War II.* New York: Hill and Wang, rev. ed., 2004.

Daniels, Roger (ed.). *American Concentration Camps: A Documentary History of the Relocation and Incarceration of Japanese Americans, 1942–1945.* 9 vols. New York: Garland Publishing, 1989.

Daniels, Roger, Sandra C. Taylor, and Harry H. L. Kitano (eds.). *Japanese Americans: From Relocation to Redress.* Seattle: University of Washington Press, rev. ed., 1991.

de Barros, Paul. *Jackson Street After Hours: The Roots of Jazz in Seattle.* Seattle: Sasquatch Books, 1993.

DeBiase, Linda Popp. "Neither Harmony nor Eden: Margaret Peppers and the Exile of the Japanese Americans." *Anglican and Episcopal History* 70 (March 2001): 101–17.

deNevers, Nancy Clark. *The Colonel and the Pacifist: Karl Bendetsen, Perry Saito, and the Incarceration of Japanese Americans during World War II.* Salt Lake City: University of Utah Press, 2004.

Dubrow, Gail, with Donna Graves. *Sento at Sixth and Main.* Seattle: Seattle Arts Commission, 2002.

Dumond, Val. *Doin' the Puyallup: An Illustrated History of the Western Washington Fair since 1900.* Puyallup: Western Washington Fair Association, c. 1991.

Duntley, Madeline. "Japanese and Filipino Together: The Transethnic Vision of Our Lady Queen of Martyrs Parish." *U.S. Catholic Historian* 18, no. 1 (2000): 74–98.

Dye, Douglas. "For the Sake of Seattle's Soul: The Seattle Council of Churches, the Nikkei Community, and World War II." *Pacific Northwest Quarterly* (Summer 2002): 127–36.

Feeley, Francis McCollum. *A Strategy of Dominance: The History of an American Concentration Camp, Pomona, California.* New York: Brandywine Press, 1995.

Fiset, Louis. *Imprisoned Apart: The World War II Correspondence of an Issei Couple.* Seattle: University of Washington Press, 1997.

———. "In the Matter of Iwao Matsushita: A Government Decision to Intern a Seattle Japanese Enemy Alien in World War II. In Louis Fiset and Gail M. Nomura (eds.). *Nikkei in the Pacific Northwest: Japanese Americans and Japanese Canadians in the Twentieth Century.* Seattle: University of Washington Press, 2005, 215–35.

———. "MS *Gripsholm* & the 1942–1943 Diplomatic Exchange Voyages with Japan." *Postal History Journal* 140 (June 2008): 12–25.

———. "Public Health in World War II Assembly Centers for Japanese Americans." *Bulletin of the History of Medicine* 73 (1999): 565–84.

——. "Redress for Nisei Public Employees in Washington State after World War II." *Pacific Northwest Quarterly* 88, no. 1 (1997–98): 21–32.

——. "Thinning, Topping and Loading: Japanese Americans and Beet Sugar in World War II." *Pacific Northwest Quarterly* 90, no. 3 (1999): 123–39.

Fiset, Louis, and Gail M. Nomura (eds.). *Nikkei in the Pacific Northwest: Japanese Americans and Japanese Canadians in the Twentieth Century.* Seattle: University of Washington Press, 2005.

Flewelling, Stan. *Shirakawa: Stories from a Pacific Northwest Japanese American Community.* Auburn, Wash.: White River Valley Museum, 2002.

Friday, Chris. *Organizing Asian American Labor: The Pacific Coast Canned Salmon Industry, 1870–1942.* Philadelphia: Temple University Press, 1994.

Fujita-Rony, Dorothy B. *American Workers, Colonial Power: Philippine Seattle and the Transpacific West, 1919–1941.* Berkeley: University of California Press, 2003.

Girdner, Audrie, and Anne Loftis. *The Great Betrayal: The Evacuation of the Japanese-Americans During World War II.* London: The Macmillan Company, 1969.

Gorfinkel, Claire (ed.). *The Evacuation Diary of Hatsuye Egami.* Pasadena: Intentional Productions, 1995.

Grodzins, Morton. *Americans Betrayed: Politics and the Japanese Evacuation.* Chicago: University of Chicago Press, 1949.

Hansen, Arthur A. (ed.). *Japanese American World War II Evacuation Oral History Project: Part III—Analysts.* Munich: K. G. Saur, 1994.

Helphand, Kenneth L. *Defiant Gardens: Making Gardens in Wartime.* San Antonio: Trinity University Press, 2006.

Hentoff, Nat. *Peace Agitator.* New York: Macmillan, 1963.

Hewes, Laurence. *Boxcar In the Sand.* New York: Alfred A. Knopf, 1957.

Hirabayashi, James A. "Four Hirabayashi Cousins: A Question of Identity." In Louis Fiset and Gail M. Nomura (eds.). *Nikkei in the Pacific Northwest: Japanese Americans and Japanese Canadians in the Twentieth Century.* Seattle: University of Washington Press, 2005, 146–70.

Hosokawa, Bill. *JACL: In Quest of Justice.* New York: William Morrow and Company, Inc., 1982.

——. *Out of the Frying Pan: Reflections of a Japanese American.* Niwot: University Press of Colorado, 1998.

Houston, Jeanne Wakatsuki, and James D. Houston. *Farewell to Manzanar.* Boston: Houghton Mifflin Company, 1973.

Ichioka, Yuji. "A Study in Dualism: James Yoshinori Sakamoto and the *Japanese American Courier,* 1928–1942." *Amerasia Journal* 13, no. 2 (1986–87).

——. "Japanese Immigrant Labor Contractors and the Great Northern Railroad Companies, 1898–1907." *Labor History* 21 (1980): 325–50.

——. *The Issei: The World of the First Generation Japanese Immigrants 1885–1924.* New York: The Free Press, 1988.

Ichioka, Yuji (ed.). *Views from Within: The Japanese American Evacuation and Resettlement Study.* Los Angeles: UCLA Asian American Studies Center, 1989.

Irons, Peter. *Justice At War.* New York: Oxford University Press, 1983.

Ito, Kazuo (ed.). *Issei: A History of Japanese Immigrants in North America.* Seattle: Japanese Community Service, 1973.

Kashima, Tetsuden. *Judgment Without Trial: Japanese American Imprisonment in World War II.* Seattle: University of Washington Press, 2003.

Keefer, Louis E. *Italian Prisoners of War in America, 1942–1946.* New York: Praeger, 1992.

Kimmett, Larry, and Margaret Regis. *The Attack on Pearl Harbor: An Illustrated History.* Kingston, Wash.: Navigator Publishing, 1991.

Kingsbury, Martha. *George Tsutakawa.* Seattle: University of Washington Press, 1990.

Kitano, Harry H. L. "The Effects of Evacuation on the Japanese Americans." In Roger Daniels, Sandra C. Taylor, and Harry H. L. Kitano (eds.). *Japanese Americans: From Relocation to Redress.* Seattle: University of Washington Press, rev. ed., 1991, 151–58.

Kohlhoff, Dean. *When the Wind Was a River: Aleut Evacuation in World War II.* Seattle: University of Washington Press, 1995.

Krammer, Arnold. *Nazi Prisoners of War in America.* Chelsea, Mich.: Scarborough House, 1991.

Kumamoto, Bob. "The Search for Spies: American Counterintelligence and the Japanese American Community 1931–1942." *Amerasia Journal* 6, no. 2 (1979): 45–75.

Lee, Shelley Sang-Hee. "'Good American Subjects Done through Japanese Eyes': Race, Nationality, and the Seattle Camera Club, 1924–1929." *Pacific Northwest Quarterly* (Winter 2004): 24–35.

Lehman, Anthony L. *Birthright of Barbed Wire: The Santa Anita Assembly Center.* Los Angeles: Westernlore Press, 1970.

Linke, Konrad. "Tanforan: A Microhistoric Study of Social Patterns and Resistance in an American Assembly Center for Japanese Americans during World War II." Unpublished master's thesis, Friedrich-Schiller-University Jena, 2007, www.google .com/search?hl=en&q=konrad+linke+tanforan&btnG=Search.

Magden, Ronald E. *Furusato: Tacoma-Pierce County Japanese 1888–1977.* Nikkeijinkai: Tacoma Japanese Community Service, 1998.

Maki, Mitchell T., Harry H. L. Kitano, and S. Megan Berthold. *Achieving the Impossible Dream: How Japanese Americans Obtained Redress.* Urbana: University of Chicago Press, 1999.

Malone, Michael P. *James J. Hill: Empire Builder of the Northwest.* Norman: University of Oklahoma Press, 1996.

McKivor, June Mukai. *Kenjiro Nomura: An Artist's View of the Japanese American Internment.* Seattle: Wing Luke Museum, 1991.

Miyamoto, S. Frank. "Reminiscences of JERS." In Yuji Ichioka (ed.). *Views from Within: The Japanese American Evacuation and Resettlement Study.* Los Angeles: UCLA Asian American Studies Center, 1989.

————. *Social Solidarity among the Japanese in Seattle*. Seattle: University of Washington Press, 3rd ed., 1984 [c. 1939].

Modell, John (ed.). *The Kikuchi Diary: Chronicle from an American Concentration Camp: The Tanforan Journals of Charles Kikuchi*. Chicago: University of Illinois Press, 1993.

Naske, Claus-M. "The Relocation of Alaska's Japanese Residents." *Pacific Northwest Quarterly* 74 (1983): 124–32.

Niiya, Brian (ed.). *Encyclopedia of Japanese American History: An A-to-Z Reference from 1868 to the Present, Updated Edition*. New York: Checkmark Books, 2001.

Nisei Veterans Committee. *Uncommon American Patriots*. Seattle: Nisei Veterans Committee, 1991.

O'Brien, Robert W. *The College Nisei*. Palo Alto: Pacific Books, 1949.

Ochsner, Jeffrey Karl (ed.). *Shaping Seattle Architecture: A Historical Guide to the Architects*. Seattle: University of Washington Press, 1994.

Okamura, Raymond Y. "The Myth of Census Confidentiality." *Amerasia Journal* 8, no. 2 (1981): 111–20.

Okihiro, Gary. *Storied Lives: Japanese American Students and World War II*. Seattle: University of Washington Press, 1999.

Polks Seattle City Directory, 1941, 1942.

Prange, Gordon N. *At Dawn We Slept: The Untold Story of Pearl Harbor*. New York: McGraw Hill Book Company, 1981.

Prebish, Charles S., and Martin Bauman (eds.). *Westward Dharma: Buddhism Beyond Asia*. Berkeley: University of California Press, 2002.

Prothero, Stephen (ed.). *A Nation of Religions: The Politics of Pluralism in Multireligious America*. Chapel Hill: University of North Carolina Press, 2006.

Robinson, Greg. *By Order of the President: FDR and the Internment of Japanese Americans*. Cambridge, Mass.: Harvard University Press, 2001.

Sakoda, James Minoru. "Minidoka: An Analysis of Changing Patterns of Social Interaction." PhD dissertation, University of California, 1949.

Sale, Roger. *Seattle, Past to Present*. Seattle: University of Washington Press, 1976.

Schmid, Calvin F. *Social Trends in Seattle*. Seattle: University of Washington Press, 1944.

Schmid, Calvin F., Charles E. Nobbe, and Arlene E. Mitchell. *Nonwhite Races, State of Washington*. Olympia: Washington State Planning and Community Affairs Agency, 1968.

Seltzer, William, and Margo Anderson. "The Dark Side of Numbers: The Role of Population Data Systems in Human Rights Abuses." *Social Research 68, no. 2* (Summer 2001): 481–513.

Shimabukuro, Robert Sadamu. *Born in Seattle: The Campaign for Japanese American Redress*. Seattle: University of Washington Press, 2001.

Shorett, Alice. "A history of the Pike Place marketing district." Unpublished manuscript, 1972.

Shorett, Alice, and Murray Morgan. *The Pike Place Market: People, Politics and Produce*. Seattle: Pacific Search Press, 1982.

Sims, Robert C. "Japanese Americans in Idaho." In Roger Daniels, Sandra C. Taylor, and Harry H. L. Kitano, (eds.). *Japanese Americans: From Relocation to Redress*. Seattle: University of Washington Press, rev. ed., 1991, 103–11.

———. "The 'Free Zone' Nikkei: Japanese Americans in Idaho and Eastern Oregon in World War II." In Louis Fiset and Gail M. Nomura (eds.). *Nikkei in the Pacific Northwest: Japanese Americans and Japanese Canadians in the Twentieth Century*. Seattle: University of Washington Press, 2005, 236–53.

Smith, Jason Scott. "New Deal Public Works at War: The WPA and Japanese American Interment." *Pacific Historical Review* 72, no. 1 (2003): 63–92.

Smith, Susan. *Japanese American Midwives: Culture, Community, and Health Politics, 1880–1950*. Urbana: University of Illinois Press, 2005.

Sone, Monica. *Nisei Daughter*. Seattle: University of Washington Press, 1982 [1953].

Spickard, Paul F. "Injustice Compounded: Amerasians and Non-Japanese Americans in WW II Concentration Camps." *Journal of American Ethnic History* 5 (1986): 5–22.

———. *Mixed Blood: Intermarriage and Ethnic Identity in Twentieth-Century America*. Madison: University of Wisconsin Press, 1989.

Takahashi, Rita. "Japanese Americans in the Pacific Northwest: The Impact of Incarceration on Non-incarcerated Persons." Paper presented at the University of Washington Center for the Study of the Pacific Northwest conference "The Nikkei Experience in the Pacific Northwest," Seattle, Washington, May 4–5, 2000.

Takami, David. *Divided Destiny: A History of Japanese Americans in Seattle*. Seattle: Wing Luke Asian Museum, 1998.

Takezawa, Yasuko I. *Breaking the Silence: Redress and Japanese American Ethnicity*. Ithaca, N.Y.: Cornell University Press, 1995.

Taylor, Quintard. *The Forging of a Black Community: Seattle's Central District from 1870 through the Civil Rights Era*. Seattle: University of Washington Press, 1994.

Taylor, Sandra C. "Evacuation and Economic Loss: Questions and Perspectives." In Roger Daniels, Sandra C. Taylor, and Harry H. L. Kitano (eds.). *Japanese Americans: From Relocation to Redress*. Seattle: University of Washington Press, rev. ed., 1991, 163–67.

———. "The Federal Reserve Bank and the Relocation of the Japanese in 1942." *Public Historian* 5 (1983): 9–30.

———. *Jewel of the Desert: Japanese American Internment at Topaz*. Berkeley: University of California Press, 1993.

Tsuchida, John Nobuya (ed.). *Reflections: Memories of Japanese Women in Minnesota*. Covino, Calif.: Pacific Asia Press, 1994.

Tsutakawa, Mayumi. "The Political Conservatism of James Sakamoto's Japanese American Courier." Unpublished Master's thesis, University of Washington, 1976.

Tsutakawa, Mayumi, and Alan Chong Lau (eds.). *Turning Shadows Into Light*. Seattle: Young Pine Press, 1982.

Whitehead, Don. *The FBI Story: A Report to the People.* New York: Random House, 1956.

Wilcox, Walter. *The Farmer in the Second World War.* Ames: Iowa State College Press, 1947.

Williams, Duncan Ryuken. "Camp Dharma: Japanese-American Buddhist Identity and the Internment of World War II." In Charles S. Prebish and Martin Bauman (eds.). *Westward Dharma: Buddhism Beyond Asia.* Berkeley: University of California Press, 2002, 191–200.

———. "From Pearl Harbor to 9/11: Lessons from the Internment of Japanese American Buddhists." In Stephen Prothero (ed.). *A Nation of Religions: The Politics of Pluralism in Multireligious America.* Chapel Hill: University of North Carolina Press, 2006.

Zabilski, Carol. "Dr. Kyo Koike, 1878–1947: Physician, Poet, Photographer." *Pacific Northwest Quarterly* 68 (1977): 2–79.

U.S. Government Documents

Commission on Wartime Relocation and Internment of Citizens. *Personal Justice Denied.* Washington, D.C.: U.S. Government Printing Office, 1982.

Congressional Record, 77th Congress, Appendix, December 8, 1941.

United States. Commission on Wartime Relocation and Internment of Civilians, Boehm, Randolph (ed.). *Papers of the U.S. Commission on Wartime Relocation and Internment of Civilians. Part 1, Numerical File Archive.*

U.S. Bureau of the Census. *Sixteenth Census of the U.S., 1940, Population,* vol. 2.

U.S. Code Congressional Service, 1943, P.L. 507, 77th Congress, 2nd Session (S2208).

U.S. Congress. House, *Hearings before the Select Committee Investigating National Defense Migration, Part 30 Portland and Seattle Hearings.* Washington, D.C.: U.S. Government Printing Office, 1942.

U.S. Department of Commerce, Weather Bureau, "Climatological Data Washington Sector," vol. 46 (nos. 4–9), 1942.

U.S. Department of State. *Papers Relating to the Foreign Relations of the United States, 1939–1945.* Vol. I.

U.S. Department of the Interior. *Community Government in War Relocation Centers.* Washington, D.C.: U.S. Government Printing Office, 1946.

———. *The Evacuated People: A Quantitative Description.* Washington, D.C.: U.S. Government Printing Office, 1946.

———. *WRA: A Story of Human Conservation.* Washington, D.C.: U.S. Government Printing Office, 1946.

U.S. War Department. *Final Report: Japanese Evacuation from the West Coast, 1942.* Washington, D.C.: U.S. Government Printing Office, 1943.

Wingate, Roy. "Housing Survey of Evacuation Centers," July 31, 1942, CWRIC Reel 6:709–11.

Archives and Personal Papers

Hoover Institution, Stanford University, Stanford, California: Edward N. Barnhart
Papers. Joseph Conard Collection. Karl R. Bendetsen Papers.
National Archives, Washington, D.C.: Records of the War Relocation Authority.
Records of the Immigration and Naturalization Service.
National Archives, College Park, Maryland: Records of the Western Defense Command and 4th Army. Records of the Wartime Civil Control Administration.
University of California at Berkeley, Bancroft Library: Japanese American Evacuation and Resettlement Records.
University of Washington Libraries, Special Collections: Emery E. Andrews Papers.
Church Council of Greater Seattle Records. Norio Higano Papers. Hiroyuki Ichihara Papers. Ring Family Papers. Calvin F. Schmid papers. James Y. Sakamoto
papers. Iwao Matsushita Papers. Eddie Sato Camp Harmony Sketchbook and
Drawings.
Washington State Archives, Olympia: Arthur B. Langlie Papers. Western State Hospital Records.

Newspapers

Anchorage Daily Times
Boise Capital News
Caldwell, Idaho News-Tribune
Camp Harmony News-Letter
Catholic Northwest Progress
Engineering News-Record
Fairbanks Daily News Miner
Great Northern Daily News
Idaho Free Press
Japanese American Courier
Minidoka Irrigator
North American Times
Northwest Enterprise
Seattle Post-Intelligencer
Seattle Star
Seattle Times
Tacoma News Tribune
The New Republic
The Pacific Citizen
University of Washington Daily

Interviews and Oral Histories

Aburano, Sharon (Tanagi), audiotaped interview with the author, Seattle, Washington, August 10, 1995.
Akutsu, Jim, audiotaped interview with the author, Seattle Washington, July 25, 1995 and November 29–30, 1999.
Hosokawa, Bill, audiotaped interview with the author, Powell, Wyoming, May 20, 1995.
Ishikawa, Shigeto, audiotaped interview with the author, Powell, Wyoming, December 21, 1999.
Kazama, Sally (Shimanaka), audiotaped interview with the author, Seattle Washington, August 16, 1995.
O'Brien, Robert W. interview with Howard Droker, April 24, 1975, University of Washington Libraries Special Collections, Accession 2420.
Okuda, Kenji, audiotaped interview with the author, Seattle, Washington, August 9, 1995.
Sasaki, Shosuke, audiotaped interview with the author, Seattle, Washington, August 17, 1995.
Tazuma, Elmer, audiotaped interview with the author, Seattle, Washington, August 1, 1995.
Tokuda, Tamako (Inouye), audiotaped interview with the author, Seattle Washington, November 18, 1998.
Uno, Shigeko (Sese), audiotaped interview with the author, Seattle Washington, August 14, 1995.
Yasuda, Margaret (Baba), audiotaped interview with the author, Seattle, Washington, December 6, 7, 1999.

Websites

Camp Harmony News-Letter www.lib.washington.edu/exhibits/harmony/Newsletter/.
Densho: The Japanese American Legacy Project www.densho.org/.
 Mary Hirata, transcript of videotaped interview, March 22, 1998.
 May K. Sasaki, transcript of videotaped interview, October 28, 1997.
Lim, Deborah K. "Research Report prepared for Presidential Select Committee on JACL Resolution #7," 1990 (aka "The Lim Report"). www.resisters.com/study/LimTOC.htm.
Pearl Harbor Attack: Hearings Before the Joint Committee on the Investigation of the Pearl Harbor Attack, part 39: www.ibiblio.org/pha/pha/roberts/roberts.html.
Seltzer, William, and Margo Anderson. "After Pearl Harbor: The Proper Role of Population Data Systems in Time of War." www.uwm.edu/~margo/govstat/integrity.htm.
Tacoma Buddhist Church History, www.tacomabt.org/history.htm.

Index

ation, 89–90. *See also* American Friends
Service Committee
Braun, T. W. (Ted) (press relations consul-
tant), 72, 129
Buckner, General Simon B., Jr., 85, 86, 180n17;
killed on Okinawa, 180n15
Bureau of the Census, 55. *See also* Dedrick,
Dr. Calvert L.

Cain, Harry P., 42, 179n62
Camp Harmony, xiii–xiv, 5–6; advance volunteers to, 84–85; banishment of residents,
149–56; compared to other assembly
centers, 5–6; evacuation from Seattle, 87,
89–90; first day at, 98–100; food preparation at, 122–23; Gordon Hirabayashi and,
82, 84; graduation ceremonies, 140; inmate
workers, 136–38; layout of center, 63–66,
101; lending library, 139; moving in, 96–97;
population, 97, 98, 108, 112, 113; receives
Alaska contingent, 87; receives nickname,
5, 66; religious life at, 105–6, 134–36; sanitary conditions, 125–26; seasonal work
leave, 116; sports, 138; student resettlement,
116–20; vacation school, 139; WPA staffing,
106–7; youngest person inducted into, 92.
See also health care at Camp Harmony;
Puyallup Assembly Center (Washington);
recreation program at Camp Harmony
Camp Harmony News-Letter, 107, 136; censorship, 129; content, 129, 131; lapses in publication, 130; reports results of plebiscite,
147; souvenir edition, 122, 130, 157; speculation on move to Tule Lake, 156; sports
news, 138
Chase, Clark, 52, 118; guarantees safety of Japanese American workers, 116; "rat" speech
and impact, 115–16
Chin, Frank, 167
Chinese community, 2, 6, 9, 10, 15; businesses,
15; mixed-marriages, 92; population in
Seattle, 15
Chinese immigration, 2, 15
Chinese laborers, 2, 10
Civil Affairs Division (CAD), of WCCA, 49,
77
Civil Control Stations, 58, 77, 84. *See also en-
tries for specific sites*
Civilian Exclusion Orders (CEO), 14, 48, 55,
82, 120; deferments and, 91–92; list of, 58;
No. 1, 56, 57
Coffee, John M., 32, 38

contract laborers, 2–3
"cross-town" district, 16, 17, 170n7. *See also*
African American community
curfew, 49–50, 80; and Gordon Hirabayashi,
82–83; at Camp Harmony, 136, 141, 142,
146–47, 149

Dedrick, Dr. Calvert L., 55–57, 176n55
deferments from evacuation: permanent,
92–94; temporary, 90–92
Desimone, Joe, 31
DeWitt, General John L., 86; advocates martial law, 133–34; authorizes seasonal work
leave, 114; issues public proclamations, 48,
49, 50, 80; orders construction of assembly
centers, 64, 71; and proposed resettlement
projects, 53–54; U.S. Public Health Service
and, 70; and WCCA, 49, 106
disposal of property, 73–79
dissension, 141–55

Eisenhower, Milton S., 53, 54, 114
Emergency Defense Council (EDC), 6, 33, 42;
cooperation with WCCA, 68–70; members
of, 33–35
Evacuee Administration Headquarters, 33,
147; organization of, 68–70
Executive Order 8802, 95
Executive Order 9066, 40, 41, 44, 61, 95, 134;
and Alaska's Nikkei, 85, 180n17; impact
on Japanese community, 45–46, 47, 48, 51,
120, 153

Farm Security Administration (FSA), 15,
76–78, 115
Federal Bureau of Investigation (FBI), 31,
39, 44, 70, 82, 151–52; arrests of Buddhist
priests, 105; arrests of enemy aliens, 25–29;
Kibei Survey and, 148; Nisei informants
and, 34, 36, 152, 166; second wave of arrests, 45–46; students and, 119
Federal Reserve Bank (FRB), 73, 76–77
Federal Security Agency, 83–84, 114
Filipino community, 6, 9, 10, 15; farmers, 78;
labor pool, 16; mixed marriage exemption
from incarceration, 92; Seattle census, 15;
and Seattle's Maryknoll School, 103
Fleming, Samuel, 44
food, 108; field rations, 122; food poisoning,
110–11; menu, 123; shortage, 100; Vienna
sausages, 100, 110
Ford, Leland M., 37–39

LOUIS FISET is the author of *Imprisoned Apart: The World War II Correspondence of an Issei Couple* (University of Washington Press, 1997) and coeditor of *Nikkei in the Pacific Northwest: Japanese Americans and Japanese Canadians in the Twentieth Century* (University of Washington Press, 2005). He has published numerous essays on Japanese Americans and the internment, including topics on medicine and health care in the assembly centers. He has appointments in the University of Washington's dental and medical schools, where he helps train Alaska Natives to provide midlevel dental services in Bush Alaska.

The University of Illinois Press
is a founding member of the
Association of American University Presses.

Composed in 10.5/13 Adobe Minion Pro
at the University of Illinois Press
Manufactured by Cushing-Malloy, Inc.

University of Illinois Press
1325 South Oak Street
Champaign, IL 61820-6903
www.press.uillinois.edu